To:

....

From:

....

Date:

....

ISBN 978-1-63609-930-9

Cover Design: Greg Jackson, Thinkpen Design

Published by Barbour Publishing, Inc., 1810 Barbour Drive, Uhrichsville, Ohio 44683, www.barbourbooks.com

Our mission is to inspire the world with the life-changing message of the Bible.

Member of the
Evangelical Christian
Publishers Association

THE
Gutsy Girl's
GUIDE TO PRAYER

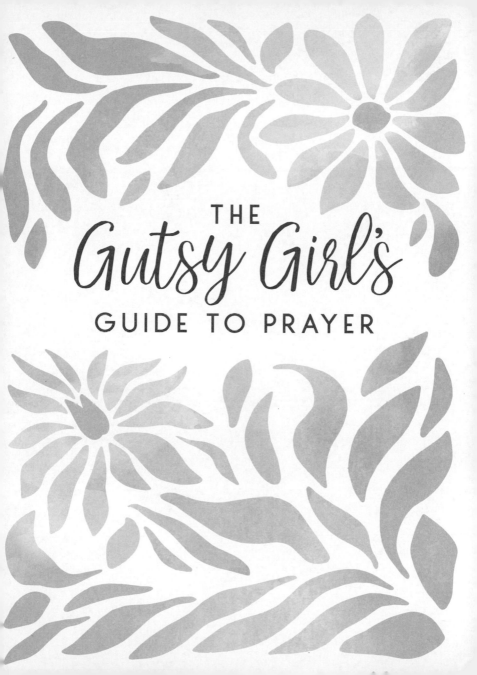

CAREY SCOTT

THE
Gutsy Girl's
GUIDE TO PRAYER

6 MONTHS OF FEARLESS
CONVERSATION WITH GOD

BARBOUR
PUBLISHING

Introduction

God has called you to be strong and courageous. He wants you to be confident in Him as you walk through the ups and downs of life. God has made it clear that His presence is with you always to guide, direct, and comfort. Yet many believers live each day tangled in stress, worry, and fear.

What if you could find a way to be brave even when your circumstances are scary and unsettling? What if you were able to find peace as you navigate heartbreaking situations? What if you felt fearless walking through the unknowns life often brings your way? Friend, God is calling you to be a gutsy girl of faith, and He will show you how through time in His Word. . .*and in prayer*.

Prayer is a powerful tool in the hands of a believer. It's how the Lord reveals Himself and how you find comfort in challenging times. It is an act of worship and obedience, allowing you to express gratitude. Prayer provides a way to share your life with God. And it reminds you that He is in control, so you don't have to be. Nothing happens without God knowing about it because He is sovereign.

Let that truth strengthen you! If the Lord is in control, then you don't have to be knotted up by stressful situations or messy moments. Instead, you can go directly to God in prayer with honesty. You can pray with a hopeful heart full of expectation. You can pray with thanksgiving for the ways He will straighten your crooked path. You can pray boldly and at any time, day or night. And you can exhale, knowing that no matter what, God's will. . .will be done. Stand strong. Hold on to the Lord, and rest.

Generational Faith

That precious memory triggers another: your honest faith—and what a rich faith it is, handed down from your grandmother Lois to your mother Eunice, and now to you! And the special gift of ministry you received when I laid hands on you and prayed—keep that ablaze! God doesn't want us to be shy with his gifts, but bold and loving and sensible.

2 TIMOTHY 1:5–7 MSG

Be bold as you pray for a meaningful faith to be passed down through the generations of your family. Because scripture reveals a precedent has been set for this to happen, recognize it is something that's available to you today, in the here and now. And then begin asking God to deepen your belief as you choose to live it out loud. Ask Him to open the eyes and ears of your children and grandchildren to see your faith in action through the way you live your life. Let them notice the ways your faith is present every day.

From challenges to celebrations, be transparent as you trust the Lord. Rather than worry about the futures of those you love, pray for Him to strengthen them to navigate the dark valleys and exciting mountaintops. Let them see you do it! Be willing to talk with them in age-appropriate ways so they can live in expectation of God's goodness. Invite them to join you in prayer, and wait for His answers together.

Was this your experience growing up? Did you have a faith-filled parent or grandparent who shared their love of the Lord? Did you have deep conversations about the ways He showed up in their circumstances, and were you prompted to look for Him in yours? Were you encouraged to live with a hopeful heart? If so, what a gift!

If this was not your experience, take heart. The truth is it's never too late to start. That means you can choose today to be the fire starter in your family. You can be the catalyst that sparks a group of true believers within your home and beyond. You can cultivate an honest and rich faith to pass down to those you love. Friend, you can be the start of a generational blessing of godliness that helps to create confident and fearless followers.

Ask God to help you become bold in the way you live to glorify Him. And ask for strength and wisdom to create faith that will forever mark your family tree.

DEAR LORD, HELP ME FACILITATE A FAITH-FILLED FAMILY
TREE. SHOW ME WAYS I CAN IMPACT THOSE I CARE ABOUT
WITH A DEEP LOVE FOR YOU. IN JESUS' NAME. AMEN.

The Courage to Obey

*"You need only to be strong and courageous and to obey
to the letter every law Moses gave you, for if you are
careful to obey every one of them, you will be successful
in everything you do. Constantly remind the people
about these laws, and you yourself must think about
them every day and every night so that you will be sure
to obey all of them. For only then will you succeed."*

JOSHUA 1:7–8 TLB

While God gave Moses the law on tablets of stone to share with
the Israelites, today's believers have been given commands to
follow that are found in His Word. Those in Bible times had to
provide sacrifices to atone for their sins, but Jesus was the sacrificial lamb for us. His death on the cross paid the penalty for our
every sin—past, present, and future. But no matter the year on
the calendar, the Lord's desire is for all His children to be strong
and courageous as we pursue righteous living.

The problem is that we often forget to look to the Word for
guidance. We simply don't dig into scripture for help and hope.
Rather than experience victorious living God's way, we limp
through life trying to figure things out on our own as our Bibles
collect dust on the shelf. Friend, unless we understand what His
will is, how can we focus our words and actions to bring Him glory?

Today's passage of scripture reminds us that we desperately need God's Word each day. Not only does it tell us His expectations and hopes, but it also serves as the believer's playbook. The Bible teaches us how to live with passion and purpose. It keeps us on the right path forward. It gives us the courage to follow our Father. And the more we dig into its pages, the more we learn how to be obedient. Be it encouraging stories of those who came before us or direct commands for godly living, as we meditate on its teaching, we will discover how to live to glorify the Lord.

We may try to live holy lives in our own strength. We may decide it is up to us to figure out the formula to follow God's will. We may even set our plans in place each day, trying to manage our efforts to be obedient. But the Bible is there to help us know the Lord's commands and meditate on them, setting us up to experience peace and joy through our faith.

DEAR LORD, GIVE ME THE COURAGE EACH DAY TO
SPEND TIME IN YOUR WORD AND OBEY YOUR WILL.
LET MY LIFE PLEASE YOU! IN JESUS' NAME. AMEN.

Encouraged by God's Presence

"Be strong. Take courage. Don't be intimidated.
Don't give them a second thought because GOD,
your God, is striding ahead of you. He's right there
with you. He won't let you down; he won't leave you."

DEUTERONOMY 31:6 MSG

In this passage, Moses was talking to the Israelites, letting them know that in God's timing and authority, leadership was being transferred from him to Joshua moving forward. This amazing man of God was 120 years old and unable to continue physically. Most importantly, he was taking this time to remind them of God's presence, which would keep them safe from opposing nations as they continued toward the promised land. Moses knew the value of reiterating that promise once again.

Let's apply this reminder to us, especially considering the times we feel oppressed by others. Each time we purpose to take positive steps forward, we often find ourselves in need of encouragement to remember God is always with us. Are you in one of those seasons right now? Is there someone who makes you feel intimidated and unsure of yourself? Are you worried about their potential reaction to a hard conversation on the horizon?

Do you feel alone navigating a group of people who are being mean-spirited? Are you scared about the state of some important relationships?

God's clear command to the Israelites back then and to us now is to be strong and courageous. He says to not even give "them" a second thought because His presence is with us always. For believers, the Lord goes before us in every situation, making a way. He is next to us, walking alongside us in support. And God will not abandon us in our time of need, nor will He let us down. His presence will be a constant companion every step of the way.

How does this truth encourage you today? How does it shift your perspective and give you much-needed hope? How does it fortify you to keep moving forward even through tough and uncomfortable circumstances? God's promise to be with us is an absolute game changer. And once we truly understand that it affords us access to strength, courage, and confidence, we will experience a new level of faith that makes us fearless.

DEAR LORD, THANK YOU FOR BEING WITH ME
EVERY DAY. KNOWING I'M NEVER APART FROM YOU
BRINGS ME SO MUCH COMFORT. KEEP MY EYES FOCUSED
ON YOU IN DIFFICULT TIMES SO I DON'T GIVE IN TO
INTIMIDATION AND FEAR. IN JESUS' NAME. AMEN.

Not a Suggestion but a Command

"This is My command: be strong and courageous. Never be afraid or discouraged because I am your God, the Eternal One, and I will remain with you wherever you go."

Notice in today's verse that God isn't *asking* Joshua to be strong. It is not a mere *suggestion* that he choose to be courageous moving forward. The Lord isn't *hoping* Joshua will muster the grit for the job so he can complete it. He is not simply *proposing* for him to be fearless and bold so he won't cower under the weight of worry. Instead, God is *commanding* it. And friend, He's commanding us to be strong and courageous too.

As believers, we are to be confident in our Father. He would never ask us to do anything that He didn't also include provision for. Just as God promised to Joshua, His presence in our lives is constant and will supernaturally strengthen us no matter what path we're walking. Whether we're leading a Bible study, volunteering in our child's classroom, choosing a new career path, supporting our husband's ministry, stepping out of our comfort zone, or caring for aging parents, we can trust God for the tools to do so. We can be strong and courageous because we know the

14

Lord will supply us with everything necessary for the task at hand.

Friend, what is He asking of you today that feels too big? Where is the Lord calling you to a higher level of trust? Is He stretching your faith in ways that make you feel unqualified? Are you overwhelmed by what you believe God is asking of you? If this describes you right now, take heart—you are not alone! Every follower is challenged at one time or another in ways that require a strong belief that God will deliver on His promises.

So don't be afraid to ask the Lord for what you need to obey. Be it wisdom, perseverance, hope, guidance, peace, or a greater measure of faith, He will supply you with exactly what you need. Remember to cling to the truth that God is always with you. And let your anxious heart be still as you trust that He will provide with each step.

DEAR LORD, IT DOES MY HEART GOOD TO REMEMBER
THAT EVERY ONE OF YOUR COMMANDS COMES WITH THE
SUPERNATURAL ABILITY TO WALK IT OUT. IN YOUR GREAT
LOVE AND COMPASSION, YOU NEVER EXPECT ME TO
THRIVE IN MY OWN STRENGTH. IN JESUS' NAME. AMEN.

Waiting, Hoping, and Expecting

*Bless the Eternal! For He has revealed His gracious
love to me when I was trapped like a city under siege.
I began to panic so I yelled out, "I'm cut off. You no
longer see me!" But You heard my cry for help that day
when I called out to You. Love the Eternal, all of you,
His faithful people! He protects those who are true to Him,
but He pays back the proud in kind. Be strong, and live
courageously, all of you who set your hope in the Eternal!*

PSALM 31:21–24 VOICE

It takes real grit to be courageous when life hits hard. Showing you have courage doesn't mean you're not scared. It means you take that next step despite your knees knocking. You obey what God is asking even though you're sweating with anxiety from head to toe. It's an intentional choice to be brave while your heart is pounding out of your chest. And most would agree that few things can shut us down and render us ineffective faster than fear.

But, friend, letting your heart take courage is no small feat. And while you may be gutsy for a bit in your own strength, there always comes a point when you feel your courage slipping away. You've lost your nerve. Your boldness fades away. And your determination to stand strong wavers. This is usually where we cry out to God in desperation for His help. This is when we recognize the limitations we have as humans. Are you there right now?

The entire chapter of Psalm 31 is a lament from David, who is seeking the Lord's help. Like you may feel today, he is worn out from life's troubles and praying for God to encourage and strengthen him. He has reached the end of himself and is looking to his heavenly Father to restore and replenish, knowing of His goodness and graciousness. And in this last section of the chapter, he reminds us to be courageous in faith and to anchor our hope in the one who promises never to leave or forsake us. Even when we feel all alone, scripture reveals the beautiful truth that we are seen and heard.

DEAR LORD, THANK YOU FOR ALWAYS SEEING ME AND HEARING MY CRIES FOR HELP. YOU ARE WHY I CAN TAKE HEART AND STAND STRONG. YOU ARE WHY I CAN BE ASSURED OF PROTECTION. YOU ARE WHY I CAN BE FEARLESS NO MATTER WHAT COMES MY WAY. IN JESUS' NAME. AMEN.

Courageous and Caring

Listen, stay alert, stand tall in the faith, be courageous,
and be strong. Let love prevail in your life, words, and actions.
1 CORINTHIANS 16:13–14 VOICE

When Jesus becomes our Savior, a supernatural transformation takes place. We begin to desire righteous living and pursue it with passion. Our old leanings no longer feel good since we are now equipped to better discern right from wrong. The Holy Spirit within every believer nudges us so we learn how to live and love in ways that glorify God and bring divinely inspired benefits our way.

What's more, faith brings a sense of fearlessness as we begin to trust that the Lord truly is our provider and protector. God's desire is that we recognize and understand it is not up to us to figure things out on our own. While we're called to be watchful, we are not called to battle alone. God wants us to be strong, but we're not expected to face challenges in our own strength. We are to be alert, but the Lord stands with us through every difficulty.

Sometimes—whether by default or by decision—we find ourselves carrying burdens on our own shoulders without His help. We don't feel confident or brave or attentive. Instead, we feel weak and worried. Even though the Word clearly tells us that the Lord is in control, old habits die hard. And when we're a mess, it's almost impossible to let love prevail. We are simply too self-focused, preoccupied with playing god rather than praying to God.

So how can we consistently live today's verse out loud? Start by spending time in the Lord's presence, boldly asking for courageous faith. Ask Him to strengthen your mind so you're able to take every anxious thought captive. Share your heart with God, inviting Him into what is troubling you. Let Him know your deep desire for love to prevail in your words and actions—and how fear keeps that from happening. It's only through the Holy Spirit's help that we can be courageous and caring, strong and sympathetic, and alert and adoring. And each time we ask Him to meet those needs, He will.

DEAR LORD, I CONFESS THE TIMES I'VE TRIED TO BE MY OWN GOD INSTEAD OF LOOKING TO YOU FOR HELP. FORGIVE ME. MOVING FORWARD, I WANT TO LOOK TO YOU FOR COURAGEOUS FAITH AS IT STRENGTHENS ME TO STAND TALL. I WANT TO LOVE IN WAYS THAT MATTER FOR YOUR KINGDOM. IN JESUS' NAME. AMEN.

The Discipline of Waiting

I am expecting the Lord to rescue me again,
so that once again I will see his goodness to me here in the
land of the living. Don't be impatient. Wait for the Lord,
and he will come and save you! Be brave, stouthearted,
and courageous. Yes, wait and he will help you.

PSALM 27:13–14 TLB

It takes grit to wait on the Lord, especially because we live in a microwave society, meaning we want what we want right now. Think about it. Do you get annoyed when there's a line at the coffee shop drive-thru or when you're put on hold calling the electric company? Do you opt for email delivery for bills and other correspondence because snail mail is just too slow? Maybe you choose to check in for doctor visits online so that no time is wasted at the office. We want to be in and out of there as fast as possible, right? The reality is there are countless ways the world feeds our need for immediate gratification. But that's not how things work in God's economy.

All throughout His Word—including today's passage of scripture—we read about the value of waiting. And if you take a moment to look back at your life, you can see a perfect track record of God showing up. Maybe it wasn't how you had hoped, but it was how it needed to be. In that moment, you may have been confused, but now you are able to see His goodness clearly. These are the experiences we draw on that secure in our hearts the Lord's promise to once again rescue, heal, and help.

Let your prayers be full of expectation, friend! Be fearless in asking for His hand to move mightily in your circumstances. As you talk with God, do so with a hopeful heart. Present your desires with anticipation, trusting He will meet your every need in the right way and at the right time. And boldly ask for an extra dose of patience as you wait for His faithfulness to shine into your life in meaningful ways. It may take all you've got to hold on, but be brave and take a deep breath. Soon you will see His goodness once again in the land of the living.

DEAR LORD, I KNOW YOU ARE TRUSTWORTHY AND WILL NOT LEAVE ME STUCK. BUT PLEASE HELP ME TRUST YOUR TIMING AND YOUR PLAN AS I WAIT TO SEE YOUR HAND MOVING IN MY SITUATION. IN JESUS' NAME. AMEN.

You're Never Truly Alone

"I'm telling you these things while I'm still living with you.
The Friend, the Holy Spirit whom the Father will send
at my request, will make everything plain to you. He will
remind you of all the things I have told you. I'm leaving
you well and whole. That's my parting gift to you. Peace.
I don't leave you the way you're used to being left—feeling
abandoned, bereft. So don't be upset. Don't be distraught."

JOHN 14:25–27 MSG

Chances are you have felt abandoned a time or two. Maybe it was a parent who walked out on your family, a friend who proved to be untrustworthy, a coworker who called you out in a group setting, an event coordinator who left you off the invite list, or a church employee who didn't help when you needed it. Regardless of whether the abandonment was on purpose or by accident, it left a scab that gets picked now and then. And with that familiar feeling comes a flood of emotions that rob you of peace.

But the truth is that as believers, we are never truly abandoned. God promises never to leave or forsake us. Once we decided to follow Jesus, we received the gift of the Holy Spirit who is loyal and devoted to our spiritual development. Scripture calls Him a *friend*. And the Spirit becomes a constant companion who brings revelation, helping us to grow deep roots of faith. He equips. He

22

reminds. He guides. He grows us. God thought of everything, didn't He?

With this gift comes access to peace that makes no sense to the world. It's a satisfying peace that digs in its heels and sticks. And it can soothe even the most anxious heart that keeps us stirred up with fear and worry.

In contrast, earthly peace is conditional and elusive. It is fragile and easily depleted, and if you happen to find comfort in it, it's short-lived and unsatisfying. But the peace given to us by the Lord will settle our spirit even when the scab of abandonment is picked. Why? Because the Holy Spirit is quick to usher in a quiet stillness, bringing a calm remembrance that the Father deeply loves us.

DEAR LORD, THANK YOU FOR THE HOLY SPIRIT
AND THE MAGNIFICENT ROLE HE PLAYS IN MY LIFE.
HELP ME TO BE KEENLY AWARE OF HIS PRESENCE AS
I LEARN TO REST IN THE PEACE PROVIDED BY YOUR
HOLY PRESENCE. IN JESUS' NAME. AMEN.

Trusting the Lord Completely

If you want favor with both God and man, and a
reputation for good judgment and common sense,
then trust the Lord completely; don't ever trust yourself.
In everything you do, put God first, and he will
direct you and crown your efforts with success.

PROVERBS 3:5–6 TLB

It is so easy for us as women to multitask and move the pile forward each day. Our to-do list is no joke! Some of it is home and family management, like carpooling, grocery shopping, laundry, homework help, sporting events, and a healthy meal on the table at the end of the day. But other items that populate the list may be a combination of volunteer work, job responsibilities, aging parents, daily exercise, and the like. And too often we tackle them in our own strength. But have you ever invited God into the mix, asking for wisdom and strength to finish well?

Scripture clearly tells us not to lean on our own understanding but instead to trust the Lord completely. We may be educated, savvy, well-versed, and fully capable of handling daily tasks ourselves, but the Bible is not conditional that way. There's no caveat. When it says we should seek God's direction in all we do, it means *everything*. Regardless of the task at hand, we are to ensure it's for our good and His glory. And we can do that by putting God first.

Maybe giving the Lord first place in your life is a challenge to walk out. Do you struggle to start your day in prayer, asking for His help and guidance? Are there circumstances you'd prefer to oversee on your own rather than seeking God's thoughts? Do you think the grind of your daily to-do list doesn't warrant His time or effort? What keeps you from trusting the Lord completely?

Let's create a legacy of faith that will bless those around us. How? Today's verse reminds us that if we truly trust God with every detail of our day, others will see it. They will watch how we consistently include the Lord in everything we do, from meal prep to boardroom presentations to caring for the less fortunate. And not only will it leave a lasting impression on them but also we'll experience a measure of favor too. Start your conversation with God before your feet hit the floor, and then carry it on throughout your day.

DEAR LORD, HELP ME TRUST YOU COMPLETELY BY INVITING YOU INTO EACH DAY. GUIDE MY STEPS SO I USE SOUND JUDGMENT AND GOOD SENSE. IN JESUS' NAME. AMEN.

The Good Shepherd

The Eternal is my shepherd, He cares for me always.
He provides me rest in rich, green fields beside streams
of refreshing water. He soothes my fears; He makes me
whole again, steering me off worn, hard paths to roads
where truth and righteousness echo His name.

PSALM 23:1–3 VOICE

. . . .

Sometimes we just need a gentle reminder that life will get better. This world can be brutal on every level, leaving us feeling shattered and beaten down. And while nothing here will change for the better, God in heaven remains faithful in His promise to show care and compassion to the brokenhearted.

The Twenty-Third Psalm brings comfort in the most meaningful ways, especially when we're waiting for God's intervention with hopeful hearts. It reminds us that we have a Good Shepherd who knows us and loves us. He sees everyone in His flock with complete clarity yet offers individual attention to them too. It is a supernatural blessing we cannot explain.

It means we don't have to wait in line for His kindness. When life hits hard, we never have to worry He missed it. We are not left to find our way back alone or to do battle on our own. And as our protector, God knows exactly what we need to settle our spirits. He recognizes our fear and understands our anxiety. The

Bible is clear when it says we *will* have trouble in this life, but the Lord promises never to leave the figuring out to us. As believers, we will never be separated from His presence.

Being a gutsy girl means you consider prayer to be a lifeline. You understand it's a direct channel of communication between you and your caring Shepherd. And when you ask, you are confident He will meet your needs and bring much-needed refreshment to your weary soul. You're certain He will reset your mind as He soothes the stressful thoughts that threaten to pull you under. And you have no doubt God will restore you in powerful ways and redirect your feet to follow paths of righteousness. Yes, friend, you are hopeful because you have a deep conviction inside, knowing the Lord is with you.

DEAR LORD, I AM SO GRATEFUL THAT YOU ARE MY CARING SHEPHERD WHO UNDERSTANDS THE COMPLEXITY OF WHAT I NEED, EVEN WHEN I DON'T. THANK YOU FOR YOUR UNWAVERING COMPASSION AND FAITHFULNESS IN SHOWING ME FAVOR EVERY DAY. IN JESUS' NAME. AMEN.

Dark Moments

Even in the unending shadows of death's darkness,
I am not overcome by fear. Because You are
with me in those dark moments, near with Your
protection and guidance, I am comforted.

PSALM 23:4 VOICE

Take a moment to reread that first sentence, friend, because if we can adopt this faith-filled mindset, it will change our lives. And since we will all experience dark times in those valley experiences, clinging to God will give us a renewed perspective. We will realize we don't have to be gripped by fear any longer. It's not that our circumstances will never be scary. It's that His presence will bring us perfect peace and comfort.

What dark moments are you facing today? Is your job unstable because of new ownership? Have you started conversations with your husband about the option of divorce? Are you facing the reality of bankruptcy? Is your child buying into an agenda that is not healthy or holy? Has there been a diagnosis that seems hopeless to manage or overcome? Are you grieving the loss of someone incredibly special and struggling to find your footing? Has counseling brought up some difficult memories to process? Did you move to a new town and it's not all you hoped for? Is the state of the world stirring up anxiety? Friend, what shadows are being cast into your life right now?

Scripture tells us that even in these dark moments, we can be strong. We don't have to let them shut us down like we have in the past. Through spending time in prayer and digging into the Word daily, we are constantly reminded that our God is ever-present and we are not alone. We can begin to pray boldly, asking for His protection. We can choose to believe the Lord will guide us through to the other side. And we can confidently exhale with relief, knowing comfort in the chaos is possible.

Talk to God and bare your heart. Share with Him the burdens keeping you afraid. Open up about the unending shadows that won't go away. Ask the Lord to shine His light of hope into your circumstances.

DEAR LORD, I'M IN THE VALLEY OF DARKNESS TODAY
AND IN NEED OF THE COMFORT ONLY YOU CAN BRING.
PLEASE HELP ME PROCESS THE EMOTIONS PLAGUING ME.
OPEN MY EYES TO SEE YOUR GUIDANCE. SETTLE MY HEART
WITH THE REVELATION OF YOUR PROTECTION. BUILD MY
FAITH AS I LEAN INTO YOU. IN JESUS' NAME. AMEN.

God's Protection
and Provision

*You spread out a table before me, provisions in the midst of
attack from my enemies; You care for all my needs, anointing
my head with soothing, fragrant oil, filling my cup again and
again with Your grace. Certainly Your faithful protection and
loving provision will pursue me where I go, always, everywhere.
I will always be with the Eternal, in Your house forever.*

PSALM 23:5–6 VOICE

This section of Psalm 23 transitions from a shepherd-and-sheep
dynamic to something a bit more personal. The mention of certain
elements like a table, anointing with oil, a cup, and the Lord's house
signifies that the believer is now a guest for a meal in the Lord's
home. And while we can feel like sitting ducks for our enemies
here on earth, at the heavenly table in God's presence, they are
powerless. Our adversaries cannot stop the fellowship between
us. They cannot stop His goodness, graciousness, and generosity.
The Father's protection and provision confirm His unending love
that will last forever. What a beautiful picture.

Let this picture bring comfort to your fearful heart, friend.
Let it remind you that this life is but a breath and that the hope
of eternity awaits us. And in that eternity, you are safely tucked

away with God. Right now, certain people and situations may have you feeling destabilized. And some days you may feel the enemy's arrows more than others. But in the end, they will lose every bit of power over you.

The good news is that you can experience perfect protection even now. You don't have to wait for heaven because God is also your protector and provider today and tomorrow. So when you're feeling overwhelmed by difficulties on every level, let that feeling drive you to your knees.

When parenting your teenager feels like a combat zone, pray. When a fight with your best friend has you in the trenches, pray. When your marriage feels more like a battlefield, pray. When you feel targeted at work, pray. When you're wrongly accused, pray. When you would rather hide in the bunker than face the day, pray. Go ahead and be bold in your requests for God's help. Ask with confidence for tangible reminders of His protection and provision. And pray with expectation because His promises for you are forever.

DEAR LORD, WHAT A BLESSING TO KNOW THAT
YOU UNDERSTAND WHAT I'M UP AGAINST AND HAVE
WHAT IT TAKES TO KEEP ME SAFE. I CAN REST IN YOU
AND BE COMFORTED. IN JESUS' NAME. AMEN.

Keeping Your Eyes on Jesus

*"You won't have to put up with our questions anymore.
We're convinced you came from God." Jesus answered them,
"Do you finally believe? In fact, you're about to make a run
for it—saving your own skins and abandoning me. But I'm
not abandoned. The Father is with me. I've told you all this so
that trusting me, you will be unshakable and assured, deeply
at peace. In this godless world you will continue to experience
difficulties. But take heart! I've conquered the world."*

JOHN 16:30–33 MSG

Did you notice the qualifier in today's verse regarding peace?
Jesus had just told His disciples a change was coming—one that
would affect them deeply—but to stay focused on Him so peace
would prevail. Peace and confidence would be guaranteed if their
trust was put into action. They would be unshakable. Trusting
Jesus would also assure them of His promises as they navigated
unsettling and challenging times.

Today, our world is even more godless, and it seems like a
peaceful heart is difficult to achieve and maintain. There are more
opportunities to face joy-draining and spine-weakening trials,
tribulations, toils, and troubles. From world events to relational
heartbreak to financial upheaval to health scares, living on planet
Earth feels like a setup for discouragement and disappointment.

But it shouldn't be for a believer.

God's command is for us to take heart. We are to be of good cheer. Faith should be what helps us stand with courage and confidence through the ups and downs. We should be undaunted by what life brings our way because our eyes are focused on the Lord and not our circumstances. How are you doing with that today?

When Jesus says He has conquered the world, He simply means He has defeated it. He has deprived it of power to take you down. And this kind of inner peace is only available through a personal relationship with Jesus. We must rely on Him to get us through worry and fear, hatred and oppression, transgression and temptation, grief and death, and the enemy's arrows. Pray with the bold belief that in Him you can experience peace amid the problems.

DEAR LORD, HELP ME ALWAYS TO KEEP MY EYES AND
EARS TRAINED ON YOU SO I CAN FIND THE PEACE
AND CONFIDENCE NECESSARY TO GET THROUGH
LIFE IN VICTORY. HELP ME TRUST YOU EVEN WHEN MY
CIRCUMSTANCES LOOK DIRE. IN JESUS' NAME. AMEN.

Settled in Your Mind

He does not fear bad news, nor live in dread of
what may happen. For he is settled in his mind
that Jehovah will take care of him. That is why
he is not afraid but can calmly face his foes.

PSALM 112:7–8 TLB

Let this be your prayer every morning. Before your feet hit the ground, ask the Lord to strengthen your faith so that whatever the day throws your way, you will be able to stand unrattled—not because you're some sort of superwoman but because your trust in God is super strong. And He's the one who steadies your sprit in the battle.

What shocking news has come your way? Did you lose your job? Has your medical condition worsened? Is the increase in cost prohibitive? Were you denied a claim? Has paperwork been filed against you? Did the door of opportunity close suddenly? Were you not included? Did someone share confidential information?

What are you afraid might happen? Are you worried about being rejected again? Does a change in their opinion scare you? What if they judge you harshly? What if they walk away without explanation? What if you're wrongfully blamed? What if the word gets around? Could it negatively affect your relationships? Might it hurt your chances?

Regardless of what threatens to knock you off balance, a strong, mature faith will stabilize you. Once you accept Jesus as your Savior, the work of the Holy Spirit begins. But understand that it takes time to develop a faith that is settled. So every time you see God show up in your circumstances, it builds trust. Seeing Him provide and protect strengthens your faith. Watching His goodness materialize stirs up gratitude toward the Lord. And recognizing that you are experiencing God's kindness and generosity gives you the grit to believe in Him again. Eventually, you will become settled in your mind that He will take care of you, and the fear that has gripped you in the past. . .no longer will.

Choose to partner with the Spirit's work in your heart. Be committed to pray for courage and confidence in faith. Have a hopeful heart for God's will and ways. Ask with expectation because you believe that God is good and that the will of God will be done. And thank the Lord now for how He is already working in your life.

DEAR LORD. IT'S SETTLED. THERE IS NOTHING TO
FEAR BECAUSE I KNOW YOU WILL TAKE CARE OF
ME WITHOUT FAIL. IN JESUS' NAME. AMEN.

Keeping a Clear Conscience

The wicked are edgy with guilt, ready to run off
even when no one's after them; honest people
are relaxed and confident, bold as lions.

PROVERBS 28:1 MSG

Today's verse is all about our conscience. Those who are wicked and living in opposition to God have an edginess in their spirit that makes them tense and jumpy. It may manifest as nervousness. Impatience. They may be quickly agitated and full of anxiety. It's there partly from their uneasy conscience that continues to remind them of the natural consequences they may face if their questionable actions don't change. The other reason is a fear of God's response. They clearly know they're not following His lead but instead are focused on satisfying their own selfish desires. And from what we read in the Bible, we know His judgment is nothing to scoff at.

In stark contrast, those who value honesty are relaxed. They have a humble confidence, knowing they are safe in God's hands. These believers aren't discouraged by tough times. They don't battle disappointment. They don't feel disheartened by difficult circumstances. Challenging times are not marked by unreasonable sadness. They don't live offended or obsess over their emotional woundings. Since their conscience is clear—not because of their perfection but rather because of their purposeful living—their spirit is at rest. They live with a profound understanding that they are safe in God's arms. Their faith in His provision and protection is rooted deep. They stand bold in the truth.

Sin has a way of making people cowards. Because of the constant expectation of the other shoe dropping, their days are filled with worry. The internal alarms keep going off. In contrast, when we commit our life to righteousness, we move forward in peace.

Friend, where are you today? Take an honest assessment of your life, digging to see if you are fearing God's judgment or living in the freedom Jesus came to give. Is your conscience clear, or are you weighed down by guilt? And then talk to God about it either way.

Maybe you need to confess your sinful ways and ask God to forgive you. Take this time to tell Him where you need strength and wisdom going forward. Or maybe you need to thank the Lord for helping you stand strong in your faith like a lion, bold and uncompromising.

DEAR LORD, KEEP ME ON THE PATH THAT LEADS TO YOU. LET ME MAKE THE RIGHT CHOICES THAT AFFORD ME A CLEAR CONSCIENCE SO I CAN LIVE RELAXED AND CONFIDENT IN YOU. IN JESUS' NAME. AMEN.

Are You Holding On to Discontentment?

I've learned by now to be quite content whatever my circumstances. I'm just as happy with little as with much, with much as with little. I've found the recipe for being happy whether full or hungry, hands full or hands empty. Whatever I have, wherever I am, I can make it through anything in the One who makes me who I am.

PHILIPPIANS 4:12–13 MSG

Paul is so bold in this passage, describing a level of contentment we think we can only imagine. But, friend, this radical contentment is available to you right now. Today. But it's a gutsy decision because many of us have reasons for holding on to a heart of discontent. Do you?

Let's just be honest with one another for a minute. There's no condemnation or judgment here, but let's be candid. Can we admit there are times when we don't want to say we are okay? Maybe we're not comfortable declaring that we're content because it feels like a setup, like we're challenging the enemy to come after us. If we don't expect satisfaction, then we can't be let down again. Right?

Maybe our identity lies in being the victim. Too often we receive certain benefits from being "messy" and unhappy. It may

38

bring attention our way, meeting a need where we feel lacking. It may help us feel loved and cared for on the regular. It may even help us get financial discounts, free services, and access others do not have. And while we all may need this kind of support from time to time, embracing a victim mentality as a way of life doesn't honor the Lord God.

When we take our eyes off our circumstances and instead focus on the Lord and His goodness, our hearts will change. It will allow us a 30,000-foot perspective and get us out of the weeds of worry and anxiety. And as we spend time in the Word and in prayer, God will settle our spirits with peace. We will be reminded that He is our provider and protector, and that truth will comfort in ways the world never can.

Ask the Lord to bring contentment to your heart in every area. Ask Him to keep you from latching on to a victim mentality. And ask Him to help you focus on eternal satisfaction rather than letting the world meet your deepest needs. Doing so will reset your heart to find joy in Jesus, regardless of what's happening around you.

DEAR LORD, LET MY CONTENTMENT BE SECURED
IN YOU AND NOT ANYTHING THE WORLD
HAS TO OFFER. IN JESUS' NAME. AMEN.

Trusting God's Presence

It is the Lord Who goes before you; He will [march] with you;
He will not fail you or let you go or forsake you; [let there be
no cowardice or flinching, but] fear not, neither become broken
[in spirit—depressed, dismayed, and unnerved with alarm].

DEUTERONOMY 31:8 AMPC

If you truly believed the Lord was always walking ahead of you, clearing the path and making a way, what would you be encouraged to do? If you knew He wouldn't let you fall flat on your face, would you be more willing to say yes? Would knowing you are safe and secure in God's hands from this day forward free you up to try something new?

Today's verse unpacks these truths perfectly. The Lord goes before you, ensuring you won't ultimately fail or be rejected or abandoned. These power-packed promises are why you can be a gutsy girl. Go ahead and grab on and let them sink deep into your heart. Let them strengthen your resolve to have an adventurous kind of faith that is not stifled by fear.

The reality is that if we allow our fear to go unchecked, we'll be rendered ineffective. We can say we trust God, but our responses to life's circumstances will always give us away. They will expose what we really think. And when the rubber meets the road, we'll quickly learn if we believe Him or not.

When the phone call comes, will you trust God to untangle your emotions? When hard conversations need to happen in your relationship, will you faithfully say what needs to be said? When the opportunity presents itself, will you step out in faith? When you must take a stand rather than compromise, will you have the confidence to do it? When you feel His prompting to let something go because it's becoming a crutch, will you trust God's help?

You have a decision to make. And it will take a good measure of grit to walk it out. But once you embrace the truth that the Lord's presence in your life cannot be removed no matter what happens, you won't let fear keep you stuck any longer.

DEAR LORD, I CONFESS THAT FEAR HAS BEEN A HUGE ISSUE THAT HAS KEPT ME FROM EXPERIENCING TRUE FREEDOM IN YOU. MAKE MY FEAR DISSIPATE SO IT NO LONGER CONTROLS MY LIFE. AND HELP ME TO HAVE AN UNSHAKABLE FAITH IN YOUR PRESENCE, TRUSTING YOU ARE WITH ME FOREVER. IN JESUS' NAME. AMEN.

Battling Fear

*Take my side, God—I'm getting kicked around, stomped on
every day. Not a day goes by but somebody beats me up;
they make it their duty to beat me up. When I get really
afraid I come to you in trust. I'm proud to praise God;
fearless now, I trust in God. What can mere mortals do?*

PSALM 56:1–4 MSG

There is no doubt our hearts will get kicked around in this lifetime.
We will experience moments when we are emotionally beat up by
the words of others. Yes, we will have seasons when our feelings
get stomped on daily. These are the times we want to raise the
white flag, crawl under the covers of our bed, and hide from the
world. No doubt you've already had to manage these instances.
We all have. But today's verse offers a divine perspective that will
help us refocus and reengage with grit.

If you are trying to navigate the mountaintops and valleys on
your own, you're missing out on God's goodness in them both.
Regardless of where you are right now, He is with you. Countless
passages of scripture throughout the Word remind us of this
powerful truth. And if the Lord—the one who declares His provision and protection—never leaves our side, why do we battle
with fear? Great question.

Maybe we struggle with giving up control and instead trusting in a God we cannot see or touch. With so many heavy issues going on in this crazy world, maybe we don't think our problems warrant His attention. Maybe we get so wrapped up in the circumstances we are facing that we genuinely forget the Lord is ready and willing to intervene. Or maybe we let these tough situations pull us down and we give up altogether. Friend, don't forget God is faithful! And when you cry out for help, He hears you.

The understanding that because He is for us, nothing can be against us is a game changer. A fresh confidence strengthens us. We are able to see with greater clarity, understanding God's sovereignty. And we're able to look at what's spooking us with spiritual eyes as we learn to adopt a divine point of view. Trusting God makes us brave and gutsy.

DEAR LORD, FORGIVE ME FOR GIVING IN TO FEAR AS I HAVE. HELP ME UNDERSTAND THAT TRUSTING YOU WITH MY FEAR IS LIFE-GIVING AND ESSENTIAL. IN JESUS' NAME. AMEN.

The Blessing of Community

Most important, live together in a manner worthy of Christ's gospel. Do this, whether I come and see you or I'm absent and hear about you. Do this so that you stand firm, united in one spirit and mind as you struggle together to remain faithful to the gospel. That way, you won't be afraid of anything your enemies do. Your faithfulness and courage are a sign of their coming destruction and your salvation, which is from God. God has generously granted you the privilege, not only of believing in Christ but also of suffering for Christ's sake.

<small>PHILIPPIANS 1:27–29 CEB</small>

Simply put, today's verses tell us to stay together and love one another through the ups and downs of life. Countless benefits come from being in a godly community, including much-needed encouragement when life gets hard. This kind of support helps us stand firm and united. It surrounds us with people who show us genuine care and compassion. It blesses us with deep companionship with others who may be facing similar struggles. It challenges us to make choices that are good for us and glorifying to God. And a community of people who love the Lord is quick to remind us of His goodness just when we need it as well as refocus our heart to better understand the privilege we have to suffer with Christ. Few things can beat the power of meaningful relationships.

Who are your people? What kind of company do you keep? Are you surrounded by friends and family who share your faith? Are you a good champion for others? If not, what needs to change?

Community is a divine creation to support believers as they take this journey of faith. Spending time with others is essential to mental and emotional health in countless ways. And if you're lacking togetherness, ask God to bring the right people into your life. Be open and willing to put yourself out there, even if it feels risky to your heart. Let the Lord populate your life with those who will bless your heart. And let Him help you find ways to bless them right back.

DEAR LORD, THANK YOU FOR THE GIFT OF COMMUNITY. YOU KNOW WHERE I'M LACKING AND WHERE I'M FULL. WOULD YOU PLEASE FILL IN THE GAPS WITH THOSE YOU'VE CHOSEN TO STAND WITH ME? IN JESUS' NAME. AMEN.

It's a Big Deal

*Fear not [there is nothing to fear], for I am with you;
do not look around you in terror and be dismayed, for I am
your God. I will strengthen and harden you to difficulties,
yes, I will help you; yes, I will hold you up and retain you
with My [victorious] right hand of rightness and justice.*

ISAIAH 41:10 AMPC

There is no way to insulate ourselves from the pain and heartache this life will bring. We will struggle in marriage or struggle because singlehood isn't what we want. We will grapple with a myriad of issues that come up in our friendships. Work will undoubtedly be like a roller coaster ride, full of unforeseen ups and downs, twist and turns. Finances will stir up all sorts of fears that are difficult to quiet. Our health will present challenges that cause anxiety to skyrocket. We'll have to navigate delicate and disheartening concerns as we raise kids in today's world. And grief, jealousy, insecurities, and perfectionism will threaten to knock us to our knees. But God.

We may not fully understand this side of heaven, but the Lord knows the power of His presence. When He tells us throughout the Word that we are not alone and He's with us continually, it's a big deal. In fact, it's such a monumentally big deal that God's presence *alone* should shut down any fear we're facing. So when we get stirred up and anxious, simply remembering the Lord is there brings peace. Quickly stilling your worry through prayer will bring comfort. But, friend, that's not all.

Trusting the Lord for peace in chaos also leads to a strengthening of your resolve. It makes you steadfast. It creates a determination to be an overcomer. You will find courage and confidence to manage the hard circumstances rather than being rendered ineffective. And while your normal response has been to wilt under pressure, you will find supernatural perseverance to stand strong in Him.

Boldly pray for a revelation of God's presence. Pray in expectation that He will hold you up with His holy hand. And pray without ceasing, especially when you find yourself on the front lines of trouble.

DEAR LORD, I CONFESS THERE ARE TIMES WHEN FEAR
GETS THE BEST OF ME. SOMETIMES I STARE AT SCARY
SITUATIONS WHEN MY EYES SHOULD BE ON YOU.
HELP ME RISE UP IN STEADFAST FAITH, KNOWING YOU
ARE WITH ME ALWAYS. IN JESUS' NAME. AMEN.

Until You See Jesus

When I pray for you, my heart is full of joy because of all
your wonderful help in making known the Good News about
Christ from the time you first heard it until now. And I am
sure that God who began the good work within you will keep
right on helping you grow in his grace until his task within
you is finally finished on that day when Jesus Christ returns.

PHILIPPIANS 1:4–6 TLB

Paul was so encouraging to those who had partnered with him to spread the gospel. He recognized their commitment and affirmed their help. Imagine what that must have done for their heart. While their motivation may have been solely to serve God, Paul's support must have built up their courage, strengthening their resolve to continue speaking truth to those around them. But then, Paul takes it one step further. In a way only he can do, Paul makes a tremendous statement designed to bolster their faith.

He reminds them that God is working in their lives and will continue to do so until they see Jesus face-to-face. Paul is confident in this. He is assured God's goodness will continue in and through them. He's certain the Lord will finish His good work. There is not one ounce of doubt that God will supply the grit and grace necessary to minister on His behalf. It was exactly what they needed to hear.

Friend, the same is true in your walk with the Lord. Because He is incapable of changing, who God was in Bible times is who He is today. And it is also who He'll be tomorrow. So we can adopt Paul's words and apply them to us right now. Yes, we can be confident God is currently working in our lives and will continue to do so until He calls us home or comes to get us.

Let the truth of God's continual work in your life motivate you to keep following His will for your life. Let it infuse your faith with unshakable trust in His plan. And let it encourage you to stay the course when you want to give up. Every day, pray for fresh bravery to help drive you forward. Ask God to open the right doors of opportunity. Let your prayer life and time in the Word be a confidence boost to trust what God has planned for you to do.

DEAR LORD, I WANT MY WORDS AND ACTIONS
TO PREACH OF YOUR GOODNESS. I WANT MY LIFE
TO POINT TO HEAVEN. UNTIL I SEE YOU, LET ME
GLORIFY YOUR NAME. IN JESUS' NAME. AMEN.

God Knows Your Limits

*But remember this—the wrong desires that come into
your life aren't anything new and different. Many others
have faced exactly the same problems before you. And no
temptation is irresistible. You can trust God to keep the
temptation from becoming so strong that you can't stand
up against it, for he has promised this and will do what
he says. He will show you how to escape temptation's
power so that you can bear up patiently against it.*

1 CORINTHIANS 10:13 TLB

Sometimes sin gets the best of us. Our fleshly desires win out.
We may love the Lord and want to follow His ways, but there are
moments when we want what we want. And rather than take
God up on His promise to show us an escape route, we grab for
what's enticing. Or we try to withstand temptation in our own
strength. . .and lose.

We don't reach out to God, but we don't ask for help from
friends either. Maybe it's because we feel ashamed. It may be
embarrassing to share what's tugging at us. We may be afraid
of coming under harsh judgment or being looked at differently
moving forward. Or maybe we think the best idea is just to handle
it ourselves. Whatever the reasoning, this kind of thinking con-
tradicts the Word. It's a bad strategy for countless reasons. The

truth is that we are not alone in these cravings. Today's passage says *many* others have faced the *exact* same problems.

But most importantly, let's praise God for recognizing our limitations! He knows how far we can be stretched and will not allow the testing to go further. It's a promise He will always make good on. We can trust it!

So what do we do when the cravings and urges start to take hold? We pray. We ask for courage. We ask for an increase in faith to stand against the enemy. We pray without ceasing and with hopeful hearts. We admit our weakness and ask for God's strength. We bring each temptation into the light, exposing it. We choose to believe He will intervene in mighty ways. We thank Him now for what He will do for us. And we connect with a trusted friend for support and prayer too.

DEAR LORD, WHAT A RELIEF TO KNOW YOU WON'T
LET ME BE PUSHED TOO FAR BY TEMPTATION. I TRUST
YOUR PROMISES AND AM GRATEFUL FOR SUCH A
COMPASSIONATE FATHER. STRENGTHEN ME FOR
THE BATTLE AHEAD. IN JESUS' NAME. AMEN.

Your Life Speaks

*For I live in eager expectation and hope that I will never
do anything that will cause me to be ashamed of myself
but that I will always be ready to speak out boldly for
Christ while I am going through all these trials here,
just as I have in the past; and that I will always be an
honor to Christ, whether I live or whether I must die.*

PHILIPPIANS 1:20 TLB

Our lives speak. How we choose to navigate the difficulties that
come our way impacts those around us. Either we can point to
God in heaven through the way we respond, or we can reveal a
lack of faith in His capabilities. Friend, it will be one or the other.

When you're struggling with insecurity or feeling frustrated
at work, how do you share it? When the pregnancy test shows
negative once again or your mother continues to be critical of your
personal choices, how do you unpack it with friends? When your
marriage is a mess or your financial debt is crushing, how do you
carry yourself? Would others say you're a complainer, or would
they see your steadfast commitment to trusting God? Would your
reactions encourage them in their own challenging circumstances?
Would they see value in having faith in the Lord for protection and
provision? Would they believe in the power of prayer?

Choose to let your words and actions preach boldly for a

relationship with God, because we all need hope. We need to know we're loved by our Father in heaven who sees and hears us. We need to see examples of faith-filled followers who've experienced His goodness in powerful ways. It's these stories that often help to settle our anxieties. These experiences encourage us to go to God and stand steadfast as we wait for His hand to move. But if we watch someone who claims to be a believer crumble and crash time and time again, that example can, unfortunately, serve as a deterrent.

The Word tells us that we will have trouble. It says life will be full of discouragement and disappointment and to expect pain, grief, and heartbreak. But as believers, we don't have to succumb to defeat. Instead, we can live victoriously because God is with us, always active and involved. And we have the privilege of being bold and hopeful in faith through all of life's challenges, honoring the Lord with how we live each day.

DEAR LORD, HELP ME NEVER TO DO ANYTHING TO DETER PEOPLE FROM FAITH. INSTEAD, LET MY WORDS AND ACTIONS ALWAYS SPEAK BOLDLY FOR YOU. IN JESUS' NAME. AMEN.

Being God's Hands and Feet

What a wonderful God we have—he is the Father of our Lord
Jesus Christ, the source of every mercy, and the one who so
wonderfully comforts and strengthens us in our hardships
and trials. And why does he do this? So that when others are
troubled, needing our sympathy and encouragement, we can
pass on to them this same help and comfort God has given us.

2 CORINTHIANS 1:3–4 TLB

God uses everything we face in life for our good and His glory.
Through each messy moment—if we will let Him—God will provide us with compassion, care, and comfort. He will strengthen
us and bring insight and perspective. Our fears will be quieted.
Each stressor will lose power. Our broken hearts will be restored.
We'll experience peace. And our parched places will be amply
quenched. Yes, God will meet us and mend us.

But have you ever considered that He uses our hardships and
trials to bless those around us too? With each healing encounter,
God equips us to provide help and comfort to others. Not only
do we understand what they're battling since we've been there
before, but we also understand how to love them through it since
God did the same for us. We are His hands and feet, nurturing

their hearts back to health.

So change your thinking. Rather than feeling hopeless when you face parenting struggles, remember God will bring you through. When being single feels overwhelming, rest in the knowledge that His plan for your life is perfect. When your medical report scares you, trust the Lord for peace. When you lose someone close and are filled with grief, ask God to heal your hurting heart. As you navigate financial strain, work frustrations, relational pain, and other hardships, ask the Lord to meet you there. And when the time is right, you will have a beautiful opportunity to help another walk the same rocky path of pain.

Think about all the hard-won wisdom you have right now. What struggles are you specifically equipped to help others navigate, based on personal experience? Who needs your support? To whom can you be a support today?

Ask God to use you according to His will. Tell Him you're ready and willing to encourage others in faith.

DEAR LORD, LET ME BE YOUR HANDS AND FEET.
OPEN THE DOORS OF OPPORTUNITY, AND I
WILL WALK THROUGH THEM WITH PASSION
AND PURPOSE. IN JESUS' NAME. AMEN.

Surprised by the Lord

But when they saw Him walking on the sea they thought
it was a ghost, and raised a [deep, throaty] shriek of terror.
For they all saw Him and were agitated (troubled and filled
with fear and dread). But immediately He talked with them
and said, Take heart! I AM! Stop being alarmed and afraid.

MARK 6:49–50 AMPC

Jesus surprised the disciples. In their exhaustion from battling the storm, the sight of Him absolutely freaked them out. These men were terrified! They were agitated and confused. Considering all the time they had spent with Jesus—witnessing miracles and listening to His teaching—their reaction may seem odd at first glance. But can't we relate?

When we're in a life storm, we're often surprised to see the Lord show up in the ways He does. We may have been diligent to ask for His help, but seeing His provision shocks us. We're amazed He acted on our behalf. And truth be told, it can sometimes be alarming to see how He's straightened our crooked path better than we could have imagined. No matter what storm we're in, God won't leave us to navigate it alone.

What storms are you in right now? Are you fighting for your child's mental health? Are you feeling tugged in too many directions and struggling to find balance? Are there issues in your marriage that feel impossible to manage? Are you unable to find your footing with your finances? Are you in counseling, trying to work through some past trauma? Are you stuck in the grieving process and unable to move forward? Are you waiting for God to intervene, but your prayers seem to bounce off the ceiling? Take heart, friend! He will show up for you!

So keep praying. Pray bold prayers. Pray without ceasing. Pray with a hopeful heart full of expectation. Pray with thanksgiving, believing God is already at work. And pray that His will be done in your stormy situation. And when you see Him, don't be afraid. Instead, grab hold of the Lord's hand and let Him lead you to safety.

DEAR LORD, IN SOME WAYS I UNDERSTAND THE DISCIPLES'
RESPONSE TO YOUR PRESENCE. I CONFESS THE TIMES I'VE
BEEN STUNNED BY YOUR HAND IN MY LIFE. BUT I WELCOME
IT! I KNOW YOU WILL NEVER LEAVE ME ALONE TO SINK
IN THE STORM. THANK YOU! IN JESUS' NAME. AMEN.

The Devil Doesn't Have to Win

And that about wraps it up. God is strong, and he wants you strong. So take everything the Master has set out for you, well-made weapons of the best materials. And put them to use so you will be able to stand up to everything the Devil throws your way. This is no weekend war that we'll walk away from and forget about in a couple of hours. This is for keeps, a life-or-death fight to the finish against the Devil and all his angels.

EPHESIANS 6:10–12 MSG

Today's verse lets us know that the devil is always looking for ways to inflict damage and discomfort. His arrows are specifically designed to bring disappointment and discouragement. He wants to see us in distress at every turn, and he is good at it. Chances are you've experienced his schemes countless times.

But God is stronger. And through Him, we have the strength to withstand the devil's attacks. He may be the prince of the world and have free rein here for a time; however, the Lord is the King over everything in the heavens and the earth. Yes, He is sovereign. And to all believers, God gives access to His holy armor as protection. We're not left to battle alone and hope for the best. Instead, we are encouraged to take hold of what He provides and stand strong. God gives us weapons to defeat the works of the devil!

This isn't a once-and-done struggle. The devil isn't going to give up that easily. Truth is, this will be an ongoing assault until you see Jesus face-to-face. It's not so much that the devil hates you as that he hates God. And since the enemy can't get to our great God, he goes after the next best thing: God's children. But keep in mind that just because the enemy has it out for you doesn't mean he will win.

Friend, where is the devil winning in your life today? Where are you feeling weak and unprotected? What struggles are wearing you down and leaving you hopeless for change? Talk to God about them right now. Be honest about your fears and failures. Be authentic with your Father and share where the battle feels out of control.

DEAR LORD, PLEASE OPEN MY EYES TO SEE ALL THE
WEAPONS AT MY DISPOSAL SO I CAN EFFECTIVELY
WITHSTAND THE DEVIL'S ASSAULT. I KNOW YOU
HAVE ME COVERED. IN JESUS' NAME. AMEN.

God's Armor

So use every piece of God's armor to resist the enemy
whenever he attacks, and when it is all over, you will still
be standing up. But to do this, you will need the strong
belt of truth and the breastplate of God's approval. Wear
shoes that are able to speed you on as you preach the
Good News of peace with God. In every battle you will
need faith as your shield to stop the fiery arrows aimed at
you by Satan. And you will need the helmet of salvation
and the sword of the Spirit—which is the Word of God.

Ephesians 6:13–17 TLB

Today's passage of scripture unpacks God's armor in detail, giving us a better understanding of what we have access to as believers. And we're told to use every piece every day so we can resist the enemy's attacks. It's a package deal because they all work together to keep us safe. And if we want to live victorious lives, we need to pray this armor on us daily.

So fasten the belt of truth around your waist, and let justice be your breastplate. Put on shoes that make you ready to share the good news of peace with others. Pick up and carry the shield of faith, which will enable you to extinguish every flaming arrow the enemy shoots your way. And lastly, don't forget the helmet of salvation and the sword of the Spirit—God's Word. This powerful combination will help you stand your ground when attacks come your way.

What piece of armor connects most with your heart right now? Is the Holy Spirit highlighting a specific piece that you've not been using? Spend some time meditating on each item and how it will help keep you safe. Ask God for insight and revelation.

We're not left unprotected and at the mercy of the devil's schemes. We don't have to navigate the ups and downs of life feeling exposed. We don't have to feel like a sitting duck or an easy target. God loves us too much to leave us defenseless. He wants us to boldly pick up each item, secure it, and use it.

DEAR LORD, YOU ALWAYS THINK OF EVERYTHING,
JUST LIKE A LOVING EARTHLY FATHER WOULD DO. I'M IN
AWE OF THE DETAILED ARMOR YOU'VE PROVIDED FOR
ME. HELP ME TO REMEMBER I ALWAYS HAVE ACCESS TO IT
AND TO PRAY IT EACH DAY. IN JESUS' NAME. AMEN.

The Power of Prayer

Pray always. Pray in the Spirit. Pray about everything in
every way you know how! And keeping all this in mind,
pray on behalf of God's people. Keep on praying feverishly,
and be on the lookout until evil has been stayed.

EPHESIANS 6:18 VOICE

Prayer is a powerful tool in the lives of believers. It's a direct line of communication to our Father in heaven. We don't have to pray through someone else or follow any specific formula. We don't have to observe any oppressive rules or save up our prayers to share at a specific time of day. And we also don't have to use big, flowery words in an effort to impress the Lord.

Anytime and anyplace, we can simply open our mouths and talk to God. We can pray silently in our minds. We can say what we need to say and ask for what we are lacking. We can pray in joy or in heartbreak. We can talk to God about the trivial and the tragic. The worries and the wins. The challenges and the celebrations. The anxieties and the aspirations. The hurt and the hallelujah. We can even pray liquid prayers, letting our tears fall from our eyes without saying a word at all. Prayer is an essential part of each day for any courageous woman of God because it keeps His presence top of mind and trains our focus on His goodness.

What about you? Are you talking to God about the clashes

you're dealing with at work? Do you talk about your struggles to love the unlovable and forgive the unforgivable? Are you unpacking with Him the deep insecurities keeping you stuck? Does the Lord hear you share your fears and worries about the future? Is He your confidant regarding your broken heart? Are you thanking Him for the open doors of opportunity? Does He get credit for a restored relationship that felt irreparable? Are you praising God for healing and restoration? There is always something to talk to Him about!

DEAR LORD, I APPRECIATE THAT I CAN TALK DIRECTLY TO YOU AT ANY TIME OF THE DAY OR NIGHT. YOU WANT TO BE MY CONSTANT COMPANION, AND KNOWING THAT NOTHING IS OFF-LIMITS TO DISCUSS IN YOUR PRESENCE IS SUCH A GIFT. FROM THE GOOD TO THE BAD, THE EASY TO THE HARD, I CAN BE OPEN AND HONEST. LET A PRAYER TO YOU BE CONSTANTLY ON MY LIPS. IN JESUS' NAME. AMEN.

Renewed by God

"Yes, indeed—God is my salvation. I trust, I won't
be afraid. GOD—yes GOD!—is my strength and song,
best of all, my salvation!" Joyfully you'll pull up buckets
of water from the wells of salvation. And as you do it,
you'll say, "Give thanks to GOD. Call out his name.
Ask him anything! Shout to the nations, tell them what
he's done, spread the news of his great reputation!"

ISAIAH 12:2–4 MSG

In this passage, we can see that God gave His people a renewed confidence. He gave them a new purpose. In His graciousness, they were recharged with newfound strength and determination. And they felt a revived connection to the Lord. Sometimes what we need the most is a holy reboot to get us back on track and ready to move forward.

Can you recall a time when you experienced this kind of joy, enthusiasm, and fresh revelation? Maybe it came from a healing or a restored sense of purpose. Maybe you finally experienced true peace and comfort in a messy situation. Or maybe God showed up in such a mighty way that you had a glimpse of His breathtaking glory in action.

Such a reboot can manifest in different ways. It could be a jolt to the system, making you excited about your faith once more. It may humble you speechless. It may give you great love for God and compassion for others. Or it may let you see God in a different light, sparking an attitude of gratitude. Regardless, it is good.

So often we just scoot through life relying on our own strength. We rest in our own wisdom, which is flawed and shortsighted. We mindlessly put one foot in front of the other to get through our day, hoping to avoid any blowups or slipups. This isn't victorious living in Christ.

Ask the Lord to infuse your heart and mind with a fresh renewal of faith. Ask boldly and with great expectation. Ask and let His kindness wash over you. Ask for His generosity to fill any empty places. Because every good thing comes from God's hands.

DEAR LORD, I'M SO GRATEFUL FOR YOUR GOODNESS
THAT BLESSES ME THROUGH FAITH. WOULD YOU RENEW
MY DESIRE FOR YOU? WOULD YOU REKINDLE MY
ENTHUSIASM FOR FOLLOWING YOUR WILL AND WAYS?
WOULD YOU REMIND ME OF WHY I FELL IN LOVE WITH
YOU IN THE FIRST PLACE? IN JESUS' NAME. AMEN.

Knowing Who God Is

You are my rock and my fortress—my soul's sanctuary!
Therefore, for the sake of Your reputation, be my leader,
my guide, my navigator, my commander. Save me from the
snare that has been secretly set out for me, for You are my
protection. I entrust my spirit into Your hands. You have
redeemed me, O Eternal, God of faithfulness and truth.

PSALM 31:3–5 VOICE

Friend, have you ever felt this way? You've tried and tried to manage things your way and have come to the end of yourself. You've made decisions based on your limited wisdom, and it hasn't been serving you well. You've stood in your feeble human strength and failed. Why do we ever try to go it alone? Why do we do anything without asking God for help? The psalmist knew the power of faith. Whether out of desperation or experience—or both—he had a clear understanding of who the Lord is and what He can do.

This passage tells us that God is our rock. He is our fortress. He's a sanctuary for our soul. And this is why we can trust Him to lead us through every difficulty. We can look confidently to Him as our guide through this life. He is our navigator to lead us through the storms, our commander when we need direction.

The Lord sees all and knows all. No wicked plan forged

against us will escape His purview, because He is our infallible protector. We can believe in His care and compassion because His love never fails. We are blessed to be in relationship with the God of faithfulness and truth.

Are you struggling to find the courage to let the Lord lead? Is it too hard to give up control to an invisible God because you can't see or touch Him? Does it feel safer to let someone else guide you through tricky situations, like a husband, friend, or parent? Do you worry that God may miss something dire in your circumstances and let you down?

Search your heart and ask the tough questions. Let God open your eyes to the reasons that trust is so challenging. Listen with expectation for His prompting. Look for new paths of healing and direction. And then boldly adopt the psalmist's revelation of who God is and walk it out with purpose.

DEAR LORD, HELP ME TRUST YOU MORE THAN ANYONE
OR ANYTHING ELSE. IN JESUS' NAME. AMEN.

The God Who Gives

But thanks be to God, Who gives us the victory [making us conquerors] through our Lord Jesus Christ. Therefore, my beloved brethren, be firm (steadfast), immovable, always abounding in the work of the Lord [always being superior, excelling, doing more than enough in the service of the Lord], knowing and being continually aware that your labor in the Lord is not futile [it is never wasted or to no purpose].

1 CORINTHIANS 15:57–58 AMPC

We each have a calling, something God planned in advance for us to accomplish. Maybe yours is to be a speaker or writer. Maybe it's to teach or command. It could be a call to serve halfway around the globe or be a stay-at-home mom. His plan may even be to start a company, lead a movement, or manage a ministry. Whatever it is, keep your eyes focused on God, who will give you all you need to do it well.

Will it be hard? Following His path often is, because the devil will try to derail you at every turn. *Will it take you out of your comfort zone?* Probably! What God asks usually takes His strength and wisdom to walk out. But, friend, faith is an adventure, and with Him is the safest and best place to be.

He will make us conquerors. Through God we will find victory. As we look to Him for protection and provision, the Lord will make us steadfast and immovable. He will enable us to do the work set forth with passion and purpose. And we can rest knowing God will waste nothing we experience, instead using it for our good and His glory.

Bathe each day in prayer, asking God to strengthen you in the right ways and at the right times. Ask for discernment to know what is true and right, and for the wisdom to adhere to it without fail. Approach the Lord in expectation, believing His heart for you is pure. Praise Him for all He will enable you to accomplish through His hand. Be bold in your requests, for you are His daughter and He delights in giving good things to those who love Him.

DEAR LORD, THANK YOU FOR CALLING AND EQUIPPING ME TO SERVE YOU IN MEANINGFUL WAYS. HELP ME TO TRUST YOU AS I STEP OUT AND FOLLOW YOUR LEAD. WHAT AN HONOR TO LET MY LIFE POINT TO YOU IN HEAVEN. IN JESUS' NAME. AMEN.

Tongue-Tied

*Because of Me, naysayers and doubters will try to make
an example out of you by trying you before rulers and
kings. When this happens—when you are arrested,
dragged to court—don't worry about what to say or how
to say it. The words you should speak will be given to
you. For at that moment, it will not be you speaking;
it will be the Spirit of your Father speaking through you.*

MATTHEW 10:18–20 VOICE

Have you ever been worried about how you will navigate a hard conversation? Sometimes the anxiety can be so strong that we're tempted to avoid talking altogether! It can be scary to open up to someone because it often brings up all sorts of insecurities. On occasion, quite a bit of stress arises when we want to share God with others. What if we say too much or say it the wrong way? What if we get tongue-tied? What if we forget the point we're trying to make?

Today's verse is Jesus talking to His apostles, preparing them to go out and share the good news on their own. He was reminding them they would be empowered to know what they should say and encouraging them to do the work at hand. It was a pep talk of sorts but also a commission to be strong, brave, and confident. And to trust that the right words would come at the right time through the help of the Holy Spirit. Their obedience would be rewarded.

Since we read it was the Spirit's job to give them the right words to speak, we can be assured He will do the same for us as believers. A precedent has been set. That means when we're overcome by fear or struggling to find the words, we can trust the Holy Spirit to intervene. It's not up to us alone. What a comfort to know He will speak through us.

Have you seen this happen in your life? Can you remember a time you said the perfect thing and it caught you off guard? Have you felt the words come when the second before you had nothing? Friend, ask God to settle your nerves, and then simply trust Him.

DEAR LORD, HELP ME REST IN YOUR PROMISE TO PROVIDE ME WITH THE WORDS TO SPEAK. I DON'T NEED TO WRITE THE SCRIPT OR STRESS ABOUT IT. INSTEAD, I CAN TRUST YOU'LL AWAYS EQUIP ME WITH EVERYTHING I NEED TO SHARE YOUR GOODNESS. IN JESUS' NAME. AMEN.

God's Got You

"Count on it: Everyone who had it in for you will end up
out in the cold—real losers. Those who worked against
you will end up empty-handed—nothing to show for their
lives. When you go out looking for your old adversaries
you won't find them—not a trace of your old enemies,
not even a memory. That's right. Because I, your GOD,
have a firm grip on you and I'm not letting go. I'm telling
you, 'Don't panic. I'm right here to help you.' "

ISAIAH 41:11–13 MSG

How does it bless your heart to know that God's firm grip on you won't falter? He promises never to let go of you, friend. His presence is continuous, and His love is steadfast. You are held in both good times and bad times and every time in between. And when you feel panic begin to rise from inside because of shaky situations, remember these beautiful truths. They will be a game changer.

While we will face a variety of grim times here on planet Earth, rest assured that those who have worked against you will pay a price. They will stand before the Lord and answer for what they've done. But with God's help, you will be an overcomer. You may sustain a few bumps and bruises along the way, but you will be left standing. The Lord will ensure that you are cared for and comforted. Your difficult days won't ever go unnoticed.

Let go of the offenses keeping you up at night. Release the anger that has taken up residency in your heart. Don't let bitterness rob you of peace any longer. Instead, lay them at the feet of the Lord and rest in His very capable hands. Your job is to believe and trust that He will act. You are to hope and persist in God's goodness. And you're to surrender the painful past to Him to sort out and bring healing.

Friend, God has you and He's not letting go. Through prayer and time in the Word, your faith will become a source of real strength. It will create in you a courage and confidence to be a fearless woman of God, bold in her belief and settled in her spirit.

DEAR LORD, I KNOW YOU'VE GOT ME AND WON'T LET ME FALL. I KNOW I AM HELD. IN JESUS' NAME. AMEN.

Wanting Heaven
over Earth

The One who has worked and tailored us for this is God
Himself, who has gifted His Spirit to us as a pledge toward our
permanent home. In light of this, we live with a daring passion
and know that our time spent in this body is also time we are
not present with the Lord. The path we walk is charted by
faith, not by what we see with our eyes. There is no doubt that
we live with a daring passion, but in the end we prefer to be
gone from this body so that we can be at home with the Lord.

2 CORINTHIANS 5:5–8 VOICE

How many times have you wished for Jesus' return, especially when life has felt overwhelming? Maybe it's because everyone is acting crazy or the state of the world is stressing you out. Maybe it's due to financial frustrations that never seem to go away. Does it feel like you're fighting an uphill battle in your marriage, or are you tired of navigating singlehood? Does a sense of hopelessness define your mood most of the time? Yes, we're all ready to be home with the Lord, and it makes sense.

When we became believers, a beautiful transformation took place. Slowly but surely, the things of this world began to lose their sparkle. Our spiritual eyes allowed us to see the decay here while our heart started longing for eternal things instead. What once felt good and right no longer satisfies because of our faith! And we long to be with God in heaven rather than in a fallen and broken world. But we are still here for a reason.

Don't forget we have a holy calling to walk out on earth. So let us be gutsy because we have the Holy Spirit as a guarantee and a guide. We can stand boldly through the trials and tribulations, knowing God's presence is always with us. We can live by what we know is true and righteous, even though we can't see the Lord Himself before us. With Him, we can be comforted during our time here. We can experience peace every day. Ask God to help you live with a daring passion here while also balancing a deep longing to be home with Him.

DEAR LORD, SOMETIMES I WANT TO GIVE UP AND JUST BE AT HOME WITH YOU. BUT I HAVE THE HOLY SPIRIT WHO BRINGS ME COMFORT AND ENCOURAGES ME TO BE STRONG IN FAITH. HELP ME LIVE WITH HOPE AND GREAT EXPECTATION UNTIL I SEE YOU FACE-TO-FACE. IN JESUS' NAME. AMEN.

The Balance Is Shifting

So, with confidence and hope in this message, strengthen
those with feeble hands, shore up the weak-kneed and
weary. Tell those who worry, the anxious and fearful,
"Take strength; have courage! There's nothing to fear. Look,
here—your God! Right here is your God! The balance is
shifting; God will right all wrongs. None other than God
will give you success. He is coming to make you safe."

ISAIAH 35:3–4 VOICE

If you are struggling with worry, anxiety, and fear today, let the passage of scripture above be just the encouragement you need to stand strong. If your hands are tired and your knees are weak, let the Holy Spirit minister to you right now.

God's goodness is yours for the taking. His splendor is on full display! So when you feel overwhelmed and underwater, be intentional to take each negative thought captive and remember who He is. God must be where you go for hope and comfort.

With the Lord on your side, Isaiah says the balance will shift. In those times when you feel oppressed by hard circumstances, sweet relief is coming. Where you have been frustrated, peace will soon abound. As you navigate disappointing relationships, clarity will fill your mind and wisdom will reveal the right path forward. Where you've been undone by life, He will heal and restore. Where you have felt the sting of rejection or abandonment, the Lord will impress on you your unmatched value. Full acceptance by God will override all those times you feel shut down or shut out. The King delights in His creation!

So stand up, sweet one. Let this message embolden you to stand even taller. You are fully known and fully loved, and the balance in those hard situations is shifting. In an act of obedience and surrender, start placing every heartbreak at God's feet. One by one. Day by day. Release every anxious thought. Yield every fearful feeling. Open your spiritual eyes and see that your God is right here with you. Immovable. Fixed. Permanent.

DEAR LORD, I CONFESS I'M FEELING FEEBLE
AND WEAK-KNEED. I'M PLAGUED WITH WORRY,
ANXIETY, AND FEAR. PLEASE STRENGTHEN ME AS I
MEDITATE ON YOUR PROMISE TO NEVER LEAVE NOR
FORSAKE ME. COMFORT ME WITH THE KNOWLEDGE
THAT YOU WILL RIGHT EVERY WRONG. I TRUST
YOUR LOVE AND CARE. IN JESUS' NAME. AMEN.

The God Who Satisfies

Stay away from the love of money; be satisfied with what
you have. For God has said, "I will never, never fail you
nor forsake you." That is why we can say without any
doubt or fear, "The Lord is my Helper, and I am not
afraid of anything that mere man can do to me."

Hebrews 13:5–6 tlb

The world uses countless distractions to lure us away from God. So many things are designed to steal our attention and keep us looking for hope in all the wrong places. This world has a way of making sin look good and necessary. And it offers solutions that do little, if anything, to nurture the hearts of believers. The truth is that we will never find real satisfaction from a counterfeit savior. But we certainly try.

To be clear, nothing is wrong with enjoying this life. Money in and of itself isn't bad. Spending your resources on a fun vacation with family and friends is about bonding. Outfitting your college student's dorm room is a way to show that you care. A trip to the salon isn't an act of selfishness, because buying what you need or want isn't wrong or bad. And even splurging from time to time won't land you in a divine time-out.

But when we love money more than we love God, and when we look to it to settle an anxious heart, we're crossing a line.

Why? Because that's what the Lord offers to do for us, and He is a jealous God. More than anything else, we're to look to Him as our provider. Rather than depending on anything this world offers, we should be seeking satisfaction in His presence alone. Peace, contentment, and comfort come from the Lord, not from retail therapy or from anything money can buy.

It takes guts to overlook earthly treasures and store up ones in heaven instead. Be intentional as you pray, asking God to keep your eyes focused on Him. Pray earnestly and unceasingly. Share your struggles with authenticity. And do your part by consistently bringing your heart back into alignment with His. Keep a tight rein on what you crave, always turning those longings back to the one who can satisfy.

- -

DEAR LORD, I CONFESS THE TIMES I'VE ASKED THE WORLD TO HELP ME FEEL BETTER. I'VE INVESTED TIME AND TREASURE THERE, HOPING TO REACH A CERTAIN LEVEL OF COMFORT AND EASE. BUT I KNOW YOU ARE THE ONLY ONE WHO CAN MEET MY EVERY NEED IN THE RIGHT WAYS. IN JESUS' NAME. AMEN.

A Good Life

*I will bless the Eternal, whose wise teaching orchestrates
my days and centers my mind at night. He is ever
present with me; at all times He goes before me. I will
not live in fear or abandon my calling because He
stands at my right hand. This is a good life—my heart
is glad, my soul is full of joy, and my body is at rest.*

PSALM 16:7–9 VOICE

If we choose to let it be true, fear will no longer have the upper hand. It will lose its grip on us when we are intentional to keep our mind trained on God for help. Every time we open the Word and soak in its teachings, especially in those fearful moments, our anxious hearts will be settled. It's a supernatural process with lasting effects. You see, faith has a powerful way of quashing fear. So whether we need God's calming once a day or once an hour, we're invited to seek His presence at any time.

The Bible is alive and active. It reveals to us who God is and who He is not. And if we take it seriously—opening it every day and meditating on what it has to say—we'll notice a difference in our days. Spending concentrated time in its pages, soaking in key scriptures that speak directly to our hearts, will help keep our minds clear during the night hours too. The Word holds life-changing truths that meet us right where we are, giving us exactly what we need to be comforted and compelled.

Reading the Bible also makes us keenly aware of God's presence. It's often when we feel the closest to Him. Whether we're engaging with the poignant stories of Bible characters, the comfort found in the Psalms, the wisdom shared in Proverbs, or the relevant teachings of Jesus, sitting in the Word creates deeper connections with the Father. It aligns our heart with His. It gives us a fresh perspective on the struggles we're facing. It equips us and guides us as we move forward. It helps us understand that God is with us. And it emboldens us with courage and confidence to take that next step of faith.

So, friend, let's rejoice that we have a God who wants us to know He is with us and promises to give us hope and help. Let's be grateful that He makes us bold. And let's choose to spend time with God in the Word and in prayer every day.

- -

**DEAR LORD, THANK YOU FOR THIS GOOD
LIFE WITH YOU! IN JESUS' NAME. AMEN.**

Praying with Thanksgiving

Thank you! Everything in me says "Thank you!" Angels
listen as I sing my thanks. I kneel in worship facing your
holy temple and say it again: "Thank you!" Thank you for
your love, thank you for your faithfulness; most holy is your
name, most holy is your Word. The moment I called out,
you stepped in; you made my life large with strength.

PSALM 138:1–3 MSG

There's something powerful about saying "Thank you." To shift
your attitude from one of entitlement or expectation to one of
genuine appreciation changes the atmosphere. The psalmist knows
this full well. Do we?

Think about your prayer life for a moment. Do your conversations with the Lord consist of request after request? Do they
come off as demanding? Are you often desperate and begging
for Him to show up? Do you lack the faith that He hears you or
that He will respond? Do you pray from fearful places, worried
and full of anxiety? While we are invited to go to God at any time
and with any and every concern, what if we shifted our focus?

Friend, let's remember to pray from a place of confidence
instead of chaos. Why not praise the Lord at the front end of
your struggle, telling Him you know He is at work in mysterious
and wonderful ways. Tell God you trust His plans. Thank Him

for having your back without fail. Show gratitude that He always knows what's best, even if it's not what you prayed for.

Reworking our prayers this way not only blesses God but also reminds us that He is trustworthy. It strengthens us by assuring us we have someone on our side who fully understands the challenges we're facing. It allows our hearts to rest and find peace. It enables us to hope with expectation! It quiets doubt and worry. And it sets us up to believe that the will of God will be done at the right time and in the right ways.

So how about it? Be gutsy and change things up. Let every prayer be filled with gratitude for our magnificent Father. Talk to Him from a place of thanksgiving. Be full of genuine and sincere appreciation. And feel the shift in your heart as fear is silenced.

DEAR LORD, ALL I CAN SAY IS THANK YOU FOR
ALWAYS WORKING FOR MY GOOD AND YOUR GLORY.
I'M PROFOUNDLY GRATEFUL. IN JESUS' NAME. AMEN.

Reaping and Sowing

*Make no mistake: God can't be mocked. What you give
is what you get. What you sow, you harvest. Those who
sow seeds into their flesh will only harvest destruction
from their sinful nature. But those who sow seeds into
the Spirit shall harvest everlasting life from the Spirit.
May we never tire of doing what is good and right before
our Lord because in His season we shall bring in a great
harvest if we can just persist. So seize any opportunity
the Lord gives you to do good things and be a blessing to
everyone, especially those within our faithful family.*

GALATIANS 6:7–10 VOICE

The concept of reaping and sowing is a constant in God's Word. According to today's passage of scripture, *what you sow, you harvest.* Think about that for a minute. If you're focused on satisfying your flesh—cooperating with things that don't point to God—that is what will manifest in your life. It will be marked by sin, negativity, and godlessness. And the price of that kind of life is heavy.

On the other hand, if you are sowing into your faith and being purposeful to do what is right and just in God's eyes, righteous fruit will come from it. You will feel energized to follow the Lord's leading as your relationship with Him deepens. And you'll receive a blessing for being obedient.

In both scenarios, the reality is that we *will* have trouble. The Bible clearly says demanding times are inevitable because we live in a sinful and broken world. Thinking this life will be easy or problem-free is an unrealistic expectation. We *will* battle fear and worry. There *will* be anxiousness and stress. There *will* be pain, grief, and disappointment. There *will* be chaos in our hearts and minds. Yes, anticipate these!

But when we are faithful to stay in a posture of surrender to the Lord, we'll experience His presence through all of life's difficulties. No, we won't be spared from the hardships of this life; however, our faith will keep us strong. It will keep us from giving up and walking away. It will make us bold and confident as we trust God's plan. And it will make us hopeful.

DEAR LORD, GIVE ME WISDOM AS I CHOOSE
WHERE TO SOW MY TIME AND ENERGY. GIVE ME
COURAGE TO INVEST IN THE KINGDOM OVER
EVERY FLESHLY DESIRE. IN JESUS' NAME, AMEN.

When Fear Keeps You Quiet

Now the leaders were surprised and confused. They looked at Peter and John and realized they were typical peasants— uneducated, utterly ordinary fellows—with extraordinary confidence. The leaders recognized them as companions of Jesus, then they turned their attention to the third man standing beside them—recently lame, now standing tall and healthy. What could they say in response to all this? Because they were at a loss about what to do, they excused the prisoners so the council could deliberate in private.

ACTS 4:13–15 VOICE

This amazing account from Acts should be of great comfort to those fearful of speaking about God's goodness to others. You might think you're not smart enough or you might be confused on what to say. Maybe you're insecure about sharing your faith, afraid you'll get tongue-tied. Or maybe you're worried you'll look or sound silly. When you step out in faith to do God's work, you will be given what's necessary to do it well.

You see, God doesn't call the equipped. He equips the called. And just like Peter and John experienced, the time spent in the presence of the Lord has far-reaching benefits. The disciples weren't well educated. They didn't come from wealth or have excessive money to spend. Chances are they had little to no experience speaking to crowds. Scripture says they were unschooled and ordinary. But what they had was time invested in their Lord.

Rest assured, the same is true for you. Every Bible study you work through matters. Those early mornings poring over God's Word before the rest of your family rises? They matter. Spending time in godly community, encouraging one another in the faith, makes a difference. Talking to the Lord in prayer regularly, and then listening and looking for His answers, sows seeds of faith.

So when you're put in a position to speak truth to others, these habits and practices will come to fruition. And like God's followers back in the day, you'll be given extraordinary confidence as you trust Him for it. Your fear will melt away as you minister through His help.

DEAR LORD, I'M SO ENCOURAGED TO READ ABOUT PETER AND JOHN AND HOW YOU FILLED THEM WITH WORDS AND AUTHORITY. KNOWING YOU WILL EQUIP ME AS NEEDED ALLOWS ME TO STEP OUT IN FAITH AND TRUST YOUR PROVISION IN THE MOMENT. HELP ME TO LIVE WITH SUCH CONFIDENCE EVERY DAY. IN JESUS' NAME. AMEN.

Even a Little Faith

*Because you have so little faith. I tell you this: if you had even
a faint spark of faith, even faith as tiny as a mustard seed,
you could say to this mountain, "Move from here to there,"
and because of your faith, the mountain would move. If you
had just a sliver of faith, you would find nothing impossible.*

MATTHEW 17:20 VOICE

. . . .

According to Jesus, we don't need a venti-sized faith to navigate
this life. It's not the dimensions of our belief that matter, because
we have a God who is limitless. He is the one who honors the faith
we do have. And even if ours is small, it's backed by the Father,
whose presence is immeasurable. But we still must have it.

In what areas are you afraid to trust God today? What challenges are you struggling to release into His hands? It's often
difficult to give up control over a tender circumstance. If we've
been burned by people in the past, that negative experience hin-
ders our ability to have faith in a Father we can't see. And it can
prevent us from taking that leap and placing our heart in His care.

Faith is a choice. It's choosing to have confidence in something
or someone. And it's a decision we must make every day.

Great encouragement can be found in the Bible. As you read
the stories of Noah, Abraham, Joseph, Esther, Daniel, and Job,
you'll see God's faithfulness on full display. Their willingness to

trust Him proved to be a solid decision. In their lives, the Lord had a perfect track record. If you haven't checked yet, take a moment to see His perfect track record in your life too.

Think of the relationship He restored that looked forever broken. Recall the resources that showed up at the right time. Do you remember praying for new opportunities, and then they came? Did you ask for healing, and it happened? Even a little faith was honored by God.

Don't let fear keep you from taking a step toward trusting Him. Refuse to partner with the desire to handle life's problems in your own strength. Instead, embrace God's promises to love and guide you each day. Make a conscious decision to believe He is who He says He is.

DEAR LORD, THANK YOU FOR HONORING EVEN
A LITTLE FAITH. I KNOW THE HOLY SPIRIT WILL
CONTINUE TO MATURE ME SO I CAN TRUST
YOU EVEN MORE. IN JESUS' NAME. AMEN.

Nothing Can Separate

"For I am convinced that nothing can ever separate us from his love. Death can't, and life can't. The angels won't, and all the powers of hell itself cannot keep God's love away. Our fears for today, our worries about tomorrow, or where we are—high above the sky, or in the deepest ocean— nothing will ever be able to separate us from the love of God demonstrated by our Lord Jesus Christ when he died for us."

ROMANS 8:38–39 TLB

In this life, love is conditional. We may think nothing can break the bond we have with another person, but then we learn just how fragile it is. We've had personal experiences of terrible heartbreak again and again. And the truth is that for most, the commitment level in relationships is shaky at best, challenging us to trust love at all.

What a relief to know we can't lose God's love. There's nothing unstable about it. He chooses to love us with a steadfast commitment that cannot be broken. It's unshakable. And that's a good thing, because we are imperfect in all we do.

When you take out your anger on God, His love stands. When you turn your back in rebellion, His love sticks. When you're reckless with your relationship, His love never wavers. When you cling to sin rather than the Savior, His love remains uncompromised.

When you are consumed with fear, God is with you. When worry and anxiety get top billing, He is still with you. When insecurities take all your energy and time, He's right there with you. When you're a complete mess and can't seem to find your emotional footing, the Lord's presence is with you.

Scripture says that nothing will ever be able to separate us from the love of God. Meditate on that truth for a moment. He can't be deterred from being a part of your life. Nothing you say or do will keep the Lord from loving you any more or any less than He does right now. Your human condition will never scare Him off.

You are fully and completely loved. You are fully seen and fully known. God knows every flaw and imperfection and limitation. So fear not, friend. For there is nothing about you that will ever discourage Him from delighting in His creation.

DEAR LORD, IT FEELS ALMOST IMPOSSIBLE TO BELIEVE
IN YOUR STEADFAST LOVE. HELP ME EMBRACE IT
AND THRIVE IN IT. IN JESUS' NAME. AMEN.

The Lord Knows Every Detail

If you want the truth, this is what the Eternal has to say:
"You will remain in Babylon for 70 years. When that time
is over, I will come to you, and I will keep My promise
of bringing you back home. For I know the plans I have
for you," says the Eternal, "plans for peace, not evil,
to give you a future and hope—never forget that."

JEREMIAH 29:10–11 VOICE

For context, this is a portion of the letter that the prophet Jeremiah wrote from Jerusalem to the elders, priests, prophets, and others who had been taken to Babylon by King Nebuchadnezzar. It was a letter from God to those He had exiled, telling them to make themselves at home because they'd be there a while. And then His plans moving forward are revealed in today's verse.

The takeaway is that the Lord knows exactly where He's leading us. He has full knowledge of what this time looks like and why it's important we experience what's ahead. God's blueprints are well thought out, each detail arranged for maximum effect—which means we can trust they are always for our good and His glory. Friend, we can be confident that God's plans bring peace, not evil, so we can have hopeful hearts. And because His promises cannot be broken or derailed, we can stand strong and embrace them wholeheartedly.

We may not have access to the particulars, but we can know who has lovingly created them. His intentionality is trustworthy. We can put our fears to rest and wait in expectation for His goodness to prevail. Our worries don't have the power to undo God's purpose. We can thank Him for orchestrating events today that will grow our trust muscles and make us more like Christ. We can pray for a greater measure of faith to believe that the will of God will be done. We can ask for a boldness that keeps us steady.

Just as God promised, the Israelites returned home seventy years later. Jerusalem's wall was rebuilt, and worship was reestablished in the city. Let these truths encourage you today. You can be courageous in your faith because He is continually faithful.

DEAR LORD, HELP ME STAND STRONG IN MY FAITH, KNOWING YOUR WORD IS UNWAVERING. LET MY HEART BE CONFIDENT TO REST IN YOU AS I WAIT FOR YOUR WILL TO BE DONE. IN JESUS' NAME. AMEN.

Knowing God Hears You

"At that time, you will call out for Me, and I will hear.
You will pray, and I will listen. You will look for Me
intently, and you will find Me. Yes, I will be found by
you," says the Eternal, "and I will restore your fortunes
and gather you from all the nations where you've been
scattered—all the places where I have driven you. I will
bring you back to the land that is your rightful home."

JEREMIAH 29:12–14 VOICE

Today's passage of scripture directly follows the one we discussed in the previous devotional. God is forecasting ahead for the Israelites through a letter from Jeremiah, letting them know about their captivity and coming release to return home. And in this section, the Lord says some especially encouraging words to them. . .words that also bolster us as believers today.

Do you ever wonder if God hears you cry out for help? Sometimes we might feel as if our prayers don't make it all the way up to heaven. We may pray repeatedly, asking and begging Him to bring relief, but nothing seems to change. In our fear and frustration, we just give up and take matters into our own hands. But let God's words bring comfort and truth to your heart right now.

Just as He promised to hear His people call out from Babylon, He also promises to hear us. When we pray, God will listen. When we look for Him wholeheartedly, we will find Him. And because He vowed restoration and followed through with it, a precedent has been set. That means we can ask Him to do it again. We can remind God of past works through prayer.

So be gutsy in your belief. Be a courageous woman of faith who knows God's heart for her is good. Pray often and honestly. Pray with expectation, certain He recognizes your voice and is listening with intent. Be full of thanksgiving because you have 24-7 access to the Creator. And pray with peace, trusting that no matter what, God's plans for your life will come together in miraculous ways.

DEAR LORD, WHAT A BLESSING TO KNOW YOUR
EYES AND EARS ARE TRAINED ON ME. THANK YOU
FOR BEING SUCH AN ATTENTIVE FATHER. HELP ME BE
PERSISTENT AND PATIENT IN PRAYER AS I WAIT FOR
YOUR PLANS TO BE REVEALED AT THE RIGHT TIME.
THERE IS NO OTHER LIKE YOU. IN JESUS' NAME. AMEN.

Where Is Your Allegiance?

Shadrach, Meshach, and Abednego replied,
"O Nebuchadnezzar, we are not worried about what will
happen to us. If we are thrown into the flaming furnace, our
God is able to deliver us; and he will deliver us out of your
hand, Your Majesty. But if he doesn't, please understand, sir,
that even then we will never under any circumstance serve
your gods or worship the gold statue you have erected."

DANIEL 3:16–18 TLB

The faith of these three young men is remarkable. Not only were they snatched from their beloved homeland and exiled to Babylon, but they also were expected to fall in line with the pagan customs. There were strict expectations for Shadrach, Meshach, and Abednego in their new living situation, including rejecting their God and worshipping golden statue gods, appeasing the king of the land by showing a switch in allegiance. Remarkably, they stood strong with the Lord.

They knew God had the power and authority to deliver them from the fire. They fully believed He was capable of rescue. But they also recognized that God's plan might be different from their personal hopes, and these men chose to trust Him regardless. They showed guts and grit, fueled by steadfast faith.

Every day, you get to make the same choice. You may not

face an actual fire for your beliefs, but you will be bombarded with false gods nonetheless. You will find yourself facing expectations and demands that feel overwhelming. Different people and circumstances will fight for your allegiance. And often, without meaning to, you will give it to them.

So, friend, are you paying attention? Is your faith steadfast? Think about the people, pleasures, and projects that top your list. Who or what gets your focused time and energy? Where does God fit into your day as you take time to read the Word and talk to Him? The truth is that unless we make a conscious decision to start with God, invite Him to help us navigate our to-do list, and close our eyes at night with fresh prayers on our lips, worshipping worldly idols becomes easier. Wrong priorities will zap us of energy and joy. And we'll lack the resolve to trust God, whether He intervenes in our ways or His.

DEAR LORD, I RECOGNIZE THAT MANY THINGS ARE
PULLING ON ME. THERE ARE PEOPLE WHO EXPECT MY
TIME AND SITUATIONS THAT DEMAND MY ATTENTION.
HELP ME KEEP FOCUSED ON THE RIGHT PRIORITIES SO MY
FAITH REMAINS STEADFAST IN YOU. IN JESUS' NAME. AMEN.

Removing the Shame

Don't be afraid, for there is no one to shame you.
Don't fear humiliation, for there is no one to disgrace you.
The shame of your younger years and the sorrow of your
widowhood are over. You'll forget those days as if they
never happened. Because the One who made you will be
your husband; the One called Commander of heavenly
armies will set you right again, the Holy One of Israel.
It's not for nothing that He is called "God of all the earth."

ISAIAH 54:4–5 VOICE

God is our source for true confidence and courage. Through Him, we can have lasting grit to stand assured about our worth. We no longer only hope for it. We don't have to muster it up on our own. Instead, we can know we're loved unconditionally by our heavenly Father, who is always working to bring much-needed restoration to our brokenness. The Lord will give us a clean slate—a fresh start—as He lovingly sets us right again.

Do you carry the heavy weight of shame for things you've done? Are you afraid of being judged by others for your shortcomings? Has sorrow infiltrated your mind relentlessly? Is the humiliation of your past eating you alive? Talk to God about it.

Friend, the Lord promises to heal your heart and remove the burden of what has been if you'll ask. He will remove embarrassment over your bad choices. He won't let you drown in humiliation, even if others are trying to bring it on you for whatever reason. Ask God to strengthen your resolve and solidify your belief that you have value. As much as you may try to handle it yourself, the reality is that this is something only the Lord can do. And He will do it.

Where do you need God to erase the disgrace? Be bold and honest as you talk to Him about what's tangling your heart. Be persistent in your requests, praying without ceasing as you wait for the Lord to answer. Ask with expectation because you believe God heals and restores those who love Him. Pray with thanksgiving, knowing He won't leave you where you are. And have unshakable faith that the will of God will be done at the right time and in the right ways.

God wants you to be free! Believe it and ask for it!

DEAR LORD, I KNOW YOUR HEART FOR ME IS GOOD AND
THAT WHEN I ASK FOR HEALING AND RESTORATION,
YOU WILL BRING IT. THANKS FOR LOVING ME IN THE
MOST PERFECT WAYS. IN JESUS' NAME. AMEN.

The High Waves

Then Peter called to him: "Sir, if it is really you, tell me
to come over to you, walking on the water." "All right,"
the Lord said, "come along!" So Peter went over the side
of the boat and walked on the water toward Jesus. But
when he looked around at the high waves, he was terrified
and began to sink. "Save me, Lord!" he shouted.

MATTHEW 14:28–30 TLB

. . . .

Aren't you thankful that God included this story about Peter in the Bible? Knowing that even this man could lose faith at times brings much-needed encouragement to us today. Think about it. Peter walked with Jesus throughout His ministry. He saw the sick healed in significant ways. He was in the inner circle of trust with just a few others. He spoke on behalf of Jesus and performed miracles in His name. Peter had a front row seat to all that Christ did while on earth. He believed Jesus was who He said He was. And still, Peter's faith faltered.

Our human condition is messy. It pulls us away from faith because we're innately flawed and easily deceived. We're predisposed to selfishness and pride because we often think we're our own saviors. And even though we may have a close relationship with Jesus—one we nurture every day—there will be times we sink as we focus on the storms surrounding us. If it happened to a man like Peter, it can happen to us too. But chin up!

Let's remember that God isn't looking for perfection from us. Instead, He's looking for purposeful living. We're not expected to get it right every time. It's just not possible! God isn't waiting for us to save ourselves. We can't. When our faith fails and we begin to sink, it's a privilege (not a burden) to cry out for God to save us once again. And He will.

The reality is that we *will* face high waves in this life. It may be a marriage on the rocks or the challenge of parenting a child who isn't thriving. It may be financial stress from job loss or anxiety caused by a medical diagnosis. It may stem from therapy dealing with past trauma or fresh suffering. But if we keep our eyes on the Lord through it, we'll have the guts and grit to walk through the tumultuous seas of life.

DEAR LORD, HELP ME KNOW I AM SAFE WITH YOU.
BE MY ANCHOR SO I CAN STAND THROUGH THE
HIGH WAVES OF LIFE. IN JESUS' NAME. AMEN.

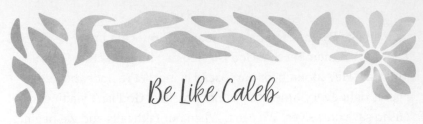

Be Like Caleb

This was their report: "We arrived in the land you sent us to see, and it is indeed a magnificent country—a land 'flowing with milk and honey.' Here is some fruit we have brought as proof. But the people living there are powerful, and their cities are fortified and very large; and what's more, we saw Anakim giants there! . . ." But Caleb reassured the people as they stood before Moses. "Let us go up at once and possess it," he said, "for we are well able to conquer it!"

Numbers 13:27–28, 30 TLB

Let's be like Caleb! It may take everything we have, but let's be gutsy women of faith who know the strength and power we have through the Lord.

Yes, we may be scared. We may face intense intimidation tactics that make us want to run and hide. As we peek at what we're up against, it may look impossible to defeat. We may feel hopeless. Victory may feel far away. And as we focus our attention on the giants—be they people or circumstances—we'll turn away scared and overwhelmed. But we weren't created to be afraid. In one form or another, the Bible tells us over 360 times not to be fearful. God doesn't want us to cower but to stand in strength through Him. We're to be like Caleb.

How would your life be different if you were able to embrace this truth? How would it change your mindset moving forward? What would it embolden you to do? Ask God to meet you in those fearful moments and help you be courageous. Ask for timely reminders that He is your strength and shield. Let Him grow your faith in meaningful ways so you're not starved for His goodness. Let Him settle your spirit with His unwavering love, because the result will be a supernatural power to look past the giants and see hope.

When fear threatens to overtake you, ask God to help you be like Caleb. He chose to see all the land could offer rather than those standing in the way. He trusted God's declaration that this was their land. He looked with his faith rather than his fear. And you can do the same thing when the giants begin to intimidate you.

DEAR LORD, HELP ME FIND THE COURAGE TO BE BOLD
AND HOPEFUL SO I DON'T GIVE IN TO WHATEVER GIANTS
ARE STANDING IN MY WAY. IN JESUS' NAME. AMEN.

Your Problems
Have Purpose

*We can rejoice, too, when we run into problems and trials,
for we know that they are good for us—they help us learn to be
patient. And patience develops strength of character in us and
helps us trust God more each time we use it until finally our
hope and faith are strong and steady. Then, when that happens,
we are able to hold our heads high no matter what happens
and know that all is well, for we know how dearly God loves
us, and we feel this warm love everywhere within us because
God has given us the Holy Spirit to fill our hearts with his love.*

ROMANS 5:3–5 TLB

The simple truth? In God's economy, our problems have a purpose. He never wastes anything, even the joy-stealing and spine-weakening trials we face. Is parenting a teen about to do you in? There's purpose! Are your aging parents driving you nutty? God is using it! Have your friends and family been stressing you out at times? He's up to something good! Does your daily to-do list overwhelm you, or are work challenges stirring up fear? God is growing you!

Be quick to go right to the Lord and ask for His insight. Let Him reveal His purposes. Ask for His perspective so you can rest in the knowledge that He'll use all for your good and His glory. You may not know when or how, but you can boldly believe it. And today's passage of scripture reveals it. Friend, that means you can trust God to be intimately involved in the difficulties of life. You can trust Him to bring purpose.

He may use tough times to teach you patience, build your character, or strengthen your trust muscles. The end game could be your faith, making it stronger and more resilient. Maybe it's hopefulness to keep you steady. Or it could be something more specific that God wants you to have for the road ahead. Regardless, we can know all is well because He is in charge. We can trust God's love because we know His heart for us is always good.

So stand strong, friend. This season will pass, and it will leave us with blessings.

DEAR LORD, WHAT A GIFT TO KNOW YOU WILL USE
EVERY PROBLEM FOR A PURPOSE. HELP ME TRUST YOU
IN THE MESSY MOMENTS. IN JESUS' NAME. AMEN.

Perfect Peace

He will keep in perfect peace all those who trust in him,
whose thoughts turn often to the Lord! Trust in the Lord God
always, for in the Lord Jehovah is your everlasting strength.

ISAIAH 26:3–4 TLB

As believers, we can have perfect peace even when life is rapidly hurling curveballs in our direction. We can find restful spaces as we're navigating the chaos and confusion of our circumstances. Our hearts can be settled despite the craziness surrounding us. And as we commit our hearts and minds into God's hands, He'll help us exhale stress and anxiety. But we must trust the Lord.

That means we cling to Him when the upsetting phone call comes. When we discover the betrayal, we go straight to God for comfort. When the medical treatment doesn't work, we open the Word of God and let scripture soothe us. As the devastating details of the situation are revealed, we pray for hope and help. And each messy moment that threatens to rob us of peace drives us to our knees and into His presence. God becomes our default button—the place we go for the relief we need.

In all things and in every way, the Lord promises to be our rock. He is our strong tower and safety net. His love provides stability when all else feels shaky. As we struggle to trust others to handle our tender hearts, God is faithful without fail. And He promises to be with us unceasingly. He plays the long game and is in it for keeps. Friend, we can trust in the Lord always.

How have you seen God's perfect peace manifest in your life? Can you remember a moment when a beautiful sense of calm washed over you when you should have been freaking out instead? Or maybe you've watched a friend or family member stay cool and collected in an incredibly challenging situation. Let the memories of these moments drive you back to the Lord every time, standing in truth and believing He is your everlasting strength.

DEAR LORD, HELP ME TO TRUST IN YOU ALWAYS
RATHER THAN LOOKING TO THE WORLD FOR COMFORT.
SCRIPTURE SAYS THAT IF MY FAITH IS SECURE IN YOU,
I WILL EXPERIENCE YOUR PERFECT PEACE EVEN IN THE
MOST DIFFICULT SITUATIONS. YOU ARE MY STRENGTH
AND THE ONE I LOOK TO FOR REASSURANCE THAT ALL
WILL BE OKAY IN THE END. IN JESUS' NAME. AMEN.

Doing It Scared

"In preparation for my audience with the king, do this: gather together all the Jews in Susa, and fast and pray for me. Intercede for me. For three days and nights, abstain from all food and drink. My maids and I will join you in this time. And after the three days, I will go in to the king and plead my people's case, even though it means breaking the law. And if I die, then I die!"

ESTHER 4:16 VOICE

Esther embraced her fear and used it to fuel her faith. Rather than shut her down, it catapulted her into action. Her courage is admirable because she approached the king without knowing how he would respond. She had no illusion her husband would accept her bold move. Yet Esther prepared her heart through fasting and prayer and then walked into the king's chamber with confidence. Even knowing that punishment by death was a possible outcome, she held her chin high and pleaded for her people.

We may not be facing a death sentence here and now, but there are certainly situations we must walk out that help us understand her fear. We may have to be whistleblowers for questionable activities at the office. We may have to speak honestly to answer a tough and pointed question from a superior. We may be called into hard conversations with an adult child who is exhibiting risky behaviors. We may have to call out a friend for a betrayal that is jeopardizing their reputation. Or we might be called to the witness stand in court to tell the hard truth about someone we care about deeply. It's not always easy to be on the front lines in life.

Had Esther not gone to the king and revealed Haman's diabolical plans, the results could have been catastrophic. She clearly understood the stakes and chose to be obedient anyway. She knew the king could choose to take her life, and by law, it would have been warranted. She realized the need to be honest about who she really was. And because she was gutsy and said yes, God used her in mighty ways to reveal evil and shut it down.

Tell the Lord you are willing and ready to be a modern-day Esther. Ask for doors to open and opportunities to present themselves. And ask Him for the guts and grit to take a stand for what is right.

DEAR LORD, MY ANSWER IS YES TO WHATEVER
PLANS YOU HAVE FOR ME TO SPEAK UP AND
SPEAK OUT. IN JESUS' NAME. AMEN.

No Reason to Fear God

We need have no fear of someone who loves us perfectly;
his perfect love for us eliminates all dread of what he
might do to us. If we are afraid, it is for fear of what
he might do to us and shows that we are not fully
convinced that he really loves us. So you see, our love
for him comes as a result of his loving us first.

1 JOHN 4:18–19 TLB

Sometimes we become fearful of God, worried He's mad at us for the sins we've committed. We think He's frustrated that we're still circling the same mountain, unable to gain footing on an issue. And that fear drives a wedge between us. Rather than going to Him in prayer and asking for help, we shut down communication, certain He doesn't want to hear it again. Friend, take heart. It's common to put human feelings and emotions on our Father and expect Him to respond as we would. But God's ways are not our ways, and His thoughts are not our thoughts. Thank goodness!

Where God's love is, no fear can exist. And you are fully and completely loved by the Father. Are you embracing this truth in your life today? It's this perfect love that supernaturally takes away our fear, freeing us up to make mistakes and live imperfectly without wondering and worrying if God still loves us. Our human condition doesn't get under His skin. And if you're second-guessing this, scripture says you're not fully convinced of His unconditional love for you.

Take inventory of your fearful feelings to see how they are interacting with God's truth. Do they interfere with your faith? Is fear stirring up an uneasiness or anxiousness that keeps you from talking with the Lord? Are you worried He's judging you and keeping score? If so, ask God for a greater understanding of His love for you. Let Him convince you in meaningful ways of how much you delight His heart, even when you mess up and make bad choices.

God's love isn't conditional in any way. You're simply adored by the one who created you according to His plans.

DEAR LORD, REMOVE ANY FEAR THAT GETS IN THE WAY
AND DISTORTS MY FAITH IN YOU. I DON'T WANT TO BE
AFRAID OR WORRIED. INSTEAD, I ALWAYS WANT TO BE
IN AWE OF YOUR GOODNESS. IN JESUS' NAME. AMEN.

A Christian's Call to Action

Believe in the Eternal, and do what is good—live in the land He provides; roam, and rest in God's faithfulness. Take great joy in the Eternal! His gifts are coming, and they are all your heart desires! Commit your path to the Eternal; let Him direct you. Put your confidence in Him, and He will follow through with you. He will spread out righteousness for you as a sunrise spreads radiance over the land; He will deliver justice for you into the light of the high sun.

PSALM 37:3–6 VOICE

This passage of scripture issues quite a call to action to Christians. We're to *believe* in God, *do good*, and *grow* where we're planted. We are to *roam* and to *rest* in Him. We're to *have joy* in the Lord and *commit* ourselves to Him. God wants us to *follow* Him with *confidence*. For most, this is a tall order because it requires surrendering what we want for what He wants. But when we find the grit and grace to do so, the benefits are hard to overlook.

As we purpose to live a righteous life, blessings start heading our way—ones that we deeply desire. God promises to follow through and make good on the perfect plans He has for our life. He'll make our goodness and fairness shine brightly into the world in significant ways.

Knowing the goodness that God wants to give each of us

according to His plan, why do we often choose our selfish ways instead? Maybe because righteous living is just plain hard, and it feels like an impossible scenario. For a while, we may be fully capable of embracing faithful living, but then we falter and fall back into old habits. We can function in our own strength for a season, but we can't sustain it for long. And while we may genuinely want our lives to be marked by sweet obedience, the reality looks vastly different. We simply don't have what it takes to live righteously. That's exactly why we need God's help every day.

Ask Him to make you a bold believer, fully dependent on the Lord's help to live in the ways that bless you and glorify Him.

DEAR LORD, I UNDERSTAND MY HUMAN LIMITATIONS
MAKE ME INCAPABLE OF RIGHTEOUS LIVING WITHOUT
YOUR FAITHFULNESS AND FORGIVENESS. THANK YOU
FOR GIVING ME BOTH. IN JESUS' NAME. AMEN.

The Wrong Kind of Anger

So turn from anger. Don't rage, and don't worry—
these ways frame the doorway to evil. Besides, those who
act from evil motives will be cut off from the land; but those
who wait, hoping in the Eternal, will enjoy its riches.

PSALM 37:8–9 VOICE

. . . .

Anger is a big deal to God. In the Word, He cautions against it often because He knows where it leads. What does anger look like in your life?

Make no mistake: there is such a thing as good anger. Righteous anger or indignation is different. How do we know if that's what we're feeling? When our anger is directed toward what angers God, we can know it's appropriate. When sin presents itself—for example, in the form of sexual immorality, idolatry, pornography, hatred of people groups, child abuse—this kind of anger isn't wrong. Even Jesus Himself showed anger, directing it at sinful behaviors and true injustices.

But we should always check our motive and attitude, making certain we're not the ones sinning in our anger. That's what today's verse reminds us to do. When we feel irritation, wrath, or rage, taking it to God in prayer is the next right step. Even entertaining worry sets us on the wrong path forward. And we know that turning from evil and embracing good pleases the Lord. As we stay focused on walking out our faith each day, we'll find that heavenly riches accompany our efforts.

So, friend, think about what anger looks like in your life. Are you easily annoyed with your kids and make sure they know it? Is any resentment building in your marriage that causes you to act in mean-spirited ways toward your husband? When things go wrong during the day, are you instantly irritated? Do you get infuriated when plans change without warning? Does your nervous energy spark wrath when someone tries to calm you down? If so, let these responses be a red flag that something else may be going on.

So often, anger is our second emotion. We feel scared and it comes out as anger. We're embarrassed and get mad because of it. We feel rejected and get riled up. Be quick to ask God to uncover what's underneath. Ask Him to show you what's really going on in your heart. And then let the Lord heal you so anger has no home.

DEAR LORD, HELP ME KNOW WHEN ANGER IS JUSTIFIED AND WHEN IT IS NOT. AND HELP ME FIND HEALTHY WAYS TO PROCESS MY EMOTIONS SO I DON'T PARTNER WITH THOSE UNWANTED FEELINGS. IN JESUS' NAME. AMEN.

Doubt

In reply Jesus said to the disciples, "If you only have faith in God—this is the absolute truth—you can say to this Mount of Olives, 'Rise up and fall into the Mediterranean,' and your command will be obeyed. All that's required is that you really believe and have no doubt! Listen to me! You can pray for anything, and if you believe, you have it; it's yours!"

MARK 11:23–24 TLB

Chances are that doubt is something we all battle; maybe you battle it too. Sometimes it's hard to just believe, because like an onion, our faith has layers.

To have faith means we choose to believe that God the Father is the true God above all other gods. It's believing that He sent His one and only Son, Jesus, to die on the cross and pay the price for our sins—past, present, and future. It's believing that God created us on purpose and for a purpose and actively following His lead. It's believing that He hears our prayers and that when we pray according to His will and timing, we can trust His will to be done for our good and His glory.

But the truth is that doubt is a part of the human condition, even if we only doubt at first or for a short amount of time. We may fully believe everything in the paragraph above, but it's common to worry or be afraid from time to time. Doubt that

God is who He says He is or that He'll do what He says He'll do can be challenging to navigate, especially when the stakes are high. But when you focus your attention on questioning things, entertaining uncertainty, or sitting in confusion, doubt infiltrates deep places in your heart. Your lack of confidence in the Lord weakens your faith in Him.

Let God help you override doubt by asking for a greater measure of faith. Make a conscious decision to believe He is willing and able to provide. Spend time in the Word so you get to know His character better. And be prayerful throughout the day, asking for spiritual eyes and ears to see His hand and hear His voice.

DEAR LORD, I CONFESS THAT I BATTLE WITH DOUBT
FROM TIME TO TIME. FORGIVE ME AND HELP ME
CHOOSE TO BELIEVE WHO YOU ARE AND WHAT
YOU PROMISE TO DO. IN JESUS' NAME. AMEN.

When Others Rise

*Be still. Be patient. Expect the Eternal to arrive and
set things right. Don't get upset when you see the
worldly ones rising up the ladder. Don't be bothered
by those who are anchored in wicked ways.*

PSALM 37:7 VOICE

The truth is that it's hard to see evil win, especially when we're
working hard to do what's right but seem to get nowhere in this
world. We point out when someone forgets to charge us for an
item at the store. We tell the truth about our working hours so
our employers pay us correctly. We admit when we've fallen
short of the goal and plans need to be readjusted. We teach our
kids to respect others and be kind whenever possible. We try to
have a servant's heart by showing compassion to those in need.
And so often, we see others rise up the ladder while we're stuck
on a bottom rung.

Our faith, however, should rest in God's timing and provision.
He's the one we should trust to be the decision maker in our life.
Scripture says He elevates and demotes. He judges what is right
and wrong, what is true and false. God can see everything we
think and everything we do because nothing gets past Him. So
we shouldn't get upset when the worldly ones beat us, because
we know God is in control. Instead of watching them, we should

stay focused on living in ways that are good for us and glorify Him.

When jealousy and envy begin to fester inside, open the Bible and let God's Word bring perspective to those feelings. Let key scriptures comfort your aching heart and heal it. Go to the Lord in prayer, asking Him to reveal the sinful places that are making you desire what others have. Ask Him to uncover discontent and to be the one who satisfies you instead.

Be still. Be quiet. Be patient. Be expectant. And watch as the Lord shows up and makes right what has gone wrong. Boldly choose to cheer others on rather than covet or crave. Cultivate a heart of gratitude for what you have. And don't forget that your faith. . .is priceless.

DEAR LORD, I CONFESS THAT MY HEART HAS BEEN UPSET WATCHING EVIL WIN. IT'S HARD TO SEE THE WICKED RISE. BUT MY HEART IS YOURS BECAUSE YOU'RE UNMATCHED. HELP ME REMEMBER THAT TRUTH. IN JESUS' NAME. AMEN.

Imminent Deliverance

Turn back; respond to me, O Eternal, my True God!
Put the spark of life in my eyes, or I'm dead. My enemies
will boast they have beaten me; my foes will celebrate that
I have stumbled. But I trust in Your faithful love; my heart
leaps at the thought of imminent deliverance by You. I will
sing to the Eternal, for He is always generous with me.

PSALM 13:3–6 VOICE

David, the writer of this psalm, is expectant for God's help. In his desperation, he is declaring his belief in the Lord's goodness. He's making sure his words reflect confidence. He's reminding Himself that the Lord will show up. David is standing boldly in his faith in God's promise of deliverance. Why do you think he would be doing this?

Sometimes when life is scary and fear is taking hold of us, what we need most is to remember the sovereignty of the Lord. We need to recognize our position next to His, knowing that we are weak but that nothing and nobody can ever come close to defeating Him. We need to vocalize our worries to Him in prayer, asking for help and intervention. We need to recall the times God has intervened in our difficult circumstances. Our anxious thoughts need to be spoken aloud so that they come out of the dark and into His light. And our prayers need to be full of expectation, believing in God's imminent deliverance.

Are you waiting for the Lord's deliverance today? Are you patiently anticipating that He will show up in meaningful ways to save, heal, and restore? Are you standing firm, even if the ground under your feet feels a little shaky at times? Great! That's a powerful mindset for those who call themselves Christians. This is exactly the attitude we should have as we pray faithfully in Jesus' name. It's how we should be living out a life of faith every day. And, friend, you can boldly trust that God sees you where you are and is working out all things for your good and His glory. It's just who He is and how He loves His children.

Yes, keep yourself in the Word and at His throne of grace. Imminent deliverance is a promise you can hope for and look for.

DEAR LORD, HELP ME. I TRUST IN YOUR FAITHFUL LOVE
AND IMMINENT DELIVERANCE. IN JESUS' NAME. AMEN.

Our Days Are Measured and Known

All their days are measured and known by the Eternal;
their inheritance is kept safe forever. When calamity
comes, they will escape with their dignity. When famine
invades the nations, they will be fed to their fill.

PSALM 37:18–19 VOICE

. . . .

The gold nugget from today's passage of scripture is knowing that our days are measured and known by God. He knew the exact moment we'd come onto the kingdom calendar, and He knows the exact moment we'll take our last breath on earth. From the very beginning, you have been planned for. The details of your life are no secret to the Lord. He lovingly thought you up, every talent and quirk. And God wasn't in a bad mood as He did so. You were created on purpose, and you're here for a purpose.

How does that powerful truth sit with you today? Is it hard to believe? Is it humbling? Does it bring you peace? Maybe it settles your anxious heart? God isn't a bystander in your life, friend. He's fully engaged from creation to eternity, working nonstop in the lives of all His children. Let this reality embolden you to live each day in freedom!

In this world we will have trouble. The Word is clear about it.

As believers, we don't get to escape the hardship, pain, and grief, because this is an imperfect world and we're imperfect people. But the Bible is also clear when it tells us that God is with us always.

His plans for us include hope and a future that brings blessing and glorifies Him. That means we can trust the Lord to get us through every challenge. We can find strength and endurance to persist through every struggle. And we can have peace since God knows every detail of our lives.

With Him, our eternal inheritance is safe, our self-worth won't be destroyed in challenging times, and our every need will be met by our loving and caring Father. So stand strong no matter what comes your way. Pray bold prayers with a hopeful heart. Tell God your needs and expect Him to answer in the best way and at the best time. And give thanks that the Lord's knowledge of you is perfect and complete, bringing comfort so you can rest in His goodness.

DEAR LORD, WHAT A BLESSING TO KNOW I'VE BEEN
CREATED ON PURPOSE AND FOR A PURPOSE. THANK
YOU FOR BEING IN CONTROL. IN JESUS' NAME. AMEN.

Sharing God's Goodness

O Lord, I will praise you with all my heart and
tell everyone about the marvelous things you do.
I will be glad, yes, filled with joy because of you.
I will sing your praises, O Lord God above all gods.

PSALM 9:1–2 TLB

Something supernatural happens in the hearts of others when we share our experiences of God's goodness with them. There is power in our testimony because it points to hope. Likewise, when we hear the testimonies of others, we're encouraged that if God showed up in such significant ways in their circumstances, He can do the same for us. Our perspective shifts from doom and gloom to encouragement. The sharing of God's goodness ignites confidence that the Lord sees us and is willing and able to intervene. And this hope strengthens us to continue another day.

Can you recall a story of faith that helped you weather a life storm? Maybe a marriage was salvaged at the last hour. Maybe a prodigal child finally returned to their good senses, showing a radical change of heart toward God and family. Maybe someone experienced unbelievable and unexpected provision in a time of great need. Maybe a friend was physically healed when all hope for recovery was gone. Or maybe a door of opportunity opened at the last possible instant. Hearing these kinds of stories helps us stay positive and expectant for God's hand to move in our messy moments.

Now think of someone in your life who could use an attitude adjustment right now. Ask the Lord to show you who needs a boost to their belief. Who needs their faith to be furthered? Who needs their hope to be heightened? Who needs their eternal focus to be enhanced? Friend, your testimony could be exactly what they need right now.

Spend time in prayer today and ask God to make you gutsy enough to reach out to bring encouragement to those He lays on your heart. Be willing to open up and share how you've experienced His comfort, healing, restoration, or provision, or to share the other timely ways God's goodness has showed up in your life. Don't keep His marvelous works a secret any longer, because we all need to hear them, especially when we're struggling and scared.

DEAR LORD, I WANT TO TELL EVERYONE ABOUT YOUR
LOVE AND COMPASSION. I WILL PRAISE YOUR NAME
AS I SHARE THE MANY TIMES I'VE SEEN YOU POUR OUT
YOUR CARE IN MY LIFE. IN JESUS' NAME. AMEN.

Right with God

If you are right with God, He strengthens you for the
journey; the Eternal will be pleased with your life.
And even though you trip up, you will not fall on
your face because He holds you by the hand.
PSALM 37:23–24 VOICE

There are solid reasons why being *right with God* should be our highest pursuit in life. And they are not trivial.

Today's verse tells us that when we live in ways that please God, we'll be strengthened for whatever life brings our way. Our journey here on earth will be supercharged by God Himself. So no matter the storms that come, the challenges that ensue, or the struggles we face, the Lord will empower us to navigate them well.

We then read that our desire for righteousness will please God. Imagine walking through each day in such a way that He smiles. Imagine delighting the Lord through the way we act and the words we speak. Think about how fulfilling it would be to close our eyes at night, knowing our choices brought God joy.

But maybe what blesses us the most is understanding that our Father isn't expecting perfection from His people. Praise the Lord for that! Instead, He recognizes our flaws. He is fully aware of our human condition and all the mess that comes with it. So often, our best intentions fall flat and we fail. But did you notice what today's verse says about that?

If we are right with God—trying to conduct our days so that His name is glorified above all else—when we trip up, He won't let us fall. Why? Because He's right with us, holding our hand every step of the way. What a relief to know our flops and fiascos won't ruin what our heart longs for most—to please God with our lives. We can make mistakes and still be fully and completely loved.

If you let it, this powerful truth will give you reasons to be even bolder in your faith. You'll reach higher. You'll dig deeper. You'll trust harder. And you'll hope with a greater measure of expectation. Be gutsy! Be confident and courageous! Live the adventure of faith without worrying that God will be disappointed. Instead, be thankful that He will be with you through the highs and lows and everything in between.

DEAR LORD, HELP ME MAKE DECISIONS THAT
ARE GOOD FOR ME AND THAT GLORIFY
YOUR NAME! IN JESUS' NAME. AMEN.

God Will Never
Let Us Down

I waited patiently for God to help me; then he listened
and heard my cry. He lifted me out of the pit of despair,
out from the bog and the mire, and set my feet on a hard,
firm path, and steadied me as I walked along. He has
given me a new song to sing, of praises to our God. Now
many will hear of the glorious things he did for me, and
stand in awe before the Lord, and put their trust in him.

PSALM 40:1–3 TLB

God is the only one who will never let us down. Our friends and family may have the best intentions, but they're simply unable to be exactly who we need every time. Their love is often conditional, and their capabilities hindered for a variety of reasons. But God sees us, hears us, and can meet each specific need fully and completely.

The next time you find yourself surrounded by difficulties, boldly go to the Lord in prayer. Don't call your bestie to complain or post something on social media, hoping for encouragement from the world. Instead, bow your head and cry out to the Lord. Let God know about the despair you're feeling. Tell Him why your heart is breaking. Be honest about the people and situations that feel overwhelming and scary. Share the insecurities that prevent you from living fully. Talk about the worrisome thoughts keeping you up at night. Ask for what you think you need while also telling Him you trust His will to be done. And then wait for God to act.

The Word once again brings comfort to our weary hearts through today's verses. It reminds us that God is always listening. He hears us. And as we humbly approach the throne room through prayer, we will find rescue and restoration.

Friend, where are you desperate for the Lord's steadiness today? Where are you seeking firm footing? Do you need a fresh spring in your step and a new song in your heart? Let God be your go-to for it all. He won't ever let you down. And in the end, you'll have a powerful testimony of His goodness to share with others, inspiring them to put their trust in the Faithful One.

DEAR LORD, YOU ARE EVERYTHING TO ME. YOU ARE
WHO I LEAN ON WHEN LIFE GETS HARD. YOU ARE MY
RESCUER AND PROVIDER. YOU ARE MY COMFORTER
WHEN DESPAIR SETS IN. THANK YOU THAT YOU WILL
NEVER LET ME DOWN. IN JESUS' NAME. AMEN.

The Faithful

The Eternal saves His faithful; He lends His strength
in hard times; the Eternal comes and frees them—
frees them from evildoers and saves them for eternity—
simply because they seek shelter in Him.

PSALM 37:39–40 VOICE

In today's passage, who does God promise to save? Who does He strengthen for the battle at hand? And who does He rescue from those with nefarious intentions? It's the faithful—the ones who confidently trust Him.

The reality is, however, that trusting the Lord is often so much easier said than done. We're strong and smart. We're able to multi-task with the best of them. We have countless life experiences to draw from. This isn't our first rodeo, if you will. We're godly women who know the Bible and love the Lord. We have good friends with great advice. And our bookshelves are filled with self-help books that promise to settle our hearts and set us on the right path as long as we follow their five simple steps. But there's no satisfactory substitution for a relationship with our Father.

When our finances are in the tank and we're stretched to pay the bills, let's pray. When the state of the world feels overwhelming and we're left scared and worried, let's look to the Eternal rather than put hope in earthly leaders. As we try to lovingly navigate the ups and downs that marriage brings or stay hopeful as we raise rebellious teenagers, let's pray with expectation. Each time we feel the familiar fear of the future creeping in, let's pray without ceasing until God's peace settles on us. And when we just don't know what to do in a tough situation, let's pray for God's will to be done, knowing we can always trust that His plan will be for our good and His glory.

If our faithfulness is the catalyst for God's goodness, then we have every reason to go directly to Him, first and fast. We don't have to be in bondage any longer to the things that have enslaved us for so long. As we spend time in His Word daily and engage with Him through prayer, we'll experience His love, strength, and protection in abundance.

DEAR LORD, HELP ME PRESS INTO YOU WHEN
I'M FEELING OVERWHELMED BY LIFE. I KNOW
THAT EVERYTHING I NEED IS FOUND IN YOU AND
THROUGH YOU! IN JESUS' NAME. AMEN.

Are You Trusting the Eternal One or the World?

Surely those who trust the Eternal—who don't trust in proud, powerful people or in people who care little for reality, chasing false gods—surely they are happy, as I have become. You have done so many wonderful things, had so many tender thoughts toward us, Eternal my God, that go on and on, ever increasing. Who can compare with You?

PSALM 40:4–5 VOICE

Why do you think we sometimes struggle to trust in God more than we trust in the powerful? There are times when it seems as if we care more about what a celebrity says regarding a current issue than what the Word says about it. We may believe the Bible to be alive, active, and relevant yet still direct our attention to the advice of politicians. We might blindly follow the latest trend or groupthink. Or maybe we choose to anchor our trust in a pastor, boss, community leader, or other authority figure, letting them direct our next steps or influence our thought process. Why are we doing this?

Friend, if our desire is to be courageous women of God, uncompromised in our faith, then we need to refocus. Our eyes need to be steady on the Lord more than anything else. We need to secure our hearts to what is true and right. Our minds need to stay engaged with His Word as we meditate on scripture throughout the day. And we should be ready to share encouragement through our testimonies, helping others refocus on what matters most—faith in Jesus.

Nothing this world can offer trumps God. Nothing. He is our hope and help. He's our shelter and strong tower. God is our provider and protector. He's our rescuer and restorer. The Lord is our giver and grower. He is unchangeable, unwavering, and unshakable. God is faithful and forgiving. He's merciful and magnificent. He gives us His care and compassion. He is good and gracious. And nothing we do will ever change that.

We don't need to seek guidance from proud and powerful people to direct our path. Instead, we need to look confidently to the Father with hope and expectation, because He has everything we need.

DEAR LORD, I CONFESS THE TIMES I'VE GIVEN TOO MUCH POWER TO THE WORLD TO SPEAK INTO MY CIRCUMSTANCES. HELP ME REMEMBER THE WAYS YOU'VE DEMONSTRATED YOUR LOVE AND CARE, AND LET THOSE REMINDERS OF YOUR GOODNESS CONTINUALLY DRIVE ME INTO YOUR ARMS. IN JESUS' NAME. AMEN.

Will You Worry or Pray?

Don't worry about anything; instead, pray about everything;
tell God your needs, and don't forget to thank him for his
answers. If you do this, you will experience God's peace,
which is far more wonderful than the human mind can
understand. His peace will keep your thoughts and your
hearts quiet and at rest as you trust in Christ Jesus.

PHILIPPIANS 4:6–7 TLB

Sometimes what we need the most is for our hearts and thoughts to find peace. We need the stirrings of chaos and fear to quiet so we can be calm. Too often, we let our minds run wild with all the what-if questions swirling. And rather than unpack our feelings with God, we sit in them. We entertain worry way too long as we sink further and further into the pit of despair.

God understands this struggle we face as women, which is in part why He inspired Paul to address it in His Word. His encouragement seems simple, but we know it's not easy to walk out in real life every day. No, not even a little.

Chances are we come from a lengthy line of worrywarts. And it's not hard to find situations and relationships that breed serious bouts of anxiety. It's an equal opportunity emotion that can knock us to our knees.

When Paul said not to worry about anything, notice that he

provided another option. We get to choose whether we will worry or pray. We choose if we sit and stew in our stress or if we sit and share with God. But recognize that the first option always brings a sense of panic and dread, while the second brings a peace the world cannot understand. Is the choice really that difficult?

When you get the hard phone call. . .when the medical report reveals a challenging diagnosis. . .when the relationship can't seem to recover. . .when the company lets you go. . .when the world feels overwhelming. . .let God meet you in the moment. Let His peace settle your heart and bring quiet to your thoughts. When you choose to manage worry this way, you'll find rest and comfort in His holy presence.

. . . .

DEAR LORD, I KNOW THAT WORRY IS A BIG ISSUE IN MY LIFE,
AND I CONFESS IT TO YOU TODAY. PLEASE HELP ME GO
RIGHT TO YOU RATHER THAN LET IT STIR ME UP. I WANT THE
PEACE ONLY YOU CAN OFFER. IN JESUS' NAME. AMEN.

Be Bold in Telling Others

I have encouraged Your people with the message of
righteousness, in Your great assembly (look and see),
I haven't kept quiet about these things; You know this,
Eternal One. I have not kept Your righteousness to myself,
sealed up in the secret places of my heart; instead, I boldly
tell others how You save and how loyal You are. I haven't
been shy to talk about Your love, nor have I been afraid to
tell Your truth before the great assembly of Your people.

PSALM 40:9–10 VOICE

Never underestimate the power of sharing your faith. It's both an encouragement to the weary and a source of hope to those struggling in life. The truth is that when life feels overwhelming, we need to know things can get better. We need a faith boost so we can stand strong and wait in expectation for God to act. We need to hear success stories because they remind us of what's possible. We simply cannot stay quiet about God's goodness.

Today's passage of scripture says we should be bold in telling others about how the Lord has showed up in our circumstances. Give the details—the before-and-after particulars. Share about your heart through it all and how it changed as you began to see God move. Talk about the things you did that brought peace, like spending time in His Word and having a robust prayer life.

Unpack the promises you saw Him make good on, promoting God's righteousness. Be honest about your doubts and struggles, and tell the ways the Lord showed His unwavering faithfulness time and time again. Talk about His loyalty to those who love Him and keep His ways. Courageously share it all!

But let's be honest. Speaking up can be hard, especially when we lack confidence or worry about being judged. As believers, we should never be shy to share about the Lord's care and compassion. Fear has no place in a Christian's heart. So every time we feel like keeping our mouths shut, let's ask God to help us boldly operate in the opposite way. Let's always be ready and willing to recount His goodness rather than keeping it hidden in secret places inside. Friend, others need to hear and be encouraged.

· ·

DEAR LORD, WHEN THE OPPORTUNITY TO SHARE
MY EXPERIENCES WITH YOU COMES, EMBOLDEN
ME TO SPEAK IN WAYS THAT CREATE HOPEFUL
HEARTS IN OTHERS. IN JESUS' NAME. AMEN.

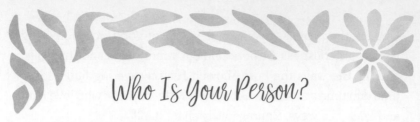

Who Is Your Person?

*Pushed to the wall, I called to GOD; from the wide open
spaces, he answered. GOD's now at my side and I'm
not afraid; who would dare lay a hand on me? GOD's
my strong champion; I flick off my enemies like flies.
Far better to take refuge in GOD than trust in people;
far better to take refuge in GOD than trust in celebrities.*

PSALM 118:5–9 MSG

Who is your person or people? When life throws you an unexpected curveball, who do you call? When your stress level reaches maximum capacity, who do you trust to make everything better? Do you rely on your husband to fix your problems? Are your parents the ones you cling to in tough times? Maybe you turn to your friends to help you figure out the next steps in a crisis. Is your go-to person your small group leader or pastor? Is it a neighbor or coworker? Maybe it's one of your kids or your favorite aunt, or maybe it's another family member altogether. Think about who you trust above all else.

The psalmist in today's scripture reveals that his person is God. When pushed to the wall with troubles, he cries out only for the Lord's help. He doesn't phone a friend or run to someone else. He prays and expects the Lord to respond in the right way and at the right time.

The reality is that there's no substitute for God's help—no one is more qualified to meet the complex needs we experience when faced with big challenges. And His response will supernaturally melt away our fear and make space for our faith to rise up. His presence will make us feel safe and secure, giving us the confidence to stay strong rather than cower. What's more, surrendering our every fear to God will embolden us in significant ways. It will remind us that He alone is our champion.

What needs to change in your life so that the Lord in heaven is your person and not anyone here? Where do you need to readjust your priorities so you're more focused on Him as your Savior alone?

Friend, God created community to help support us as we journey through life together. Our family members and friends play a vital role in our lives! But when we look to them above Him, something isn't right. Ask the Lord to make you a courageous woman of God who deeply appreciates friends and family but also has a healthy understanding of her place.

. . . .

DEAR LORD, I CHOOSE TO TAKE REFUGE
IN YOU! IN JESUS' NAME. AMEN.

When Your Sins Catch Up

Please, Eternal One, don't hold back Your kind ways from me. I need Your strong love and truth to stand watch over me and keep me from harm. Right now I can't see because I am surrounded by troubles; my sins and shortcomings have caught up to me, so I am swimming in darkness. Like the hairs on my head, there are too many to count, so my heart deserts me.

PSALM 40:11–12 VOICE

Sometimes we find ourselves in the thick of it. Sin has a way of doing that, you know. One little white lie leads to another. One reckless choice quickly snowballs. One secret indiscretion eventually becomes known, bringing with it natural consequences that hurt. And before we know it, we find ourselves in a mess. But God's heart for you is always good.

Friend, our compassionate heavenly Father will let us walk the wrong path only so long before He intervenes. He loves us too much to leave us in those barren places. And when we ask for God to stand watch and guide us into better decisions, He does.

As believers, we have the gift of the Holy Spirit who helps us pursue righteous living. He is often behind that gut feeling we experience when teetering on immoral behavior. He reminds us of key scriptures that reveal God's will with clarity. The Spirit helps us grow deep roots of faith by using life's moments to mature us in meaningful ways. And He convicts (not condemns) us of sin, leading us to repentance. Do you feel Him working in your life?

When we ignore the Spirit and instead satisfy our fleshly desires, we will inevitably find ourselves surrounded by troubles. Respectfully, this life is not about us. We're on the kingdom calendar to bring glory to God through our words and actions. Our life should point to the Father in heaven. And if we're constantly running from our sins, there will come a time when they catch up.

Let every day be another opportunity to live courageously. With confidence, choose to let your life be an advertisement for faith. Your life preaches either way, so choose wisely. And ask the Lord for the right attitude, a hopeful heart, and a godly perspective so that you can walk without reproach.

DEAR LORD, I CONFESS MY SINFUL WAYS AND THANK
YOU FOR YOUR FORGIVENESS. I ADMIT I OFTEN
LIVE IN WAYS THAT SATISFY ME WITHOUT BLESSING
YOU. HELP ME REFOCUS ON RIGHTEOUS LIVING
AS THE SPIRIT LEADS. IN JESUS' NAME. AMEN.

A Humble Heart of Gratitude

The LORD is God! He has shined a light on us! So lead the festival offering with ropes all the way to the horns of the altar. You are my God—I will give thanks to you! You are my God—I will lift you up high! Give thanks to the LORD because he is good, because his faithful love lasts forever.

PSALM 118:27–29 CEB

. . . .

When you pray, do you thank God for all He has done in your life? Do you recognize His hand at work and offer up praise in response? Are you quick to show your appreciation for His continued and perfect faithfulness? Do you draw near to the Lord with a humble heart? If you think about it, there are countless reasons to approach the Lord with thanksgiving. Without any doubt, God is good all the time.

Where have you seen Him lately? Did unexplainable peace settle in your spirit during a tumultuous event? Did you experience joy in a situation where there should have been none? Did you stand strong in a spine-weakening moment? Did the perfect words spill out of your mouth, even catching you off guard a bit? Did the timing line up perfectly for you to share encouragement with someone who desperately needed it? In your hardship, did necessary provisions show up unexpectedly?

Let these occurrences be a sweet reminder that Jesus sees you. He knows exactly where you are emotionally and mentally. He sees every need, spoken and unspoken. God knows your needs—often before you do. And He loves to bless you. So keep your eyes open and watch for the Lord's goodness to descend on your life in both small and significant ways. Then spend time in prayer thanking God.

Just like you, the Lord delights in receiving others' gratitude. Knowing our kindness and generosity have blessed another makes us feel good. And receiving a thank-you brings a smile to our face. God wants to hear from you too! Be bold in your appreciativeness, never missing an opportunity to recognize His compassion and care.

DEAR LORD, YOU ARE A GOOD, GOOD FATHER!
THANK YOU FOR BEING INVOLVED IN MY LIFE AND
ALWAYS WORKING THINGS OUT FOR MY GOOD AND
YOUR GLORY. I TRUST YOU, AND I APPRECIATE THAT
YOUR PLANS ARE TO LOVINGLY GROW ME TO BE MORE
LIKE YOUR SON EVERY DAY! IN JESUS' NAME. AMEN.

The Joy of the Lord

But may the joy of the Lord be given to everyone
who loves him and his salvation. May they constantly
exclaim, "How great God is!" I am poor and weak,
yet the Lord is thinking about me right now! O my
God, you are my helper. You are my Savior; come
quickly, and save me. Please don't delay!

PSALM 40:16–17 TLB

. . . .

When the Bible mentions the joy of the Lord, it's talking about the delight and contentment that come to those who know God. It happens when you stand strong in your faith, choosing to abide in Christ daily. It comes from being filled with the Holy Spirit and following His lead throughout your life. And joy is also a fruit of the Spirit that will take time to grow and mature in the life of a believer. Yes, it's a blessing that follows the decision to accept Jesus into your life as Savior.

The more you know God, the more joy you'll experience. It's inevitable. His Word is where He reveals Himself. He'll speak to you through scriptures that catch your eye and resonate with your soul. And as you study verse by verse and book by book, you'll get a more robust understanding of who He is, what He has done, and what He promises to do. That knowledge will comfort your heart and bring you joy.

Are you struggling to find hope and happiness? Do you lack excitement and expectation in your faith? Do you feel disappointed or defeated by life? While we may feel all of these ways from time to time, we shouldn't stay there for long. They should be fleeting emotions that lose their power through prayer. They should disappear when the initial shock fades away.

As believers, we can overflow with joy even while navigating difficult times, just as the psalmist recognized that he could be joyful while also feeling poor and weak. He experienced gladness knowing he was on God's mind. He delighted in the truth that the Lord was his helper and trusted God would save him in His perfect timing. The psalmist felt the joy of the Lord deep in his spirit. Friend, you can too.

DEAR LORD, GIVE ME BOLDNESS TO CHOOSE JOY RATHER THAN COWER IN FEAR. LET ME EXPERIENCE YOUR JOY IN MY HEART NO MATTER WHAT. IN JESUS' NAME. AMEN.

The Source of all Hope

*I pray that God, the source of all hope, will infuse
your lives with an abundance of joy and peace
in the midst of your faith so that your hope will
overflow through the power of the Holy Spirit.*

ROMANS 15:13 VOICE

Did you catch that? Paul made a powerful declaration in today's
verse. And if we believe it, cling to it, and act on it, our lives will
be transformed.

Paul pointed out that God is the source of all hope. Not just
some hope, but every bit of hope. He's the supplier of our confidence. Because of His faithfulness, we can trust and expect all
things to work out in His perfect timing and according to His plan.

The problem is that so often we anchor our hope in all the
wrong things. We believe in doctors and lawyers. We look to
medications, diets, and workout plans. We put our faith in politicians, police, and pastors. We feel confident because of policies
and procedures. We feel optimistic thanks to lofty goals and gutsy
decisions and gritty willpower. But in the end, they fail us. They
simply can't supply us with the kind of hope we need—the kind
that delivers and lasts.

But when we truly understand that God is the source of all
hope, we're able to direct our energy in the right ways. Rather than

looking at earthly options, we look only to the Eternal One. We invest our yearning in prayers rather than counting on people to deliver. We share our challenges with the one true and sovereign God instead of expecting hope to rise from worldly substitutes. Simply put, we take God at His word and trust in it.

Where do you need a dose of hope today? Where are you lacking substantial joy and craving lasting peace? How is your faith in God's provision being challenged? If not the Lord, then who are you looking to for help?

Friend, He is the source of *all* hope, so go to Him for it. Don't waste time looking in all the wrong places.

DEAR LORD, I KNOW YOU ALONE ARE
MY SOURCE. IN JESUS' NAME. AMEN.

Trusting in God Alone

But blessed is the one who trusts in Me alone;
the Eternal will be his confidence. He is like a tree
planted by water, sending out its roots beside the stream.
It does not fear the heat or even drought. Its leaves stay
green and its fruit is dependable, no matter what it faces.

JEREMIAH 17:7–8 VOICE

In yesterday's devotional, we talked about how God is the source of all hope. Today's scripture tells us that our trust should be in Him alone. Do you see the pattern, friend? He is a jealous God who wants us to place our faith in Him alone and for all things. Let's dig a little deeper.

If you are intentional to believe in God for all things, this verse says you are blessed. That means you trust His provision in financial matters, even when your situation feels hopeless. When your child walks away from the faith you so carefully modeled in your family, you rest in His sovereignty. When your health begins to falter, you keep your eyes on God first and foremost. When the betrayal of a loved one is exposed and it rocks the very foundation of your relationship, you hide in the shadow of His wings. When you're overlooked for promotion, you trust there's a better *yes* down the road. No matter what comes your way, your expectation is always for God's goodness to prevail. Even when

He allows the road to be rocky, you can rest because you trust it's for your good and His glory.

Life is hard and can shake us to the core. But when we honestly believe that God is on our side and His love for us is unwavering, we can confidently exhale the stress and worry. Our anxious thoughts don't have to tangle our hearts in fear. We can choose to believe, letting His peace override our panic. And as we put our energy toward trusting the Lord and His perfect history in our life, a calm will settle over our spirit. And we'll be able to breathe.

So before you venture out of bed in the morning, go to God in prayer. Ask for the courage to trust in Him alone. And ask for confidence in His will and ways, realizing they're often much different from our own.

DEAR LORD, GIVE ME THE GRIT TO BOLDLY
TRUST IN YOU ALONE. IN JESUS' NAME. AMEN.

A Bold and Courageous Woman

Eternal One, I am calling out to You; You are the
foundation of my life. Please, don't turn Your ear from me.
If You respond to my pleas with silence, I will lose all hope
like those silenced by death's grave. Listen to my voice.
You will hear me begging for Your help with my hands lifted
up in prayer, my body turned toward Your holy home.

PSALM 28:1–2 VOICE

To be a courageous woman of God means to pray boldly. It's praying every time the issue or person comes to mind. It's going to the Lord even when it seems as if your prayers are bouncing off the ceiling. It means not growing weary in petitioning God for His hand to move in a situation. It's going straight to the source of hope and rightly placing all your trust in Him. It's pleading your case without ceasing as you wait for Him to show up in supernatural ways. It is standing strong on the Rock.

In today's psalm, David is crying out to God. He's asking for his life to be spared while his enemies are destroyed. He battles not only with the opposition but also with some in his own family. Sound familiar? Regardless, David knows God and trusts that He will save and protect.

If you are battling with friends or family right now, take heart. Keep praying for God to strengthen you for what's ahead. You certainly don't want them destroyed, but you do want evil to be restrained. You don't want them physically or emotionally hurt, but you do want a spirit of repentance to prevail. So pray with expectation—and keep at it until you see a shift. If the Lord seems silent, keep praying with perseverance. Pray boldly. Pray often. Pray with a hopeful heart. Pray with thanksgiving. Pray with passion.

While God created community to be a blessing, the reality is that it's also pretty messy. We're imperfect people in relationships with imperfect people, trying to navigate life in an imperfect world. What could go wrong! But as bold and courageous women, we understand the power of prayer and we pray until God moves.

DEAR LORD, I WILL CALL OUT TO YOU WHEN I'M
FRUSTRATED AND DISCOURAGED BY MY FRIENDS AND
FAMILY. AND I WILL KEEP PRAYING UNTIL I SEE YOUR HAND
MOVE IN MEANINGFUL WAYS. IN JESUS' NAME. AMEN.

Total Depravity

The heart is the most deceitful thing there is and
desperately wicked. No one can really know how bad it is!
Only the Lord knows! He searches all hearts and examines
deepest motives so he can give to each person his right
reward, according to his deeds—how he has lived.

JEREMIAH 17:9–10 TLB

It's the heart that gets us into trouble. It wants what it wants and is quick to inform our actions and thoughts. It's the center of our passion, making us willing to entertain our worldly, fleshly desires. It's the home of our cravings, both good and bad. It's also the place from where we love and where we feel loved in return. But scripture tells us our heart is the most deceitful thing. It's desperately wicked, meaning it's incurable. It's a terminal condition.

For context, today's passage is about Judah's choice to give in to sinfulness despite the multitude of blessings they had received from God. This nation perfectly illustrates the problem with the human condition. We're all guilty, every one of us, of what theologians call *total depravity*. That doesn't mean we're each as bad as we could be but rather that we are a deeply sinful people with no hope for righteousness on our own. It's why we need Jesus. We need to be supernaturally transformed by His blood.

Today, surrender yourself to the Lord for inspection. Ask Him to search your heart to see where fleshiness is alive and active in your life. Friend, you may not even be aware of it all because some sins feel like second nature. You may not realize it's happening. So let the Lord bring fresh revelation. Have the courage to listen to God's report. With contrition, repent of those sinful ways. And then ask Him for spiritual eyes and ears to see and hear when depravity strikes again.

You can trust the Lord with your imperfections. As a believer, you can know without a doubt that there's nothing you can do to make God love you less. He knows the complexity of your heart because He created you. He understands the worldly things that pull you this way and that. He sees the struggle and He is the solution. So pray with hope and expectation, certain the Lord will forgive and restore you.

DEAR LORD, THANK YOU FOR ALWAYS MAKING A WAY
FOR MY DEPRAVITY TO BE FORGIVEN AND MY HEART TO
BE RESTORED ONCE AGAIN. IN JESUS' NAME. AMEN.

Resting in the Lord

The Eternal should be honored and revered; He has
heard my cries for help. The Eternal is the source of
my strength and the shield that guards me. When I
learn to rest and truly trust Him, He sends His help.
This is why my heart is singing! I open my mouth
to praise Him, and thankfulness rises as song.
PSALM 28:6–7 VOICE

Today's verse suggests the importance and value of rest. Our decision to rest, accompanied by our trust in God, triggers His help. The psalmist knows He is the source of strength and the shield that guards, but rest matters! What does it look like to rest in the Lord?

It doesn't look like stopping all activity. We are busy women with a lot to do, as well as having friends and family who are counting on us throughout the day. It's not an excuse to sleep in or take naps either, although those are not terrible things to do! Instead, God wants us to rest in Him, meaning we take a *spiritual* rest.

This kind of rest is so vital to us because it's when the Lord restores and revitalizes our weary spirit. The Hebrew translation for the word *rest* means "to be still, quiet, or calm." It's to be at peace. This is a sacred space where we can take a break from anxiousness, stress, fear, worry, and insecurities. It's where we cease striving at life and surrender to God. It is a safe place to get away from the attacks of enemies—both internal and external—that keep us stirred up and unsettled. And rest is also the choice to pray rather than panic when the storms of life hit.

As a believer, you can do nothing more important than surrender to the Lord. When life begins to feel overwhelming, let that drive you to your knees. Unload your burdens as you tell Him everything heavy in your heart. Admit where you feel weak and unable to move forward. Give God your tears and fears, uncensored. And boldly ask Him to meet you in this moment, bringing the perfect amount of healing and hope.

Then when He does, because He will, praise God through prayers of thanksgiving. For the Lord delights in His creation and is ready to give you the restorative rest you need.

. . . .

DEAR LORD, HELP ME MAKE THE TIME TO REST
IN YOU. I SIMPLY CANNOT DO ANYTHING TO
RESTORE MYSELF. IN JESUS' NAME. AMEN.

Trapped in the Snare of Fear

People are trapped by their fear of others; those who trust the Lord are secure. . . . The unjust person is disgusting to the righteous; the straight path is disgusting to the wicked.

PROVERBS 29:25, 27 CEB

If you think about it, there are really two big ways we can find ourselves trapped by fear. It can be either physical or psychological. But for most believers living in the West, we tend to be more snared by the fear of man psychologically. We simply care too much about what others think.

So how does this fear manifest in our lives? Maybe we work overtime trying to please others so they like us or approve of who we are. We may give in to peer pressure easily because we want to be respected. Maybe we choose to keep our mouths shut when we see an injustice rather than risk angering others. Maybe we abandon our morals and values so as not to be judged. And maybe, just maybe, that's why we often shy away from sharing our faith. This is one reason the Bible tells us repeatedly to trust the Lord and not our own understanding.

Friend, let's choose to muster the guts and grit to stand up for our faith. If we're going to be courageous women of God, it starts here. We must decide we care more about following His will and ways than being liked by the world. And sometimes that's a tall order.

Don't fall into the trap. While the world tells us tolerance, progressivism, and political correctness should be top priorities, the devil uses these worldly values to twist our thinking so we look away from God. Standing firm on His Word can sometimes get us labeled as narrow-minded. And while it's important for us to care about the issues happening in our world and to show compassion to others, the fear of man shouldn't be the driver.

Our top priority during this short stint on planet Earth is to be living a life of faith that glorifies the Lord. We should seek His strength and wisdom to pursue a life of passion and purpose. So go to God in prayer every day, asking Him to embolden you to do so. Don't let fear of man rob you of righteousness.

DEAR LORD, I DON'T WANT TO COMPROMISE
MY FAITH TO FIT IN. THE WORLD HOLDS NOTHING
FOR ME. GIVE ME COURAGE TO FOLLOW YOU
EVERY DAY. IN JESUS' NAME. AMEN.

Feeling Victorious in Hard Circumstances

But I pour my trust into You, Eternal One. I'm glad to say, "You are my God!" I give the moments of my life over to You, Eternal One. Rescue me from those who hate me and who hound me with their threats. Look toward me, and let Your face shine down upon Your servant. Because of Your gracious love, save me!

PSALM 31:14–16 VOICE

Let today's verses encourage you that as a believer, you can feel victorious even though you're having to navigate crushing circumstances. We don't have to walk around discouraged and disappointed. We don't have to give in or give up. Instead, we can declare God's goodness and graciousness on the front end and let it bolster our faith in significant ways as we navigate through the hard times.

In Psalm 31, we see this concept play out in David's life. He had been rejected by his friends and faced enemies scheming to take his life. So many tough things for one person to manage at the same time! Nevertheless, this man after God's own heart was steadfast in his faith even while in great emotional pain and physical agony. He trusted the Lord without fail, and his prayers reflected it. In them, he made a point of affirming God's power not only to bless God but also to remind himself of his Father's love and compassion.

Maybe you can relate to David's emotional state while he was writing this psalm because you are there today. Friend, are you dealing with some form of personal persecution? Is your heart tangled in a knot of agony or angst? Do you feel abandoned by friends or family? Are you lonely and lacking a supportive community? These are the kinds of situations that can feel so overwhelming it's hard to stay hopeful. But David knew God was with him always. We can claim that same truth today.

When we choose to follow the Lord with our heart, we can feel victorious over every joy-draining and spine-weakening circumstance that comes our way. We can pray with great expectation, knowing He will meet us there and lead us through it. We can pray with hope because God's love never fails. And we can pray with thanksgiving since we have faith that He will intervene with perfect timing.

DEAR LORD, NOTHING THAT I MUST FACE WILL CRUSH
ME IF I STAND VICTORIOUSLY IN YOU. HELP ME LIVE WITH
THIS KIND OF FAITH EVERY DAY, IN JESUS' NAME. AMEN.

Choosing Fear or Confidence

*I don't fear; I'm confident that help will come to the
one anointed by the Eternal: heaven will respond to his
plea; His mighty right hand will win the battle. Many
put their hope in chariots, others in horses, but we place
our trust in the name of the Eternal One, our True God.
Soon our enemies will collapse and fall, never to return
home; all the while, we will rise and stand firm.*

PSALM 20:6–8 VOICE

The psalms that David wrote are full of both lament and hope. What a gift that God included so many of his songs in His Word, because they have a supernatural way of bringing deep encouragement, meeting us right where we are.

The nugget we can take away from today's verses is that as believers, we have a choice. We can either be guided by fear or respond to life with confidence. We can spend our time worrying about how everything will work out, or we can rest knowing God will show up. We can let anxiety eat us alive as it steals our joy, or we can be comforted by remembering His perfect track record in our lives. But it doesn't stop there.

We can also end up putting our faith in someone other than God, certain they will bring help and hope. We may trust the government or a community movement. We may look to our husbands or parents to save us. We may expect friends to fix our circumstances or a pastor to make things right. Even with the best intentions, they're unable to meet our needs.

However, if we choose to respond by trusting the Lord above all else, we will be strengthened. Through Him, we'll find a fresh measure of faith infusing our weary bones. We'll find a peace that makes no sense to the world. Our resolve will keep us standing strong as we wait for God to answer. And fear will melt away as we have the guts and grit to believe He is our only Savior. . .no one else.

DEAR LORD, I CONFESS THE TIMES I'VE STRUGGLED
WITH FEAR. HONESTLY, IT'S HARD TO BE BRAVE IN THIS
CRAZY WORLD. BUT I KNOW THAT IF I GIVE IN TO IT OR
PUT MY FAITH IN SOMEONE ELSE, I WILL EVENTUALLY
BE LET DOWN. YOU ARE THE ONLY ONE WHO HAS
THE POWER TO SAVE. IN JESUS' NAME. AMEN.

Starting the Day with God

Do not allow this world to mold you in its own image.
Instead, be transformed from the inside out by renewing your
mind. As a result, you will be able to discern what God wills
and whatever God finds good, pleasing, and complete.

ROMANS 12:2 VOICE

How has the world tried to mold you? Has it told you how you should look to be loved and accepted by others? Has it said you should think in ways that go against God's Word? Have you been guilted or shamed into doing something in stark contradiction to your value system? Do you struggle to embrace the current societal norms pushed by those around you? Have you been ridiculed or left out for not going along with the group?

The truth is that this kind of peer pressure is never going away. Stand strong and let God lead you through these challenging times. Let Him give you courage to be faithful when it's hard. Invite Him into your thought life, asking Him to keep it perfectly aligned with His.

How can you do this? Each morning, get your mindset in the right place to start the day. Committing to this practice will set the tone for what's ahead by getting your eyes fixed on the Lord. What will your morning routine look like? Here are a few ideas.

Why not open God's Word and let Him meet you in its pages?

What scriptures is He highlighting? What encouragement do you find there? What should you meditate on throughout the day, talking about it with God and waiting for revelation to come?

Why not commit to an ongoing conversation with the Lord? Being in continual communication with Him invites Him into your day as you navigate the difficulties it brings. It keeps you intimately connected to the Father.

Why not spend time with godly friends? As long as they are devoted to deepening their relationship with the Lord, let them be a support for you. Watch as they bring hope by sharing their own testimonies of God's goodness.

Friend, choose a morning routine that starts you off strong and reaches into the rest of your day, helping you grow your faith so you don't fall prey to the world's ways.

DEAR LORD, THE WORLD HOLDS NOTHING FOR ME. EVERY DAY, PLEASE BRING TRANSFORMATION AND RENEWAL THAT SETS MY MIND ON YOU AND ALL YOU HAVE PLANNED FOR MY LIFE. IN JESUS' NAME. AMEN.

The One Who Advocates for You

Meanwhile, the moment we get tired in the waiting,
God's Spirit is right alongside helping us along. If we don't
know how or what to pray, it doesn't matter. He does our
praying in and for us, making prayer out of our wordless sighs,
our aching groans. He knows us far better than we know
ourselves, knows our pregnant condition, and keeps us present
before God. That's why we can be so sure that every detail
in our lives of love for God is worked into something good.

ROMANS 8:26–28 MSG

There's no doubt we get tired in the waiting. It's hard to stay strong waiting for a broken marriage to be restored. It's not easy to wait for a child to return to a wholesome mindset once they've gone down a terribly destructive path. Waiting for physical healing is hard when the clock is running out of time. Hanging on for the financial mess to get sorted out takes every ounce of strength. And staying focused on getting through each day feels almost impossible when the grief won't relent. Sometimes we just don't have enough left in the tank to lift up a prayer asking God for help. But the Holy Spirit does.

Scripture tells us that the Spirit is there with us, helping in ways we may not even realize. But we can be assured of this: When we can't find the words, He does the praying for us. When we don't even know what to say, He knows exactly how to express our emotions to the Father. When all we can do is grunt and groan, the Spirit advocates on our behalf. And in those messy moments when all we have are liquid words, He keeps us before God, making sure He knows what we are feeling. How can He do this when words escape us? Because the Holy Spirit knows us far better than we know ourselves.

Let this truth fan the flames of your faith. Let it embolden you to trust the Lord with every part of your life. Let God be your first thought in the morning and the last prayer on your lips at night. Talk with Him throughout the day, expectant for His love and compassion to bring you comfort. When you're feeling weary in the waiting, trust the Spirit to be gentle with you and thorough with God.

Yes, friend, you are deeply cared for by the one who created you.

DEAR LORD, THANK YOU FOR THE HOLY SPIRIT'S
WORK IN MY LIFE! IN JESUS' NAME. AMEN.

Working Together in Community

For in the same way that one body has so many different parts, each with different functions; we, too—the many— are different parts that form one body in the Anointed One. Each one of us is joined with one another, and we become together what we could not be alone. Since our gifts vary depending on the grace poured out on each of us, it is important that we exercise the gifts we have been given.

ROMANS 12:4–6 VOICE

If you're not actively working together with others in a community of believers—sharing your God-given talents and giftings—then we're all missing out! What you have to offer matters greatly. Your skill set is needed and necessary. And when the Lord thought each of us up, His special design for us included abilities meant to further His kingdom.

If we choose not to participate in the Lord's work with others, we may hinder something God has planned. Not that our refusal to take part will keep His will from being done. Not that it will stop Him from moving forward. But our unwillingness to join forces robs those around us from experiencing our friendship and camaraderie. It keeps us from discovering meaningful relationships.

And rather than growing our faith together by working toward a common goal, we become stale in our disobedience.

Today's scripture reminds us of the importance of exercising the gifts God has given us. This is how we offer our lives to Him in an ongoing act of worship. Friend, His purpose for every believer is that we serve each other in significant ways every day. When we do, what is impossible alone becomes possible together.

What giftings has God baked into you? What are you good at? What kinds of things do you like to do for others? If you're not sure, ask God for revelation. Pray with persistence until you begin to hear His whispers. Talk to your pastor or small group leader for insight. Meet a godly mentor for coffee and ask for their help. Be intentional to discern and hone the talents you've been given so you can share them in community. And then boldly step out and serve.

DEAR LORD. THANK YOU FOR CREATING ME WITH
SPECIFIC TALENTS AND GIFTS. GIVE ME COURAGE TO
EMBRACE THEM AND USE THEM TO BLESS OTHERS AND
WORSHIP YOU EVERY DAY. IN JESUS' NAME. AMEN.

No More Condemnation

With the arrival of Jesus, the Messiah, that fateful dilemma is resolved. Those who enter into Christ's being-here-for-us no longer have to live under a continuous, low-lying black cloud. A new power is in operation. The Spirit of life in Christ, like a strong wind, has magnificently cleared the air, freeing you from a fated lifetime of brutal tyranny at the hands of sin and death.

ROMANS 8:1–2 MSG

. . . .

The truth is that in our sin, there is condemnation. But when we accept Jesus as our Savior, we are no longer under it. In this letter from Paul to the Romans, he wanted to remind them of the importance of this good news for everyone who believes in Jesus for salvation. His death changed everything. Where we once were condemned by God, we are now justified by Jesus' blood. And that means the low-lying black cloud is gone forever. For believers, it's lifted. It's no longer there!

When Jesus surrendered His life and died on the cross, a supernatural exchange happened. A new power was made available to operate in us, and every bit of our deserved condemnation was transferred onto Him. Jesus willingly took the punishment we should have undergone ourselves. Our decision to believe in Him and surrender our life to Him not only removed every bit of that weighty condemnation—past, present, and future—but also gave us the gift of eternal life in heaven. The air has been cleared and sin has lost its hold.

Have you accepted Jesus into your life? Are you living a life free from condemnation? If not, you're still under the jurisdiction of sin and death. You're cut off from the blessings of God. The low-lying black cloud sits directly over your life and will stay there until the blood of Jesus removes it.

Are you ready to pray the sinner's prayer? If so, there are no magical words you need to say. It's just a declaration to God that you're choosing to rely on Jesus to be your Savior. If you're ready, make these words the prayer of your heart. . .

DEAR LORD, I KNOW I'M A SINNER AND DESERVE THE CONSEQUENCES OF MY SIN. BUT TODAY, I'M CHOOSING TO TRUST IN JESUS ALONE AS MY SAVIOR. I BELIEVE HIS DEATH ON THE CROSS AND RESURRECTION THREE DAYS LATER SECURED MY FORGIVENESS ONCE AND FOR ALL. THANK YOU THAT JESUS' BLOOD REMOVED ALL CONDEMNATION AND BRIDGED THE GAP THAT SIN LEFT. IN JESUS' NAME. AMEN.

Loving Others Well

Do not slack in your faithfulness and hard work.
Let your spirit be on fire, bubbling up and boiling over,
as you serve the Lord. Do not forget to rejoice, for hope is
always just around the corner. Hold up through the hard
times that are coming, and devote yourselves to prayer.

ROMANS 12:11–12 VOICE

Right before these verses, Paul was firm in saying that believers should be enthusiastic about trying to outshine one another. In the way we show respect and admiration to each other, we should be demonstrative. Wouldn't that alone make the world a better place?

Today's scripture piggybacks on that command, telling us not to lose our gusto. Paul was smart to bring this potential pitfall into the light, because it's normal for us to let life get in the way and slack off unknowingly. Unless we stay focused and on-task, loving others well will slip our mind. So how do we keep up our enthusiasm?

Paul goes on to say we're to let our spirit be on fire. It's to bubble up and boil over as we serve. We're to rejoice as we wait for hope. We're told to stay strong in challenging times and to pray without ceasing. Friend, do you see that in these commands, faith is a verb? Living in these active ways is how we can be gutsy as we purpose to bless others.

Today, ask God to set your heart on fire through the Spirit who lives in you. Ask Him to burn within so your desire to follow His plans and walk out kindness and generosity toward those around you stays aflame. Ask the Lord to help you stay fully connected emotionally and spiritually. Be bold and expectant in your asking, friend, and God will honor it.

Also remember that it takes great intentionality to keep other believers at the forefront of your mind. Not because you don't care but because it's easy to become overwhelmed by all that life demands from you. Between managing a home, growing a family, caring for yourself, and navigating daily responsibilities, you may have trouble remembering the needs of your Christian brothers and sisters. Each day, keep your eyes and ears open so when God brings opportunities or reminders, you're able to reengage in meaningful ways and love others well.

DEAR LORD, HELP ME NOT TO BE LAZY BUT INSTEAD
TO BE FULL OF FOCUS AND ENERGY. EMBOLDEN ME TO
LOVE THOSE AROUND ME SO THEY FEEL ENCOURAGED.
FILL ME WITH YOUR SPIRIT SO I CAN BE YOUR HANDS
AND FEET IN THE WORLD. IN JESUS' NAME. AMEN.

Learning God's Purpose and Plans

Make me hear of Your faithful love in the morning, for I trust in You. Teach me how I should walk, for I offer my soul up to You. Rescue me from my enemies, Eternal One, for You are my shelter from them. Teach me how to do Your will, for You are my God.

PSALM 143:8–10 VOICE

. . . .

Many of us are unsure about God's plan for our lives. We cry out for a lighted billboard that catches our attention. We hope for someone to tell us what our purpose is so we can move forward. We ask for His audible whisper to unveil the direction we're to walk. But God's plan is already in black and white, just waiting for us to uncover it. His plan is in the Bible.

Friend, never stop opening His Word. In its pages, you will discover how to walk in His ways. The Lord has laid out His purpose for your life, and it is beautiful. His plans are not hidden from those who genuinely seek them. As you spend time in scripture, God will speak into your heart and the Holy Spirit will guide you in the right ways at the right times. And yes, you will be equipped for everything He calls you to do.

The Bible is an immovable foundation for the believer. It's

where our trust in God begins and grows. It's where He reveals Himself so we're better able to understand His will and ways. The Word is alive and active, relevant in our lives right now. And we can't say God isn't answering our prayers if our Bible is on the shelf, collecting dust.

To learn the Lord's will and how to live it out daily, we'll find the path forward clearly laid out in the Bible. Let's become serious readers. Let's consistently dig into the Word with an open heart to hear what He has for us. Let's be bold in our faith and make time to learn what God says in the scriptures. Let's grab our pen or highlighter and mark up key passages, inwardly digesting their wisdom with an undivided heart. And as we do, the Holy Spirit will mature our faith while we grow in knowledge of our magnificent God.

His love for us is new every morning, and He'll prove it to us through His Word.

DEAR LORD, THANK YOU FOR THE GIFT OF THE BIBLE.
GIVE ME A DIVINE DESIRE TO DIG IN EVERY DAY SO I
GET TO KNOW YOU BETTER. THROUGH IT, TEACH ME
HOW I SHOULD WALK. IN JESUS' NAME. AMEN.

A Powerful Picture of Friendship

If people mistreat or malign you, bless them. Always speak
blessings, not curses. If some have cause to celebrate, join in
the celebration. And if others are weeping, join in that as well.
Work toward unity, and live in harmony with one another.
Avoid thinking you are better than others or wiser than the
rest; instead, embrace common people and ordinary tasks.

ROMANS 12:14–16 VOICE

Today's scripture paints a powerful picture of how to be a good friend. It's not a to-do list that puts you in good standing with God. Nor is it a command. Instead, Paul is simply telling us ways that we should try to walk out our faith in community.

When we accept Jesus into our life, a beautiful transformation takes place. Our character changes. Our hearts soften. Our ability to forgive expands. Our focus turns from self to others. Our desire for revenge lessens. Our craving for worldly things diminishes. And where we used to hate, we now feel compelled to love and bless.

This makeover is a gift because it allows us to experience unity on a deeper level. Peace and comfort come from living with this kind of renewed mindset, often catching us off guard. Our go-to responses—the fleshly ones that are usually self-serving—lose

174

steam. Our hardened hearts that once wanted to defend and dispute now feel the tug to extend grace and goodness. Rather than continuing to think we're above others, we begin to recognize that this life is not a competition and that we're all in it together.

Living this way requires the Holy Spirit's help. That's one reason God deposits His Spirit in us when we become Christians. He knows we battle with selfishness and sin and need supernatural strength to do what is right. Loving others well requires His power flowing through us. And as we pray in expectation and with hopeful hearts, asking for the Spirit's help daily (sometimes hourly), we will be met in the moment in significant ways.

God will help us bless our enemies through word and deed. We'll have compassion to celebrate and weep with those around us. We will pursue unity and harmony. And our heart for others will be good.

DEAR LORD, I'M SO MOVED BY THE WAYS YOU PROMISE TO CHANGE OUR HEARTS. I APPRECIATE YOUR WORK TO MAKE US MORE LIKE YOUR SON. HELP ME EMBRACE CHANGE AND LOVE OTHERS IN AND THROUGH YOU. IN JESUS' NAME. AMEN.

God Will Right
Every Wrong

God is jealous over those he loves; that is why he takes
vengeance on those who hurt them. He furiously destroys their
enemies. He is slow in getting angry, but when aroused, his
power is incredible, and he does not easily forgive. He shows
his power in the terrors of the cyclone and the raging storms;
clouds are billowing dust beneath his feet! . . . The Lord is
good. When trouble comes, he is the place to go! And he knows
everyone who trusts in him! But he sweeps away his enemies
with an overwhelming flood; he pursues them all night long.

NAHUM 1:2–3, 7–8 TLB

This is why you can rest in God's goodness, free from angst and
worry. While today's passage is from a vision He gave Nahum
regarding the impending doom of Nineveh, it's a truth we can
cling to for us too. God is jealous for those He loves, and He will
right every wrong that comes our way. So when trouble arrives,
we can run straight into His protective arms. We have a safe place
to go, a shelter from the storm.

When your husband walks out on the marriage and you're left
with a broken heart, take it directly to God. When the phone call
comes out of the blue and turns your life upside down, be quick

to cry out to the Father. Every time hopelessness sets in regarding your prodigal child, let Him bring much-needed comfort. When you find yourself out of work with bills mounting, allow God to calm your anxious thoughts. When grief overwhelms you or aging parents expect too much of you or hurtful people target you, grab hold of the Lord and never let go.

In the past, we may have tried to navigate these hard moments alone, or we may have sought advice from family or friends. Maybe we've turned to comfort food or retail therapy. Chances are we've tried self-help books or daily affirmations to strengthen us for the battle. Or we've hidden, choosing to give in and give up in fear and worry. But God sees it all and offers you a safe place to go for hope and help. The choice is yours.

DEAR LORD, MY HEART IS BLESSED TO KNOW YOU ARE JEALOUS FOR ME AND WANT ME TO TURN TO YOU ALONE IN HARD TIMES. REMIND ME TO REST IN YOU AS YOU FIGHT MY BATTLES FOR ME. IN JESUS' NAME. AMEN.

We Are Not God

Do not retaliate with evil, regardless of the evil brought against you. Try to do what is good and right and honorable as agreed upon by all people. If it is within your power, make peace with all people. Again, my loved ones, do not seek revenge; instead, allow God's wrath to make sure justice is served. Turn it over to Him. For the Scriptures say, "Revenge is Mine. I will settle all scores."

ROMANS 12:17–19 VOICE

Paul is once again reminding us that we are not God. It's not our job to plot and carry out revenge. We don't have to get even when others hurt us. Instead, when He says that revenge is His alone, the message is clear and strong: God wants to be the one to settle all scores. That means we're to let go and trust that He will ensure justice is served.

Trusting an unseen God to deal with our offenses is a gutsy choice. Why? Because we want to see evildoers pay for what they've done, and we want to see it now. So the idea of waiting for the Lord to act in His timing and in His ways is hard! But being a courageous woman of faith means we release our heartache and anger into His capable hands. We need to leave room for the wrath of God.

Our focus should be making peace with those around us. . .if doing so is within our power. The truth is that sometimes it's not. As much as we may try, we simply can't control what others choose to do. We can't make them respond in the ways we'd like them to. However, we do have complete control over our own actions and words. And while our best efforts to live in harmony may not always be received well on their end, we can still choose to be kind. Even if they respond with hate, we can choose not to engage in the same.

While community can be fun and fulfilling, it can also be a huge source of frustration. Be quick to pray for confidence to say what needs to be said in kindness. Ask for boldness to keep short accounts, letting God take it from there. And always try to do what is good and right.

DEAR LORD, HELP ME REMEMBER THAT YOU ARE GOD AND THAT I AM NOT. ENCOURAGE ME TO BRING YOUR PEACE INTO EVERY INTERACTION I HAVE. IN JESUS' NAME. AMEN.

The Foundation of a Saving Faith

By an act of faith, Enoch skipped death completely.
"They looked all over and couldn't find him because God
had taken him." We know on the basis of reliable testimony
that before he was taken "he pleased God." It's impossible
to please God apart from faith. And why? Because anyone
who wants to approach God must believe both that he exists
and that he cares enough to respond to those who seek him.

HEBREWS 11:5–6 MSG

This chapter in Hebrews is often referred to as the Hall of Faith because it's packed full of Old Testament men and women who had one thing in common. They put their full faith in God. They had complete confidence in Him, and their belief pleased Him. Enoch was one of them, as were Noah, Abraham, Jacob, Joseph, Moses, and Sarah.

Make sure you don't miss two important aspects of this passage of scripture. First, anyone who wants to approach God must believe He exists. It's not head knowledge but heart knowledge. And second, they must believe He cares enough to respond. In other words, we know He's a good God. We trust in the goodness of His character.

These two beliefs are the foundation of a saving faith. They are the anchors of a strong belief in God. They are what draw us closer to Him every day. Faith is what makes hope possible. And this is the kind of faith that pleases Him. While we may not be able to see God with our eyes this side of heaven, by faith we have confidence.

Scripture clearly tells us that Enoch pleased God. What did that look like? Knowing what the Bible says, we can assume it meant He walked with the Lord by faith each day. He talked to God, listened for His leading, and then obeyed. Friend, we can do the same thing here and now.

Faith is what helps us live in ways that please the Lord. It's why we can be bold, hopeful, and expectant for His goodness in our lives. Being a believer means we put our trust and confidence in God every day.

DEAR LORD, HELP ME BLESS YOU THROUGH MY IMPERFECT FAITH. GIVE ME THE COURAGE TO FOLLOW YOU THROUGH EVERY UP AND DOWN LIFE BRINGS. I HAVE HEART KNOWLEDGE OF YOU, AND I BELIEVE YOU WILL ALWAYS BE ACTIVE IN MY LIFE. IN JESUS' NAME. AMEN.

Just Trust Me

While he was still talking to her, messengers arrived from Jairus's home with the news that it was too late—his daughter was dead and there was no point in Jesus' coming now. But Jesus ignored their comments and said to Jairus, "Don't be afraid. Just trust me."

MARK 5:35–36 TLB

Those three little words—"Just trust Me"—are packed with a big challenge for believers. Especially when we're facing scary or heartbreaking circumstances, these words often feel too big to walk out. It seems a hopeless endeavor, even for the seasoned Christian. And if we're honest, there are times it feels almost impossible to trust an unseen God with our pain and grief. Yet that is exactly what He's asking of us.

When the dire health diagnosis comes, or our child is failing to launch, or we discover our husband's betrayal, God says, "Just trust Me." When our financial stability is failing and we don't see any relief in sight, He says, "Just trust Me." Each time we face rejection or mean-spiritedness from others, He whispers for us to trust Him—and that should be our response. When we look at world events and our spirit feels unsettled by it all, God reminds us to trust that He sees all and is in control. Our circumstances may be a bit different than those of Jairus, but no doubt we can understand being overcome by fear, insecurity, and worry. How are you doing with that, friend?

As we try to understand the hows and whys of life, we can rest in the knowledge that the Lord's faithfulness to those who love Him never changes. It never wavers. We may not have the answers in those difficult moments, but His command is and always will be: "Just trust Me."

Ask God for the strength to flex your faith muscle when troubling times come your way. Pray with expectation, believing that He will meet you in those moments to bring wisdom, peace, joy, rest, perseverance, and guidance. Have faith that His will for you will be done in His perfect timing. And cling to Him for hope, trusting He's already working things out for your good and His glory.

DEAR LORD, WHEN THE STORMS COME, REMIND ME
NOT TO GIVE IN TO FEAR BUT INSTEAD TO TRUST IN
YOUR GOODNESS AND LOVE. I KNOW YOU WILL
ALWAYS BE THERE FOR ME. IN JESUS' NAME. AMEN.

The Power of Testimony

I could speak more of faith; I could talk until time itself ran out.
If I continued, I could speak of the examples of Gideon, Barak,
Samson, and Jephthah, of David and Samuel and all the
prophets. I could give accounts of people alive with faith who
conquered kingdoms, brought justice, obtained promises, and
closed the mouths of hungry lions. I could tell you how people
of faith doused raging fires, escaped the edge of the sword,
made the weak strong, and—stoking great valor among the
champions of God—sent opposing armies into panicked flight.

HEBREWS 11:32–34 VOICE

The Bible gives us countless examples of heroes of the faith whose stories provide hope and encouragement as we navigate life today. God included them in His Word because He recognizes the power of a testimony. And the Lord understands that we need to know He was alive and active back in the day and is the same God who is moving in the lives of believers in the here and now. If He has done it before, He can do it again.

Something powerful happens in our hearts when we see how others have endured hardships and come out stronger. Remembering the ways God showed up helps us persevere with expectation through the hardest of times. It keeps us in the fight, knowing He is with us and for us. And as we pray for His help, we can respectfully remind Him that a precedent has been set and that we're asking for Him to do it for us too.

So whether you're asking for God to shut the mouths of hurtful people like He did the lions for Daniel or asking for an army of friends (even if small, like Gideon's) to help you walk through a difficult time or using a current example of His goodness in the life of someone else, be bold in your request. Let God know you trust Him to move on your behalf. Let Him know you're aware of His previous faithfulness toward believers.

God may not act in the same way as before. His timing may be different. And in His sovereignty, you may not see His answers until much later. But you can know, without fail, that the Lord hears you and will respond for your good and His glory. Your job is to ask for what you need and trust the perfection of His will and ways.

DEAR LORD, I TRUST YOU TO BE FAITHFUL ALWAYS,
NO MATTER WHAT. IN JESUS' NAME. AMEN.

God Will Fill Every Need

Know this: my God will also fill every need you
have according to His glorious riches in Jesus the
Anointed, our Liberating King. So may our God
and Father be glorified forever and ever. Amen.

PHILIPPIANS 4:19–20 VOICE

Don't be confused. In this passage, Paul isn't saying that believers won't go through challenging times. He's not suggesting we won't have moments of major need or times when we feel discouraged and desperate. If you think about it, Paul himself never had it easy as a follower. He endured trouble on the regular! He had money problems, faced persecution, landed in prison, and felt the pangs of hunger, to name a few struggles. But his spirit wasn't dampened. Why? Because Paul knew deep in his heart that God was trustworthy. He never doubted His goodness. And when he needed it, the Lord strengthened Paul for the battle.

It may be easy to *say* you trust God will fill every need you have, but when the difficulties come, do you? Consider that what we struggle with the most is having the perseverance and endurance to hold on to that truth when we feel overwhelmed. But when you look back at your life, can't you see how God has met your needs?

Maybe money showed up unexpectedly when you found

yourself in great need of it. Maybe you woke up with a heart of reconciliation and chose to make things right with that person again. Maybe a new and fresh door of opportunity opened at the perfect moment, bringing much-needed excitement for the future. Maybe you had the energy to stand up and speak up, advocating for yourself with both strength and kindness. Maybe you had a steady and hopeful heart through the medical procedure rather than drowning in worry and fear. Friend, wasn't that God meeting your complex needs in your weakest moments?

The truth is that God has unlimited tools at His disposal. That means He can access whatever He needs whenever He needs it. The Lord's resources are bottomless. So when we find ourselves in a tough place, let's boldly and humbly go right to the Source. Let's ask with expectation and thanksgiving. Through Him, we will find the grace and grit to withstand challenges and come out the other side intact. God will give us exactly what we need to go through every hardship that life brings our way.

DEAR LORD, I KNOW YOU HAVE MET MY NEEDS IN
THE PAST AND YOU WILL DO IT AGAIN EVERY TIME I
NEED HELP. THANK YOU! IN JESUS' NAME. AMEN.

Getting to the
End of Yourself

*She had suffered much from many doctors through the
years and had become poor from paying them, and was no
better but, in fact, was worse. She had heard all about the
wonderful miracles Jesus did, and that is why she came up
behind him through the crowd and touched his clothes. For
she thought to herself, "If I can just touch his clothing, I will
be healed." And sure enough, as soon as she had touched
him, the bleeding stopped and she knew she was well!*

MARK 5:26–29 TLB

She had come to the end of herself. Scripture tells us she had
suffered at the hands of many doctors who had tried to stop her
bleeding. For twelve years, they had been unable to fix what was
wrong. Their best remedies and prescribed treatments fell short.
What they offered as medicine or therapies never worked. And
in her desperation, she willingly paid them their fees, leaving her
broke and still bleeding. Imagine how much time and money
she'd spent trying to be whole again. Imagine too the emotional
toll her sickness had taken.

We may not have had to navigate the same issue she did,
but we know what it feels like to be emotionally bankrupt. We

understand hopelessness. We've spent our resources in good faith yet didn't get what we wished for. And honestly, it's not a stretch for us to relate to her persistence only to find ourselves once again. . .lacking. Broken. Just like the woman in today's passage, we get to the end of ourselves.

But she had heard about Jesus and the miracles He'd been doing in the area. And just like that, hope was restored. She dug deep and mustered the guts and grit to try one more thing in her pursuit of healing. It paid off.

She reached through the crowd and touched Jesus' garment and was healed immediately. In that very moment, the twelve years of bleeding stopped. She felt her broken body become whole.

In the same way, we can go directly to Jesus for help too. We can reach out to Him through prayer and feel His divine encouragement dry up our doubt and despair. When you come to the end of yourself, rather than look for worldly cures, find the courage to reach out to God.

DEAR LORD, HELP ME TRUST YOU TO BE MY SOURCE FOR
ALL THINGS SO I DON'T END UP EXHAUSTED AND DEPLETED
IN MY OWN STRENGTH. IN JESUS' NAME. AMEN.

We Are Overcomers

Everything that has been fathered by God overcomes the corrupt world. This is the victory that has conquered the world: our faith. Who is the person conquering the world? It is the one who truly trusts that Jesus is the Son of God, that Jesus the Anointed is the One who came by water and blood—not by the water only, but by the water and the blood.

1 JOHN 5:4–6 VOICE

Every true believer can be an overcomer. You don't have to be super spiritual or be in ministry. You don't have to log a ton of volunteer hours or have years of therapy under your belt. Victory in Jesus is not for the holy elites to enjoy alone. This isn't about our standing or our work. Scripture clearly says that if we've been born again into faith in Jesus, we are overcomers.

John goes on to say that our faith is the victory that overcomes the world. It's through this faith that we're able to give up control and put it in God's hands. It's how we're able to release our will and embrace His instead. And the only way we can overcome the influence and sway of this corrupt world is by clinging to our faith in Jesus. We hold on with all our might because we know faith in Him is the key to our victory.

How do we cling to Jesus in practical ways? We do it by reading the Bible and going to God in prayer. Scripture gives us encouragement and strength. It leaves us hopeful and comforted. And through its pages, our faith grows and matures with the Holy Spirit's help.

As we pray daily, we find hope and peace through our conversations with the Father. Our love for Him deepens. Our connection solidifies. And pouring out our worries and concerns lightens our load as we trust God with our greatest challenges.

So, friend, be gutsy in your prayers and talk to God with expectation that He will show up for you once again. Remember that you can connect with Him anywhere and anytime. And watch how these two things—scripture and prayer—will give you courage to walk through hard times in victory.

DEAR LORD, THANK YOU FOR MAKING ME AN OVERCOMER THROUGH FAITH IN YOU. THIS WORLD CAN'T HOLD ME DOWN WITH TROUBLES AND TRIALS ANYMORE. HELP ME WALK IN THAT TRUTH EVERY DAY. IN JESUS' NAME. AMEN.

Making Plans

*People go about making their plans, but the Eternal has the
final word. Even when you think you have good intentions,
He knows your real motives. Whatever you do, do it as
service to Him, and He will guarantee your success.*

PROVERBS 16:1–3 VOICE

Think of all the plans you have in the works right now. As women,
we're usually multitasking miracle workers who not only manage
our own lives but also keep all the plates spinning for others. From
husbands to kids to parents to friends, we help make the world go
around. Whether work related or personal, all kinds of things need
our attention every day. And nothing's wrong with being diligent
and making plans. Thinking ahead and being organized isn't bad
or wrong. But be sure to ask God to enable you or redirect you
according to His will, and always be prepared to pivot.

As believers, we can trust the Lord to see our hearts and know
our motives. He knows when our plans are self-seeking or others-
focused. He sees the truth of our intentions and understands the
complexities of our hearts. God knows our hopes and worries.
He recognizes the struggle to find balance. And as we commit
our work to the Lord and look to Him for help, He will bring our
plans to fruitfulness in His perfect way and in His perfect time.
We can expect this from our loving Father.

Be prayerful about the plans you're making. Talking to the Lord about all the decisions ahead, both small and big, is always a smart way to go. Ask for His guidance. Ask for direction as you move forward so you can be sure you're honoring Him. And as you feel His Holy Spirit leading you in a certain way, boldly and humbly follow. If you're going to err, always err on the side of faith and trust that He will change your course if necessary.

You can also commit to spending time in the Word, making sure your plans align with His will. Is anything you're working toward in direct opposition to the Bible? Has a precedent been set in its pages that you can bring to Him in prayer? This kind of diligence will help you achieve true success.

Every day and in each plan we make, let's purpose to please Him. And then let's trust that He will work all things for our good and His glory.

DEAR LORD, AS I MAKE PLANS, I TRUST YOU TO
BLESS OR REDIRECT. HELP ME TO BE FLEXIBLE
AND FAITHFUL. IN JESUS' NAME. AMEN.

Let Nothing Separate

I have written this to you who believe in the Son of God
so that you may know you have eternal life. And we are
sure of this, that he will listen to us whenever we ask
him for anything in line with his will. And if we really
know he is listening when we talk to him and make our
requests, then we can be sure that he will answer us.

1 JOHN 5:13–15 TLB

John authored the letter of 1 John so that we might believe in the Son of God. All of his writings are designed to point us to Jesus so that we can be certain of eternal life. He wants us to know that with Christ, our life can be wonderful and abundant even as we navigate its choppy waters at times. And along with that promise comes the assurance of His love. The truth is that we can't be loved any more or any less than we are right now. We can have confidence in who God is and who we are to Him, and this confidence helps to quiet that pesky doubt that often makes us second-guess our security and value in Him.

But when our standing with Him hasn't been settled in our hearts, we may feel a sense of anxiety that has a way of washing away our confidence, creating waves of fear. Even though we're told over 360 times in the Bible not to be afraid, we are. We let fear shut us down and make us ineffective in our calling. We let it make us feel small and insignificant. We forget about the abundant life Jesus' death on the cross has afforded us. Fear weakens our faith, causing us to feel ashamed. And worst of all, we stop talking to God and decide to go about each day in our own strength and understanding.

Friend, be careful that you let nothing separate you from the Father. When feelings of fear or shame come flooding in, they should serve as a huge red flag. If we desire to be gutsy girls who love God with all our hearts, we need to stay close to Him no matter what. That means as we feel the wedge beginning to grow, we go straight to the Lord in prayer and talk about it. Let's share our feelings boldly because He is listening. Let's pray with hopeful, thankful hearts. And as we confess, let's ask God to remove the barriers that sin has erected. We can be certain He will because this request always lines up with His will.

DEAR LORD, HELP ME STAY CLOSE TO YOU ALWAYS. IN JESUS' NAME. AMEN.

Changing Our Perspective on Trials

Don't run from tests and hardships, brothers and sisters.
As difficult as they are, you will ultimately find joy in
them; if you embrace them, your faith will blossom under
pressure and teach you true patience as you endure.
And true patience brought on by endurance will equip
you to complete the long journey and cross the finish
line—mature, complete, and wanting nothing.

JAMES 1:2–4 VOICE

In today's passage of scripture, James is encouraging us to evaluate how we see tests and hardships in life. He's asking us to shift our perspective and look at these trials in a different way: from God's point of view. And rather than run from them or try to insulate ourselves from pain, we should press into the Lord for strength and peace.

The truth is that tough times are just part of the human experience—whether you're a believer or not. They will come. We'll have to navigate the ups and downs of this life. Being a Christian does not exclude us from heartache. To expect otherwise is a setup for disappointment. But where faith is applied, we can trust that God will use every trial for our good and His glory. We can find peace in knowing He's working everything out according to His beautiful plan.

When James says we'll find joy in tests and hardships, that emotion will come from knowing every trial has the potential to produce good things in us. We can rejoice because we trust God and know something bigger is taking place under His loving direction and care. Joy may be directly opposite of our normal reaction, but we can let James' words help us change our perspective in the tough times from doom and gloom to expectation and hope.

Friend, think of these tough times as a training ground. They are building our spiritual muscles, building necessary life skills like endurance and patience. If we never faced these kinds of challenges, how would our Christian character grow? If not tested, how would our faith mature?

Being gutsy means we embrace the grim times in the moment while being grateful for what they will accomplish in us later. Ask God to give you the spiritual eyes to see Him working in your struggles. And thank Him for always working things out according to His perfect plan.

DEAR LORD, YOU ARE SIMPLY AMAZING. THANK YOU FOR HAVING A PURPOSE FOR EVERYTHING LIFE BRINGS MY WAY. IN JESUS' NAME. AMEN.

Clinging to Comforting Truth

When you go through deep waters and great trouble, I will be
with you. When you go through rivers of difficulty, you will
not drown! When you walk through the fire of oppression,
you will not be burned up—the flames will not consume you.

ISAIAH 43:2 TLB

Some days we cling to this comforting truth with all we have. It's what gets us through the unexpected breakup. It's how we find hope when it seems like the world is against us. Knowing God's presence is with us is why we're able to get out of bed and function. Understanding His power to save is why we're able to put one foot in front of the other and try again. The promises in this verse are what hold us up when we'd rather wilt in defeat. But as believers, we cling to the truth because we know the Lord God is mighty to save.

The Bible is crystal clear when it tells us that we will face difficulties. Chances are you have firsthand experience wading through murky, deep waters. We will most certainly encounter trouble of every kind while living and breathing here on planet Earth. The rivers of difficulty—be they relational, financial, emotional, or physical—will threaten to pull us under and wash us away. We'll find ourselves walking through the fire, feeling the flames lapping at our peace and hope. These trials are part of living in a fallen and broken world. But God is the game changer.

The presence of the Lord within us makes these difficulties bearable. Even more, it transforms them into opportunities for us to experience victory—the kind Jesus Christ came to give! As believers, we don't have to fall prey to hard times. Instead, we can find ourselves secure and stable. And no matter what comes our way, with God's Spirit within us we're able to cling to the truth that brings freedom to our hearts and minds. His presence changes everything.

DEAR LORD, THANK YOU FOR BEING WITH ME AS I NAVIGATE THE MESSY MOMENTS OF LIFE. HELP ME REMEMBER THAT WHEN THE DEEP WATERS OF LIFE THREATEN TO DROWN ME, I CAN CLING TO YOU AS MY ANCHOR. NO FIRE WILL CONSUME ME. YOUR LOVE IS SIMPLY AMAZING. IN JESUS' NAME. AMEN.

Our Wisdom Isn't Enough

If you don't have all the wisdom needed for this journey,
then all you have to do is ask God for it; and God will grant
all that you need. He gives lavishly and never scolds you
for asking. The key is that your request be anchored by
your single-minded commitment to God. Those who depend
only on their own judgment are like those lost on the seas,
carried away by any wave or picked up by any wind.

JAMES 1:5–6 VOICE

We all need wisdom to get through each day. So many decisions need to be made, some with substantial consequences attached. And while we may feel equipped to choose our own way, the truth is that we need God's wisdom to direct us. We simply don't have the ability to see the big picture, but He does.

Scripture tells us that if we feel a lack of direction or understanding, we have the freedom to ask God for it. When we need sharp discernment as we parent through a tough situation, God will give it in abundance. As we face decisions about career moves and the monetary impact that may play out, we can trust the Holy Spirit to show us the right path to follow. When a relationship feels off and we need insight to pinpoint the core issues and navigate the hard conversations that must come, He will generously provide guidance if we ask. When we come to an important crossroads and see the pros and cons of both paths, we can lessen our confusion by letting God lead our steps forward. He gives lavishly.

What sets us up for the Lord's extravagance is having a single-minded commitment to God. That means we don't cling to our own understanding. We don't depend only on our own judgment because we know it's imperfect, just as are we. Instead, we make a conscious decision to rely on the Lord over anything we come up with. We don't trust in our past experience. We don't count on insight from self-help books. We don't phone a friend.

As believers, we open the Bible and let God speak to us there. We pray boldly and earnestly, thank Him in advance, and then stand by for His direction. And until we get it, we wait in expectation.

DEAR LORD, THANK YOU FOR GIVING ME
WISDOM WHEN I NEED IT! IN JESUS' NAME. AMEN.

Through the Wilderness

*But forget all that—it is nothing compared to what I'm
going to do! For I'm going to do a brand-new thing. See,
I have already begun! Don't you see it? I will make a
road through the wilderness of the world for my people
to go home, and create rivers for them in the desert!*

ISAIAH 43:18–19 TLB

. . . .

Isaiah shared these powerful words with the nation of Israel, bringing them hope during the years of their captivity. Because they'd
wandered so far from God in their hearts, they were certain He
had disowned them. They figured He had rejected or abandoned
them, and this faulty assumption kept them unsettled.

But the Israelites had forgotten something especially important.
It's not God who condemns. That's the enemy's job. Any condemnation they were feeling wasn't divine—it was demonically inspired.
The reality is that God loves lavishly and always makes a way back
to Himself. And it's as true today as it was back then. . .God will
always make a way out of the wilderness.

God encouraged His people to look ahead, not behind. He
wanted them to know He was doing something brand-new. God
wanted them to have hope for something more.

Maybe you need that reminder too. Do you need something
new in your life? Do you need a fresh start in your marriage?

Do you need a renewed sense of value and worth after a painful breakup? Are you hoping for something different in your outlook and perspective on life? Does your faith need to be revived? Are you tired of circling the mountain and you're craving rest? Are you hoping for your courage and confidence to be restored? Where are you hoping for God to do a brand-new thing in your life?

Friend, let today's passage remind you that God is on the move in your life. He won't leave you in the mess. He won't let you get stale in your situation. Turn back to Him and ask for help in forgetting what was and focusing on what He will do—what He is doing. Because God is making a road just for you to navigate through the wilderness and come back to Him. He's waiting for you with open arms, full of compassion.

DEAR LORD, THANK YOU FOR CREATING A WAY BACK TO YOU. FORGIVE ME FOR MY WANDERING, SELF-SEEKING WAYS. PLEASE FILL ME WITH HOPE AND EXPECTATION FOR YOUR WILL TO BE DONE IN MY LIFE. IN JESUS' NAME. AMEN.

Blessed for Endurance

*Blessed (happy, to be envied) is the man who is patient under
trial and stands up under temptation, for when he has stood
the test and been approved, he will receive [the victor's] crown
of life which God has promised to those who love Him.*

JAMES 1:12 AMPC

When the frustrating times hit, we often lose sight of what is true.
We become myopic and don't see the bigger picture of what's
really going on. Rather than focusing on what God may be doing
in each difficult circumstance, we let discouragement settle into
our hearts. We become depressed. We feel hopeless. And we forget
there is always a divine purpose behind our pain and suffering.

When James writes the word for *blessed* in this scripture, it
means so much more than just being happy or envied. It's having
a secure inner joy that can't be disturbed by outward troubles. It's
choosing to trust that God is in control and resting in His goodness.
It's looking at each circumstance with an eternal perspective and
not an earthly one. And when we are patient through the trials
and don't buckle under the weight of temptation, scripture says
that we are blessed. We are highly favored.

Each time we boldly endure what life brings our way, it's a win.
Each decision to persevere when we'd rather give up reveals our
courage. James isn't suggesting that it's a blessing to face hardship.

But when we're steadfast in our faith and trust God through every struggle, His rich blessings will follow. He will honor our choice to stand strong. We'll receive the victor's crown of life for persisting. He'll assure us that our endurance hasn't gone unnoticed.

God uses trials to season us to maturity. Adversity is how we grow. And on the other side of them are personal growth and spiritual development. So we can walk through challenges with our eyes on the Lord and with an expectant heart. Truly, a hopeful mindset helps make tough times more bearable.

Friend, ask the Lord to give you an eternal perspective. Ask Him to remind you that blessings are coming. And never forget that He is at work in meaningful ways for both your good and His glory.

DEAR LORD, HELP ME TO BE PATIENT IN TRIALS AND TO STAND UP UNDER TEMPTATION. I KNOW YOU WILL BLESS ME FOR THAT KIND OF FAITH. IN JESUS' NAME. AMEN.

Asking Daily for His Protection

This I declare, that he alone is my refuge, my place of safety; he is my God, and I am trusting him. For he rescues you from every trap and protects you from the fatal plague. He will shield you with his wings! They will shelter you. His faithful promises are your armor. Now you don't need to be afraid of the dark anymore, nor fear the dangers of the day; nor dread the plagues of darkness, nor disasters in the morning.

PSALM 91:2–6 TLB

Sometimes we forget the powerful promises of God. We forget the places in scripture where He tells us of His protection. We forget that He understands the craziness of this world and the way it stirs up real fears, even in the hearts of believers. And we forget that the Lord cares about those who love Him. He will override every fear we have with His love.

What worries you today, friend? What anxieties are pressing in on you right now? Consider the fact that you may be reading this devotional today as part of God's plan because He sees your troubled heart. So why not follow the psalmist's lead and receive the Lord's comfort too? Why not re-read today's verses as a prayer and boldly make them personal to you?

Recognize that God alone is your refuge. He is your place of safety, so you can choose to trust Him. Thank the Lord for offering you rescue from the world's curses and calamities by shielding you with His wings. They will provide shelter from the storms. Show gratitude for His promises that are unbreakable and unshakable. They are the armor that surrounds you. Regardless of what life brings your way, God stands before you. Go ahead and confidently embrace these promises. Pray with expectation every day, asking Him to fortify you with His perfect presence.

Ask the Lord to defend you and give you sanctuary from whatever threatens your peace and joy. And then shower Him with praises because you know He will respond in the right ways at the right times. Friend, you are seen and heard, and your Father will be who you need Him to be.

DEAR LORD, WHAT A RELIEF TO KNOW YOU ARE MY REFUGE AND PLACE OF SAFETY. GIVE ME THE COURAGE TO TRUST IN YOU FOR HELP RATHER THAN LEANING ON MY OWN UNDERSTANDING AND STRENGTH. IN JESUS' NAME. AMEN.

Tempted versus Tested

No one who is tempted should ever be confused and say that
God is testing him. The One who created us is free from evil
and can't be tempted, so He doesn't tempt anyone. When a
person is carried away with desire, lured by lust, and when
desire becomes the focus and takes control, it gives birth to
sin. When sin becomes fully grown, it produces death.

JAMES 1:13–15 VOICE

Earlier in this chapter, James explains that as Christians, we will endure tough times. We will face temptation and testing. While the enemy drives the former, the latter is a method God uses with precision. Temptation is part of the human condition, part of living in a fallen world, but God's testing is altogether different. He applies it to believers because it produces good things in us, like perseverance. This is how our faith grows and matures.

It's this developing faith that will keep us from being crushed and overwhelmed. It will give us an eternal perspective to realize that God isn't the one tempting because He Himself can't be, and so He doesn't try to seduce believers with temptation either. He will not lead us into sin because sin is not in His nature. Absolutely nothing can entice the Lord to wickedness. And while we may be angry with God when we feel the pull into debauchery, thinking He's behind the lure, it's simply not the truth. For Him, the goal is the trial itself.

God uses trials to authenticate our faith. They are tools to help refine us. They teach us to rely on the divine Father for help rather than allow the decrepit world to hook us. Trials open our eyes to where we need to relinquish control and trust the Lord. They reveal our weak areas—the ones where we desperately need His fortification. We may not enjoy the trials that come our way, but they are an essential part of our journey with Him.

Ask God for wisdom to know the difference between temptation and testing and to respond accordingly. With God, you are not weak and unable to discern. Instead, you are safely in His hands. And when you ask, you'll have exactly what you need to navigate them both.

DEAR LORD, HELP ME SEE THE CHALLENGES THAT
COME MY WAY WITH SPIRITUAL EYES AND FULL
FAITH IN YOU. IN JESUS' NAME. AMEN.

The Power of Because

For the Lord says, "Because he loves me, I will rescue
him; I will make him great because he trusts in my name.
When he calls on me, I will answer; I will be with him
in trouble and rescue him and honor him. I will satisfy
him with a full life and give him my salvation."

PSALM 91:14–16 TLB

Did you notice the power of the word *because* in today's scripture?
It's a qualifier to God's protection and goodness, and it allows us
to see an important aspect of the role we play in our relationship
with the Lord. He gives lavishly in response to our faith. His
abundance and help answer our belief.

When we choose to love God with all our heart, mind, and soul,
He takes care of us. Every time we decide to trust in the Lord's
sovereignty, we will be rewarded for being obedient. Following
Him with passion and purpose prompts God to hear our cry and
answer it according to His perfect will. And He tells us through
the psalmist that He'll be with us no matter what troubles we're
facing. We will be rescued and honored. We will be fulfilled in this
life and then spend eternity in heaven. What amazing and awe-
inspiring promises we receive upon accepting Jesus as our Savior!

Can you remember times when you've seen this play out in
your life? Have you trusted God to act on your behalf, giving up

the relentless desire to control the situation? Have you pored over scripture, finding the courage to stand confidently in the truth of who God is and what He promises to do? Have you cried out for help and watched as the Lord orchestrated a Red Sea moment for you to escape on dry ground? These beautiful moments are *because* you have loved and trusted God with all your heart, even if imperfectly at times.

God sees you. He delights in who you are. Your faith has received His full attention. His heart for you is always good. Nothing could make Him love you any more or any less than He does right now. And when you demonstrate your steadfast faith in action, you will be blessed in meaningful and significant ways.

DEAR LORD, THANK YOU THAT BECAUSE I LOVE
AND TRUST IN YOU THROUGH THE FRUSTRATIONS
OF LIFE, YOU RESPOND IN WAYS THAT BLESS ME
AND HOLD ME UP. IN JESUS' NAME. AMEN.

Open Ears and
Closed Mouth

*Listen, open your ears, harness your desire to speak,
and don't get worked up into a rage so easily, my brothers
and sisters. Human anger is a futile exercise that will
never produce God's kind of justice in this world. So
walk out on your corrupt liaison with smut and depraved
living, and humbly welcome the word of truth that will
blossom like the seed of salvation planted in your souls.*

JAMES 1:19–21 VOICE

. . . .

Opening our ears means we're quick to listen to the whole story
or the entire opinion someone is sharing. *Harnessing our desire to
speak* means we have control over our words and don't try to share
them in haste. These concepts are easy enough to understand
but quite a challenge to walk out in real time.

How many relationships have been damaged because we
didn't take the time to let someone speak? In our anxiousness
to speak, how many times did we interrupt without hearing all
that they had to say? How many people have we hurt because
we decided what we had to say was more important than what
they had to say? James is sharing a particularly important truth
that we all would do well to embrace and live out. Think about

how this admonition challenges you today.

The reality is that we're not naturally bent this way. We often speak up first and reluctantly listen second. But with God's help, and intentionality, we can learn to be better listeners. We can train ourselves to be quick to hear and slow to speak. Doing so will allow for better and more respectful communication. And it will help us reach greater understanding so we can digest others' words rather than get angry and defensive.

Instead of grandstanding to be heard or to get our way, let's remember what the Word says about living life well and loving others with purpose. The Bible guides us away from depraved living and shows us ways we can be blessed and be a blessing. One of those is honoring others by giving them space to share their thoughts and feelings. It's letting them know that what they think and feel matters. And we can ask God for help in controlling our desire to be heard above all else.

Listening well is a gutsy move because it challenges us to drop our selfishness and see the value of those around us. Only with God's strength and compassion can we love others with such purpose. Ask Him for open ears and a closed mouth, and He'll give them to you.

DEAR LORD, HELP ME SEE THE VALUE IN
LISTENING FIRST. IN JESUS' NAME. AMEN.

When Tough Seasons Come

The LORD supports all who fall down, straightens up all
who are bent low. All eyes look to you, hoping, and you
give them their food right on time, opening your hand
and satisfying the desire of every living thing. The LORD
is righteous in all his ways, faithful in all his deeds.

PSALM 145:14–17 CEB

It takes courage to get back up after you've fallen and grit to
stand tall when life hits hard. Challenging circumstances can leave
us feeling weak. We'll face situations where our resolve fades
away. And chances are we're used to pulling ourselves together
on our own.

Repeatedly, the school of hard knocks has made us feel like
we're the only one we can truly trust. Family members usually
have the best intentions, and our friends want to support us in the
ways they can, but in the end, we feel the weight of it all. That is,
unless we go to God.

When those tough seasons come, be prayerful. Be quick to
run into the Father's arms and ask for His guidance. Put your
burdens at His feet so the pressure to fix your situation is gone.
Take Him up on His promise to be your shelter and strong tower.
Go to God in your need with a hopeful heart full of expectation.

Walk into His presence with your hands open, believing the

Lord will satisfy every desire that aligns with His will for your life. Keep your eyes trained on God, for He is your source of hope and healing, direction and guidance, wisdom and discernment, joy and peace. Because of His goodness, you will experience God's faithfulness time and time again. And with that, your confidence will grow, helping you see the value in staying true to the one who will always be there for you.

DEAR LORD, I CONFESS THE TIMES I'VE LOOKED TO SOMEONE OTHER THAN YOU TO FIX ME. THERE HAVE BEEN MOMENTS WHEN I'VE TRUSTED IN PEOPLE MORE THAN IN YOU. I'VE EVEN DECIDED IN CERTAIN SITUATIONS THAT MY WAYS AND THOUGHTS WERE HIGHER THAN YOUR WAYS AND THOUGHTS. BUT I KNOW THAT YOU ARE MY SUPPORT AND THE ONE WHO STRAIGHTENS MY SPINE. THANK YOU FOR BEING MY SOURCE, THERE FOR ME THROUGH EVERY UP AND DOWN. IN JESUS' NAME. AMEN.

Controlling Your Mouth

If you put yourself on a pedestal, thinking you have
become a role model in all things religious, but you
can't control your mouth, then think again. Your mouth
exposes your heart, and your religion is useless.

JAMES 1:26 VOICE

For many, this may be a terrifying scripture because it's not always easy to keep our tongue in check. But James is saying that if we consider ourselves to be faithful followers, we will have self-control and be able to use it. It's easy to say we love the Lord and that we walk as He guides, but what matters most is how we live. Is our life preaching truth?

What does it mean to control our mouth? The reality is that whatever we feed our heart and mind comes out in our words. This is about the condition of the heart, because it's from the heart that our words and actions spill forth. To tame a tongue, you'll need to ask God to transform your way of thinking. He'll need to breathe new life into your heart. And your faith will have to grow in the knowledge and understanding of who God is and who you are because of Him.

Our mouths are quick to betray what's going on inside. So if we decide we're role models in the faith but what we say is wicked and unloving, we're deceiving ourselves in the worst of ways. The tongue will always give us away. And when it does, our faith will be proven useless.

But take heart, friend! God is ready, able, and willing to renovate when you ask. If you need Him to change your heart and strengthen your faith, tell Him today. Ask with bold conviction, telling the Lord about whatever concerns you. Confess your shortcomings and sinful ways, asking for forgiveness and cleansing. Ask for revelation to see what may be causing your bad choices. And give God praise for do-overs and second chances. We are here to bring Him glory, and we must control our mouths (by protecting our hearts) to do so effectively.

DEAR LORD, THE TRUTH IS THAT I AM WRETCHED WITHOUT YOU. FORGIVE ME FOR FILLING MY HEART AND MIND WITH ALL THE WRONG THINGS, LEADING ME TO BE CARELESS WITH MY WORDS. MY GREATEST DESIRE IS TO LOVE YOU AND FOR MY LIFE TO POINT TO YOU AND YOUR GLORY. IN JESUS' NAME. AMEN.

The Sole Source

I look up at the vast size of the mountains—from where will my help come in times of trouble? The Eternal Creator of heaven and earth and these mountains will send the help I need.

PSALM 121:1–2 VOICE

- -

This psalm is one of the Songs of Ascent. Travelers sang it as they made their way up through the hills to the city of Jerusalem. The writer is recognizing that God is his sole source of help. He's the one who will keep watch over the nation of Israel and provide protection for His children. For us, this is a sweet reminder that God is still in control and will keep us safe as we walk through this life of faith with Him.

Our help comes from the Lord in a variety of meaningful ways that we experience every day. It's the strength we need to stand up for ourselves when we feel too insecure to speak up. It's wisdom to know the next right step to take in a demanding situation. It's the discernment necessary to separate truth from lies and right from wrong. The Lord gives us peace when our circumstances threaten to shake our confidence. Often, He fills us with joy when the situation at hand calls for worry and an unsettled spirit. It's the guts and grit we need to walk away from temptation that could lead us into sins. Whatever it is we need, looking to Him as our sole source brings blessings.

God promises to listen when we cry out and to meet our every need. He won't tire of our requests. He won't sit in frustration when we keep asking for the same things. The Lord will never change His mind about us, even when our hearts are messy, and our sins are ugly. He is unwavering, steadfast, and consistent, always ready to offer much-needed help and hope to those who love Him.

We can be confident that our God will give us what we need to navigate the difficulties that come into our lives. His help may look different than what we prayed for, and His timing may not line up with our request, but we can fully and completely trust Him with those details. Until we see Him face-to-face, our help will most certainly come from the Lord.

DEAR LORD, I STAND IN CONFIDENCE THAT YOU
WILL ALWAYS HELP ME. IN JESUS' NAME. AMEN.

What It Really Means to Be Still

*"Be still, be calm, see, and understand I am the True God.
I am honored among all the nations. I am honored over
all the earth." You know the Eternal, the Commander
of heavenly armies, surrounds us and protects us; the
True God of Jacob is our shelter, close to His heart.*

PSALM 46:10–11 VOICE

Notice that before we can understand that God is God, we are commanded to be still. In Hebrew, the word for *still* is *rapa*, which means "to cease." It's likened to two people fighting until someone intervenes and makes them drop their weapons. Once they stop, they can then find the focus to see their need to trust the Lord.

So often we think this instruction is telling us to get quiet in God's presence. That in and of itself is a helpful and wonderful practice. But in truth, this scripture is telling us to stop moving anxiously. It's saying we're to cease acting in our desperation. We are to stop living with such worry and recklessness. For believers, being still means looking to God to be our source of help and hope rather than trying to figure everything out on our own.

The word *know* in this verse means "to be aware." It's a call to truly know who God is, because when we do, we'll be emboldened to trust Him enough to stop fighting for ourselves. We'll fully believe He has our backs.

Who do you know God to be, friend? Do you believe without doubt that He's sovereign? Do you acknowledge He is all-knowing, all-powerful, and all-present? In your heart, do you trust that the Lord is holy, faithful, and loving? Is He kind and generous? Is He full of compassion for those who love Him? Is He good? Let the answer to every one of these be a resounding yes!

Ask the Lord to strengthen you to know the truth of who He is. Ask for the courage to stop fighting in your own strength to fix the problems facing you today. Pray with complete expectation that God is who He says He is and that He will do what He promises in the Bible to do. And always pray with thanksgiving because you're not alone to figure life out. You are deeply loved by the one who created you.

DEAR LORD, HELP ME BE STILL AND TRUST THAT
YOU WILL MEET ME IN EVERY CHALLENGE
AND BE GOD. IN JESUS' NAME. AMEN.

Kept Close to God

He holds you firmly in place; He will not let you fall. He who
keeps you will never take His eyes off you and never drift off
to sleep. What a relief! The One who watches over Israel never
leaves for rest or sleep. The Eternal keeps you safe, so close
to Him that His shadow is a cooling shade to you. Neither
bright light of sun nor dim light of moon will harm you.

PSALM 121:3–6 VOICE

These verses don't suggest that we won't run into trouble in life.
The psalmist isn't saying we'll be spared from hardship and live
easy, simple, predictable lives. The truth is that no matter how
much we try to secure ourselves, we will face exceedingly difficult
times. A lot of them.

Some of our deepest desires—like being married or having
kids—may be unmet in this life. We'll have breakdowns in important relationships that will leave us heartbroken. Health scares
and financial stresses will challenge us in significant ways. We'll
have to navigate times of terrible insecurity and fear regarding
our work. The state of the nation or world will unsettle our spirit
from time to time. Our children's disobedience and/or departure
from our hopes and dreams will tear us apart on the inside. Our
loved ones will pass away, their absence shaking us to the core.
Our foundation will be rocked countless times. Friend, struggles

are inevitable and should be expected.

But the psalmist is promising that as we face these moments of pain and worry, God will keep us close. He will hold us firmly in place. We won't ultimately fall and fail. His attention will be steadfast, and His interest won't drift away. God will keep us safe and will bring relief and rest.

We can be confident that the one who loved us yesterday also loves us today, and He will most certainly love us tomorrow. And even when we go through times when we feel hope is nowhere to be found, as believers we know that's not true. Our feelings aren't always facts. We can boldly trust that God is with us through it all, holding us in His holy and capable hands.

DEAR LORD, WHAT A RELIEF TO KNOW YOU HOLD
ME AND WILL NOT LET ME FALL. HELP ME TRUST YOU
EVERY DAY IN EVERY WAY. IN JESUS' NAME. AMEN.

Avoiding the Parched Places

The LORD proclaims: Cursed are those who trust in mere humans, who depend on human strength and turn their hearts from the LORD. They will be like a desert shrub that doesn't know when relief comes. They will live in the parched places of the wilderness, in a barren land where no one survives.

JEREMIAH 17:5–6 CEB

Jeremiah consistently reminds us that trusting in man is futile and encourages us throughout his ministry to look only to God for provision. And for good reason.

How can we profess faith if we're constantly turning our back on Him to lean into our own understanding? To do so is to reject the Lord. When we rely on ourselves or look to those around us to be our savior, it's like we're a desert shrub living in parched places. We'll never be properly satisfied and cared for. We'll feel a profound lack deep in our spirit and find ourselves destined to hardship and hurt. But this isn't how the Lord wants us to live!

God's greatest hope is for us to flourish in relationship with Him, experiencing the joy of the Lord no matter what life brings. He wants us to thrive rather than just survive. And when we cling to Him for our every need, we'll grow and prosper by His hand.

Trusting in mere humans is a dangerous trap because it sets us up to fail. With our limited understanding and resources, we simply cannot navigate the storms of this life in our own strength and wisdom. Trying to do so sets us up for a powerless life when instead we could claim victory through Christ. And it inevitably lands us in parched places, desperate for help and hope but seeking it from our own abilities and from those around us. We won't survive here.

We were created to be in relationship with our Creator. And as we fellowship with Him in a loving and trusting way, we'll experience His care, compassion, strength, guidance, provision, and protection. Every day, pray for the confidence and courage to live this way, avoiding the trap of parched places. Friend, no one can bloom in the barren land of the wilderness.

DEAR LORD, LET ME ALWAYS DEPEND ON
YOU OVER ANYONE OR ANYTHING ELSE.
YOU'RE ALL I NEED! IN JESUS' NAME. AMEN.

Because We Don't Live in a Perfect World

Cast your troubles upon the Eternal; His care is unceasing!
He will not allow His righteous to be shaken. But
You, O God, You will drive them into the lowest
pit—violent, lying people won't live beyond their
middle years. But I place my trust in You.
PSALM 55:22–23 VOICE

In a perfect world, we would wake up in a good mood with no lingering worries from the day before. We'd spend time in the Word and let it refocus our eyes on God. Everything on our to-do list would be easily knocked off without any hitch, and we wouldn't be exhausted by what the day required. Everyone, including us, would be punctual and affirming. Every interaction with others would leave us feeling loved and appreciated. Each of our relationships would be life-giving and without any conflict. No comfort eating or retail therapy would be needed. There'd be no reason for fear or worry. No reason for anxious thoughts or stress. And after a day of eating balanced, healthy food and happily engaging in an epic workout, we'd lay our head on the pillow and easily fall asleep. How wonderful. . .and impossible.

The reality is that we have many troubles to manage. Think of all the ones heavy on your heart right now! There's no shortage of situations that rock us to the core. We are imperfect people living in an imperfect world and dealing with other imperfect people. And we have an enemy whose sole purpose is to steal, kill, and destroy. There's no hope for an easy and seamless life. But that's okay, because we have a God willing to take every heartache and affliction for us. We're invited to take every burden off our shoulders and give it to the one who can carry it on our behalf, bringing the resolution and restoration we cannot.

As we do this, something supernatural happens. The Holy Spirit working in us provides peace and comfort. We have strength to take the next right step as He leads. And we find ourselves held and loved, empowered to stand strong as He works things out for our good and His glory.

Let prayer be always on your lips, for prayer is the way you share your burdens with God. Be bold enough to ask Him to carry each one, and then expect that He will as you surrender them into His capable hands. He's got this.

DEAR LORD, THESE ARE MY BURDENS. PLEASE TAKE
THEM FROM ME. IN JESUS' NAME. AMEN.

227

Living with Joy and Happiness

Tormented and empty are wicked and destructive people,
but the one who trusts in the Eternal is wrapped tightly
in His gracious love. Express your joy; be happy in Him,
you who are good and true. Go ahead, shout and rejoice
aloud, you whose hearts are honest and straightforward.

PSALM 32:10–11 VOICE

Today's verse is a good reminder that we were created to live joyful lives even in the midst of challenging circumstances. As believers, we should find our happiness in an abundant life of faith and not anything the world can offer. God's grace is like a tight hug that makes us feel loved and secure in Him alone. And when our hearts for God are good and we feel driven to be more like Christ in our words and actions, our spirits will settle in His love.

In contrast, when we choose to live in opposition to the Father, we'll find ourselves suffering inside. Because we're not following God's commands with passion or purpose, we won't be able to experience peace in any meaningful way and our lives won't reflect His goodness. There will be no obedience for Him to reward, as the Bible mentions repeatedly. Instead, there will be a deep emptiness that can't adequately be filled by people or things—at least not for long.

So how can we position ourselves for a life of faithfulness in which we trust God for all we need? How can we experience His gracious love, express joy, and radiate happiness? It takes intentional living every day.

Friend, commit to spending time in God's Word so you know what life should look like. Let scripture teach you what He wants and why following His ways will bring blessing into each day. Learn about the character of God as He reveals Himself throughout its pages. Read about joy and peace—and how you can experience both no matter what you're navigating.

And pray. Pray bold prayers. Pray without ceasing, asking for these qualities to be displayed in your life. Pray with an expectant heart, hopeful for His goodness to delight your spirit. Pray with thanksgiving for who He is and how He shows His kindness and generosity.

. . . .

DEAR LORD, GIVE ME THE COURAGE TO TRUST YOU
WHOLEHEARTEDLY SO I CAN EXPERIENCE YOUR GOODNESS
IN MY LIFE. KEEP ME FROM A VICTIM MENTALITY WHERE I TURN
AWAY FROM YOUR LOVE AND GRACE. IN JESUS' NAME. AMEN.

Being Inspired, Instructed, and Prepared

Every Scripture is God-breathed (given by His inspiration)
and profitable for instruction, for reproof and conviction
of sin, for correction of error and discipline in obedience,
[and] for training in righteousness (in holy living, in
conformity to God's will in thought, purpose, and action),
so that the man of God may be complete and proficient,
well fitted and thoroughly equipped for every good work.

2 TIMOTHY 3:16–17 AMPC

Simply stated, scripture is inspired. It's instructional. And it prepares. Have you ever thought how nice it would be to have a playbook to help you get through life? Have you wanted access to an instruction manual to help figure out ways to manage your circumstances? Friend, you do have such a thing. It's the Bible.

God uses this book to teach us what is right and what is wrong. It's chock-full of historical accounts and powerful parables that help us understand correct and compassionate responses as believers. It contrasts the differences between living in victory and living as a victim. It highlights God's promises and reveals His character. And the more time we spend in its pages, the more the Lord will use it to transform our hearts supernaturally.

The Bible will equip us to manage both the mountaintops and the valleys with integrity. It will show us how to love the unlovable and forgive the unforgivable. With the Holy Spirit's help, our faith will mature.

God's Word will allow us to discover how testing differs from temptation and how conviction differs from condemnation. We will understand what holy living looks like and how we can stay in God's grace.

This beautiful book will guide us in relationships, including marriage and parenting. It will unpack money issues and how they relate to heart issues. It will challenge us to see things from a unique perspective. We'll be stretched to release control and surrender our will to His.

And when you find yourself afraid and worried, the Bible will supernaturally provide comfort for your unsettled spirit. It will give you timely hope. It will strengthen you and increase your confidence, making you bold. You'll collect wisdom and discernment. And you can pray scripture back to the Lord, asking Him to bless you in the ways the Bible mentions.

God's Word is a blueprint for whatever comes your way. Let it inspire, instruct, and prepare you!

DEAR LORD, YOUR WORD IS A GIFT AND A BLESSING.
LET ME WIELD THIS SWORD OF THE SPIRIT IN MY LIFE
WITH POWER AND PURPOSE. IN JESUS' NAME, AMEN.

A Holy Way of Life

Since you are all set apart by God, made holy and
dearly loved, clothe yourselves with a holy way of life:
compassion, kindness, humility, gentleness, and patience.

COLOSSIANS 3:12 VOICE

A holy way of living and loving isn't easy. It takes intentionality for these practices to become our default because they go against our human nature. We may say we're set apart by God—fully on board with our faith—but do our everyday actions and speech line up? What are you clothing yourself with each day?

Compassion is selflessness. It's a response to those around us as well as to God, and it shows we love others by how we care for them.

Kindness is all about how we treat others. In Greek, this word is translated to mean "moral goodness or integrity."

Humility—a trait highly regarded by God—proves we understand our position in relation to His. Toward others, it means not acting as if we're better than anyone else. We treat others fairly in every way.

Gentleness (also known as meekness) is choosing not to be hard-hearted toward others. Some interpret it to mean believers should be timid or fearful, but that's incorrect. Here, Paul is telling us that gentleness is controlling our strength rather than using it to harm those around us.

Patience reveals our belief that God's timing is perfect, His love is steadfast, and His power is unceasing. True patience isn't passive but rather active. It's perseverance in the waiting. And the Lord will develop it in every believer who seeks it.

This holy way of life requires the Holy Spirit's help. If we were left to our own devices, our ability to live this way would be a series of ebbs and flows. So if we're wanting to courageously walk out a life of faith, then we must tap into God's power through prayer so we can live a life set apart by Him. Only through the Lord's help will we be able to clothe ourselves with compassion, kindness, humility, gentleness, and patience. Pray each day that God will remind you of the call to live with intentionality. And ask Him to help you make it happen.

DEAR LORD, PLEASE CLOTHE ME WITH A HOLY WAY OF LIFE. HELP ME DEPEND ON YOUR SPIRIT TO HELP ME TREAT OTHERS WELL AND LOVE YOU WITH PURPOSE. IN JESUS' NAME. AMEN.

The Power of a Praying Woman

So own up to your sins to one another and pray for one
another. In the end, you may be healed. Your prayers are
powerful when they are rooted in a righteous life. Remember
Elijah? He was a man, no different from us. He prayed
with great intensity asking God to withhold the rain; God
answered his prayers and did not allow a single drop of
rain to fall for three and a half years. It did not rain until
Elijah prayed again for God to open the skies, when the
rain came down and the earth produced a great crop.

JAMES 5:16–18 VOICE

Not only are we called to pray for others as we follow the Holy
Spirit's prompts to live a righteous life, but some believe today's
verse says we're to pray with great intensity. The thought is that
we go to God passionately. We share heartfelt prayers. Done right,
they'll sound a bit forceful at times because they're coming from
deep places of hope, love, and compassion. These are meaningful,
wholehearted prayers where we're all-in as we ask God to meet
specific needs, and the results from them won't be the same if
we pray halfheartedly.

There are others who think this verse means that praying

with intensity is talking about the outcome or the ways prayers are answered. In this view, it's not how forcefully or passionately we pray but simply that as righteous women, we do pray. The requests of the upright make a difference to God. Thus, the prayers of believers are powerful no matter how we deliver them.

Regardless, James is telling us that prayer is important. It's effective, especially when offered up by someone who strives to follow God's will. It is significant in the lives of Christians. And it should be a priority every day. We should pray earnestly and sincerely, believing that when we cry out to the Lord and our requests align with His heart for us, they are power-packed.

Just as Elijah the prophet was a godly man—*no different from us*—who prayed with remarkable results, the Lord will hear and answer us too, in the right ways and at the right times. And James commands us to own up to our sins because he knows that if not confessed, they may hinder the efficacy of our prayers.

So, friend, pray with great expectation, confessing and thanking and asking. Pray with a hope-filled heart. Your prayers matter.

. . . .

DEAR LORD, I'M COMING CLEAN WITH MY SINS AGAINST YOU
AND THOSE I'VE HURT. I'M THANKING YOU FOR YOUR POWER
AND LOVE. AND I'M ASKING WHOLEHEARTEDLY THAT YOU
HEAR AND ANSWER MY REQUESTS. IN JESUS' NAME. AMEN.

Being Ready to Forgive

Be gentle and ready to forgive; never hold grudges.
Remember, the Lord forgave you, so you must forgive
others. Most of all, let love guide your life, for then the
whole church will stay together in perfect harmony. Let the
peace of heart that comes from Christ be always present
in your hearts and lives, for this is your responsibility and
privilege as members of his body. And always be thankful.

COLOSSIANS 3:13–15 TLB

Can we agree that it's hard not to hold a grudge? Are you holding one right now? Maybe your boyfriend or husband walked away when the relationship got too difficult. Maybe your child unloaded on you for being an imperfect mom. Maybe the doctor made the wrong diagnosis, costing you precious time and money. Maybe your parents made you feel worthless and unimportant growing up and that message is still playing on repeat in your mind today. Maybe your best friend shared secrets you never wanted made public.

You have good reason to be angry about these kinds of situations. A case could be made to stay angry until the other party fixes what they've done wrong. But that isn't God's way for us. We're not to hold on to offenses, even the really bad ones. Instead, Paul reminds us to be gentle and ready to forgive. And, friend, we can only do that with the Lord's help.

It's hard to forgive when our hearts have been hurt. We want to lash out and make them pay. We want to exact revenge. But when we humble ourselves before God and are honest about our feelings, asking for healing, God will give us the ability to release the hurt into His hands as we forgive.

Our highest call is to let love guide our life, because love creates unity. Loving others wholeheartedly sets us up to experience a supernatural harmony in community. When we choose to let our faith lead us to peaceful places, even when unforgiveness taunts us, God will bless us.

Don't try to forgive on your own. Instead, be quick to pray, asking the Lord to soften your heart. Ask for a divine perspective in those tough situations. Pray with confidence because you know forgiveness is His will and He will make it possible. You may have been hurt, but inviting God into your pain is a gutsy decision that will bring peace and hope.

DEAR LORD, I ADMIT I CAN'T FORGIVE OTHERS IN MY OWN
STRENGTH. HELP ME FOLLOW YOUR COMMAND TO RELEASE
OFFENSES INTO YOUR HANDS. IN JESUS' NAME. AMEN.

Understanding the Ins and Outs of Prayer

"Don't recite the same prayer over and over as the heathen do, who think prayers are answered only by repeating them again and again. Remember, your Father knows exactly what you need even before you ask him!"

MATTHEW 6:7–8 TLB

Today's scripture says that when we pray we shouldn't fall into the habit of worthless repetition. This doesn't mean we can't bring the same request to God repeatedly. Persistence in heartfelt prayers for your friends or family, world or nation, or something you're struggling with is encouraged and perfectly acceptable. He wants to hear these!

But the idea that mindless, repetitive words make our prayers more important or motivate God to answer them faster or differently just isn't true. He's not impressed by big, fancy words or flowery monologues. We simply cannot manipulate the Lord through prayer. And if we get into mindless chants or formulaic prayers, saying the same words over and over again, the Bible tells us practices like these are rooted in pagan religion. Friend, we're told to stay away from such things.

Don't think that short and simple prayers are bad. Sometimes it's best to get straight to the point when talking to God. Don't be misled into believing that long, elaborate prayers make you sound holier. That just isn't true.

Instead, let's make prayer a time of honest conversation with our Father when we stay present and engage in meaningful sharing and listening. This time in God's presence is both sweet and powerful, so let's be intentional with words that come from deep places. Let's pray boldly, trusting Him with our hearts' desires. Let's close our eyes and keep our attention on Him, realizing prayer is an act of worship. And let's always lace it with thanksgiving because the Bible tells us to.

God's Word teaches us about prayer, both what to do and what to avoid. As women who believe, let's talk directly to the Lord and not pray through someone else. Let's pray in faith with hopeful hearts full of expectation. Let's be humble. And let's close with the words *in Jesus' name* since that's where the power comes from.

DEAR LORD, I LOVE THAT I CAN TALK TO YOU WHENEVER
AND WHEREVER. AND I APPRECIATE THE CHALLENGE TO
BE REAL AS I DO, STAYING AWAY FROM WRONG MOTIVES
AND PAGAN PRACTICES. IN JESUS' NAME. AMEN.

Letting God's
Word Change You

*Let the word of the Anointed One richly inhabit your lives.
With all wisdom teach, counsel, and instruct one another. Sing
the psalms, compose hymns and songs inspired by the Spirit,
and keep on singing—sing to God from hearts full and spilling
over with thankfulness. Surely, no matter what you are doing
(speaking, writing, or working), do it all in the name of Jesus
our Master, sending thanks through Him to God our Father.*

COLOSSIANS 3:16–18 VOICE

When Paul says that our speaking, writing, and working should
all be done in the name of Jesus, let's take that truth to heart! The
desire to do everything in Jesus' name should be the foundation
of our faith walk and the guiding principle of our interactions with
those around us.

How can we live this out? Every time we open the Word and
soak in its goodness, we're letting it take hold of us. God speaks
to us through its pages and transforms the way we think and act.
It begins to be the main source informing us. It becomes our
operating system, if you will. And as it takes root in our hearts
and shapes our character, we can be certain that the way we're
living each day glorifies Him.

As a believer who spends time in the Word, do you notice that you interact differently? Are you kinder and more encouraging? Are you more intentional with your words? Do you credit God for the good things that come your way rather than thinking it's all you or a bit of luck? Do you see the needy and want to find ways to help them? Are you more generous with your time, talents, and treasure? Do you show honor and respect for everyone, even if they don't believe what you believe? Are you less selfish and more others-focused? Does your heart break for what God's heart breaks for? This is because God's Word is at home in you, dear friend.

Be a woman of faith, filled with thanksgiving for who the Lord is, how He's blessed you with His presence, and how He powerfully transforms those who love Him. Through prayer, show gratitude that He uses your life and testimony to positively impact His kingdom in significant ways. And commit to following Him all the days afforded you here.

DEAR LORD, LET EVERYTHING I SAY AND DO BLESS YOU AND ENCOURAGE OTHERS. IN JESUS' NAME. AMEN.

Prayer Motivation

*Likewise, when you pray, do not be as hypocrites who love
to pray loudly at synagogue or on street corners—their
concern is to be seen by men. They have already earned
their reward. When you pray, go into a private room, close
the door, and pray unseen to your Father who is unseen.
Then your Father, who sees in secret, will reward you.*

Matthew 6:5–6 voice

The appropriateness of praying in public all boils down to motivation. Just as we're to give to the poor without drawing attention to ourselves, that same need for discretion is shared here. If we're honest, we'd have to confess to certain situations where we "virtue signaled" to impress others. It's something we've all done a time or two. We want to look good because it makes us feel better or more important. Yet in the process, we end up giving others a false impression of who we truly are.

In response to today's verses, the question to ask ourselves is if we're praying as a public performance. Are we praying in front of others to benefit us personally?

Friend, don't read what this passage isn't saying. Nothing's wrong with lifting your voice to God when others are around. Praying out loud for a family meal at a restaurant or at a small group meeting at church or with friends at the park is not wrong

242

or bad. That's not what is being suggested in this passage. But the Lord sees immense value in going into a private room, closing the door, and praying unseen. The warning here is to make sure you're praying to be heard by God and not praying to be elevated by those you're with or those who may be in earshot.

This is just another example of how to pray effectively so your reward will come from God and not from a worldly source. Remember that the Bible is our guide for knowing how to walk out a life of faith. And also keep in mind that it's in those sacred spaces—those times and places where you're alone with the Lord—that you are seen. You can pray courageously, expectantly, and honestly and know that you are heard.

DEAR LORD, LET MY PRAYER MOTIVATION BE
AUTHENTIC AND FAITH FILLED. LET ME PRAY ONLY
TO BE IN YOUR PRESENCE RATHER THAN TO IMPRESS
ANYONE LISTENING. IN JESUS' NAME. AMEN.

Setting Your Mind

*If then you have been raised with Christ [to a new life,
thus sharing His resurrection from the dead], aim at
and seek the [rich, eternal treasures] that are above,
where Christ is, seated at the right hand of God. And
set your minds and keep them set on what is above (the
higher things), not on the things that are on the earth.*

COLOSSIANS 3:1–2 AMPC

With all the crazy and corrupt things happening these days, this message from Paul is especially timely. It's a great reminder that where we choose to focus our mind and heart will drive how we respond to everything life brings.

In this passage, Paul is writing to the church in Colossae, which as a Roman city was wicked and depraved. As a result, the believers living there had no choice but to look only to God for direction. They may have resided in Colossae, but they were clearly instructed not to believe or behave in the heinous ways of the culture. Honestly, the same is true in our culture today, wouldn't you agree? "Seeking the eternal treasures that are above" is what will keep us in the Lord's perfect peace rather than stressed and afraid. We too should heed Paul's directive.

When he tells us to "set our mind," it's a call to be mindful of what we think about. Our thoughts affect our decisions and guide our actions. If our attention is on what the world has to offer, we'll get discouraged. We'll feel anxious and worried. So when we let all kinds of messages from news channels, internet searches, billboards and publications, social media, and idle chatter settle in our heart, we'll find ourselves destabilized. Those messages of hopelessness will worm their way into us, infiltrating our mind.

But if we spend time in God's Word and let His message capture our hearts instead, we'll have peace. He will bless us with a fresh revelation of His goodness. With our spiritual eyes and ears, we'll see the world's craziness from His perspective and be comforted. And where others are bogged down, we will have hope and joy.

As with the believers in Colossae, our address may be here, but we are clearly called to set our mind on what is above. Ask God to make you bold as you navigate this life of faith.

DEAR LORD, GIVE ME A CONFIDENT AND COURAGEOUS HEART TO KEEP FOCUSED ON YOU WHILE SURROUNDED BY THE WORLD'S CRAZINESS. IN JESUS' NAME. AMEN.

Storing Up Treasures in Heaven

"Don't store up treasures here on earth where they can erode away or may be stolen. Store them in heaven where they will never lose their value and are safe from thieves. If your profits are in heaven, your heart will be there too."

MATTHEW 6:19–21 TLB

. . . .

More than anything else—more than people, places, prizes, possessions, properties, products, or profits—we're to want God most. We are to treasure Him above everything. To do that, we must choose to commit all we have and all we do to further His kingdom on earth. The Lord must be what drives us to wake each day and live with passion and purpose for His name's sake. Friend, nothing we do in service to God goes unnoticed, whether big or small.

So whether you take a meal to a hurting family, or feed the homeless, or put dinner on the table for your family each evening, you're storing up treasures. If you volunteer at church, in your child's classroom, or at the soup kitchen, it's stored above. Every time you open the door for someone, donate to a charity, or pray with a friend in crisis, God tucks these goodies away in heaven. When you love in earnest and forgive with sincerity, He writes it on a divine sticky note. When you speak from a stage, sing in a stadium, or write on pages about the Lord's goodness, it's recorded in the heavenlies. We all have different ministries—different ways of blessing those around us and glorifying God's name—but every one of them delights the Lord God.

In contrast, we can also work for recognition and accolades here on earth. It's not far-fetched to think about climbing the corporate ladder or being recognized as an expert in our field. We may strive to have the biggest house with the classiest décor or shop till we drop to fill our closets with the trendiest fashions. We may use social media to get the attention we crave, sharing pics and posts that make our lives look perfect. Whether in regard to our marriage, our kids, or our travels, we want to be praised for being a success. And, friend, that's how we store up treasures on planet Earth.

Every day, you get to choose your heart's focus. Be gutsy, friend. Be bold in your faith. And let your life always point to God in heaven.

. . . .

DEAR LORD, I WANT TO STORE UP TREASURES IN
HEAVEN AND NOT HERE ON EARTH. HELP ME FOCUS
ON LIVING IN WAYS THAT WILL BLESS OTHERS AND
BRING YOU GLORY. IN JESUS' NAME. AMEN.

Continually Happy, Joyful, and Glad

*Be happy [in your faith] and rejoice and be glad-hearted
continually (always); be unceasing in prayer [praying
perseveringly]; thank [God] in everything [no matter
what the circumstances may be, be thankful and give
thanks], for this is the will of God for you [who are] in
Christ Jesus [the Revealer and Mediator of that will].*

1 THESSALONIANS 5:16–18 AMPC

Paul is telling the believers in Thessalonica to be happy in their faith. They are encouraged to rejoice always and to be glad-hearted continually. From this, we can see little room for misinterpretation. Regardless of what we're struggling with, we should live this way every day—happy, joyful, and glad. The way we feel or the situations we're navigating shouldn't affect this general outlook.

As believers, we need to be intentional about adopting God's perspective. This is how we live a life of victory! When we do, the trials and challenges that come our way won't interrupt our joy. We won't see these hardships in the light of humanity, feeling the weight of discouragement and disappointment. Instead, we'll look through our spiritual eyes and remember God's goodness to help those who love Him. We will recount His perfect history of showing up and bringing hope and healing. And we will stand tall, boldly waiting with expectation for the Lord to intervene in meaningful ways. We will stand with hopeful hearts because we know God keeps His promises.

We can be happy, joyful, and glad based on His past faithfulness. We can remain in this attitude today knowing God will never leave us or forsake us. . .ever. And we can stay confident in that sacred space, fully believing God will continue to be exactly what we need in the future. Always cling to the truth that He is our hope. He's our strong tower and security. He is our provider. And no matter what, the will of God *will* be done.

Friend, the choice to be faithful or fearful is ours. We can be happy or grouchy. We can be glad or testy. We can be brimming with joy or simmering with irritability. Let's choose wisely!

DEAR LORD, HELP ME REMEMBER THAT AN ATTITUDE OF GRATITUDE AND TRUST SETS ME UP FOR CONTINUAL HAPPINESS, JOY, AND GLADNESS NO MATTER WHAT I MAY BE FACING. WHEN I PRAY WITH PURPOSE AND SHOW THANKFULNESS IN SPADES, MY OUTLOOK ON LIFE WILL POWERFULLY REFLECT THOSE CHOICES. IN JESUS' NAME. AMEN.

What Will Worry Add?

"Look at the birds! They don't worry about what
to eat—they don't need to sow or reap or store up
food—for your heavenly Father feeds them. And you
are far more valuable to him than they are. Will all
your worries add a single moment to your life?"

MATTHEW 6:26–27 TLB

Friend, what worries are you carrying with you today? What is weighing you down and causing unwanted stress and anxiety? Is it a scary doctor's report from your last appointment? Is it uncertainty about your job security? Is it the economic or political unrest in the world and what the future may hold because of it? Did another month pass without you becoming pregnant? Did your relationship suddenly end when you thought it was headed toward marriage? Did you lose a parent or someone you deeply loved, and the grief is overwhelming? Are you struggling with a life change that has shaken you to the core? Is it a lack of good friendships? Is your money not going as far as it used to? Is your child failing to launch? Deep breath.

Scripture says worrying won't do anything good. It will bring no benefit to the situation. It adds nothing. Even more, the reality is that it may negatively affect your health, strain your relationships, and rob you of joy, but it will never help the situation.

As believers, we should know with conviction that God sees what's at hand and is working on our behalf. We can boldly trust that the Lord will meet our needs in the right way and in His perfect timing. Because of His great love, we are held in very capable hands.

Do you see the tension in this passage of scripture? You get to choose what path to walk when the hardships come. Will you follow distrust and worry? Or will you embrace faithfulness and believe God?

Worrying is easy, but standing in courage takes intentionality. Do you truly trust that He will make good on His promises? Do you believe you're covered? Do you know without a doubt that God has complete knowledge of every challenge you face and is acting even now? If the answer is yes, then worry can't weigh you down. If the answer is no, go to God in prayer right now and boldly ask Him to strengthen your faith and bolster your resolve to believe.

. . . .

DEAR LORD, STRENGTHEN MY FAITH SO I CAN STAND
IN THE TRUTH THAT YOU ARE MOVING IN MY LIFE EVERY
DAY AND IN EVERY SITUATION. IN JESUS' NAME. AMEN.

Being a Prayer Warrior

Pray diligently. Stay alert, with your eyes wide open in
gratitude. Don't forget to pray for us, that God will open
doors for telling the mystery of Christ, even while I'm
locked up in this jail. Pray that every time I open my
mouth I'll be able to make Christ plain as day to them.

COLOSSIANS 4:2–4 MSG

The greatest privilege we have as believers is the opportunity to talk directly to God. Through prayer, we can offer up to Him our petitions and pleas. We can bring our own challenges to Him, or we can pray for our brothers and sisters who are facing their own trials and tribulations. With a spirit of thanksgiving, we can approach the throne room anytime, anywhere. We can simply bow our heads, close our eyes, and humbly meet Him in the sacred space. Whether we pray out loud or quietly in our thoughts, He is always ready to hear what's on our hearts.

Paul was unswervingly devoted to prayer for himself and others. In this letter to the believers in Colossae, he was urging them to become prayer warriors. He was encouraging them to pray with diligence, staying alert with eyes wide open and a heart of gratitude, knowing God could and would act on their behalf. He even asked for open doors to share the gospel, whether in jail or in his travels.

Let's commit to being prayer warriors during our time here on earth. Let's persevere without giving up on our requests. Let's commit to praying even when the answer seems far off. When we're met with opposition, let's pray with a renewed sense of hope and expectation. Let's be bold as we ask God to show up in both small and significant ways. And let's be warriors who pray without ceasing until we see the Lord move.

Each day, our delight should be to have unbroken communication with our Father who treasures our words. This prayer connection keeps us from becoming lazy in our faith. It keeps us always interested in deepening our intimacy with Him. And used rightly, it becomes a powerful weapon in our hand for times of struggle.

DEAR LORD, AS I BREATHE IN THE UPS AND DOWNS OF LIFE,
LET ME EXHALE PRAYERS OF THANKS AND PETITION. LET ME
WIELD THE WEAPON OF PRAYER, KNOWING THAT IT'S ALWAYS
TIME WELL SPENT IN YOUR PRESENCE. IN JESUS' NAME. AMEN.

The God of Restoration

"Yes, GOD's Message: 'You're going to look at this place, these empty and desolate towns of Judah and streets of Jerusalem, and say, "A wasteland. Unlivable. Not even a dog could live here." But the time is coming when you're going to hear laughter and celebration, marriage festivities, people exclaiming, "Thank GOD-of-the-Angel-Armies. He's so good! His love never quits," as they bring thank offerings into GOD's Temple. I'll restore everything that was lost in this land. I'll make everything as good as new.' I, GOD, say so."

JEREMIAH 33:10–11 MSG

While Jeremiah was still a prisoner of the king—shackled in the palace courtyard and surrounded by guards—he received a second message from the Lord. God spoke to this prophet about the inevitable defeat of Jerusalem.

While many had hoped that the Egyptian army would intervene, it wasn't going to. Jerusalem's loss at the enemy's hands was inevitable. The city was going to fall, and nothing could stop it. But God gave Jeremiah the ability to see past this defeat to the city's promised restoration. He gave hope to His chosen ones through this prophet.

Today's scripture confirms that God is a God of renewal. This truth gives us hope that what is broken or destroyed won't always be that way. There may be good reasons for destruction, but ultimately God will use it for our good and His glory. From beginning to end, He will ensure it strengthens us in ways we may never fully understand this side of heaven. Though the destruction may not make sense right now, one day it will.

Have difficult circumstances in your life left you feeling empty and desolate? Do they feel final, like there's no hope of returning to what once was? Are you in parched places where there used to be plenty? Are you in a place of lack where once abundance was the norm? Since our God is a God of His word, you can live with expectation and trust that where restoration is needed, it will be given. In His perfect timing and according to His perfect will, the Lord will restore everything that was lost and make it good as new once again. Take heart! God is on the move!

DEAR LORD, WHAT A GIFT TO KNOW YOU WILL BRING
GOOD FROM EVERY HEARTBREAK AND DIFFICULTY
WE MUST FACE IN THIS LIFE. HELP ME TO TRUST YOU
MORE, WITH HOPE AND THANKSGIVING! I KNOW YOU
WILL TAKE CARE OF ME. IN JESUS' NAME. AMEN.

Watch and Pray!

When he came back to his disciples, he found them sound asleep. He said to Peter, "Can't you stick it out with me a single hour? Stay alert; be in prayer so you don't wander into temptation without even knowing you're in danger. There is a part of you that is eager, ready for anything in God. But there's another part that's as lazy as an old dog sleeping by the fire."

MATTHEW 26:40–41 MSG

In these final chapters of the book of Matthew, the time of the cross draws ever closer. Jesus fully understands the hour they're in and goes to pray. He knows this time in the Father's presence is necessary and important. But as He returns to the disciples, He sees they've fallen asleep.

Did you notice His two strong commands? Jesus told them to *stay alert* and *be in prayer*. If they didn't, temptation was ready and waiting. He needed these men to grab hold of a deeper understanding of the life of faith. Their spirits may have been willing, but their flesh was weak.

Friend, these two commands are essential for us today too. As believers, we should watch and pray, because sin will only bring us down. It will corrupt our hearts and infiltrate our minds, leading us down a path away from God. The only chance we have to live a victorious life in such a broken world is through complete dependence on the Holy Spirit's leading. That's why we're told to watch and pray. This is a bold stance to take! Without the Spirit's daily guidance—whether our reluctance to follow Him is rooted in pride or fleshly desires—we're simply incapable of avoiding a sinful life. It's just part of the human condition.

Remember that the enemy's attacks are unrelenting. And as believers, we have a giant target on our backs. So let's choose to watch and keep watching every day. As courageous women, let's pray and keep praying continually. These two commands should be the foundation of our faith because we know the hour is late. And unless we stand firm, we'll be easily influenced to go our own way. We'll fall asleep rather than be alert and prayerful. In our own strength, our spirits may be strong, but our flesh is weak.

DEAR LORD, HELP ME STAY ALERT AND PRAY
ALWAYS SO I CAN BE SOBER IN THESE TIMES
AND AVOID THE TEMPTATIONS THAT COME
MY WAY. IN JESUS' NAME. AMEN.

The Blessing of Prayer

One day Jesus told his disciples a story to illustrate
their need for constant prayer and to show them that
they must keep praying until the answer comes.

Luke 18:1 TLB

In today's verse, Luke is writing about the necessity of prayer. We're told it should be constant so that we stay in regular communication with our Father. We also learn our prayers should be persistent—we should keep approaching the throne until we see His answers. Neither of these is easy to do at first; they are holy habits we must cultivate. But beautiful things happen when we do.

A robust prayer life humbles us because we begin to see that we have needs only God can meet. It's a time when we can lay our worries at His feet, acknowledging the burden is too heavy and hard for us to carry alone. And it allows us to release control of problems we can't control in the first place.

Prayer grows our faith because we grow closer to the Gardener. It helps us understand that we are loved unconditionally. It knits our hearts to His in ways that are significant and meaningful. And the more time we spend talking to the Lord, the more our relationship with Him is strengthened. Time in prayer provides us with the blessing of resting in the hope of His goodness.

Through time invested in prayer, we learn how to listen for

His still, small voice, which is an important discipline. Sometimes we get so focused on asking that we don't hear Him speaking to our spirits. But the more we pray and spend time alone with God, soaking in His presence, the more sensitive we become to the ways He speaks to us.

Praying with perseverance builds our faith muscle by teaching us to wait with expectation. Because we've seen His hand move before, we have hope it will happen again. We've seen Him provide. We've watched Him restore. We've witnessed Him move mountains and part raging seas. All of these occasions give us confidence to ask for what we need and to trust that He will respond in His time and in His way.

Friend, God wants our prayer life to be relentless in every way. You can be bold. You can be hopeful and expectant. You can be full of thanksgiving. And you can pray anytime and anywhere.

DEAR LORD, WHAT A PRIVILEGE IT IS TO PRAY TO YOU
DIRECTLY. HELP ME TO ALWAYS HAVE A PRAYER ON MY
LIPS AND FAITH IN MY HEART. IN JESUS' NAME. AMEN.

When You Need God to Stay Close

The Eternal stays close to those who call on Him, those who pray sincerely. All of you who revere Him—God will satisfy your desires. He hears the cries for help, and He brings salvation. All of you who love God—He will watch out for you, but total destruction is around the corner for all the wicked.

PSALM 145:18–20 VOICE

Friend, where do you need God to stay close to you right now? Did your feelings get wrecked by a careless comment from a trusted family member? Did someone you deeply care about get hurt by the unexpected and reckless action of another? Are you in a season of insecurity, letting your emotions get easily tangled by those around you? Are you struggling to extend forgiveness, feeling justified in holding on to an offense instead? Scripture tells us to pray with sincerity and God will stay close.

Maybe there's a great desire within your heart you can't shake. It could be a dream job that feels unreachable or a deep craving for a meaningful relationship. It could be an intense hope for peace to preside in a volatile relationship. Maybe it's a physical healing you've been asking of the Lord for a long time. It may be a longing to be a mom, be it through birth or adoption. The psalmist says that your reverence of God prompts Him to move on your behalf.

Trying to navigate each day without Him is unwise because life is hard and messy. But as believers, we can be confident He hears our cries for help. The Lord promises to bring deliverance so we can stand tall in every trying time. Yes, we can be sure the Lord will stay close to us in each moment of distress and discouragement. So let's be bold in our faith, asking Him to save us!

When we choose to invest in our relationship with God—spending time in His Word and in prayer—He sees our love and respect. He sees our commitment to growing our faith in significant ways. The time we spend with the Lord strengthens our resolve to lean into Him as we walk through dark valleys. And it keeps us from a life of total destruction.

DEAR LORD, I CAN'T DO THIS LIFE WITHOUT YOU.
PLEASE ALWAYS STAY CLOSE TO ME—ESPECIALLY
IN THOSE MOMENTS WHEN MY HEART IS HEAVY AND
FULL OF FEAR AND WORRY. IN JESUS' NAME. AMEN.

The Reminder to Keep On

*So I say to you, Ask and keep on asking and it shall be given
you; seek and keep on seeking and you shall find; knock
and keep on knocking and the door shall be opened to you.
For everyone who asks and keeps on asking receives; and
he who seeks and keeps on seeking finds; and to him who
knocks and keeps on knocking, the door shall be opened.*

LUKE 11:9–10 AMPC

. . . .

What a beautiful call to persevere and wait with expectation for the
Lord to respond! We're to *keep on* asking when we need wisdom
to navigate difficult moments. We're to continue seeking His will
in the confusing circumstances we face—big or small. When we
feel desperate for guidance, strength, or perspective, our job is
to knock until the door opens. However long it takes, we're to
have the guts and grit to hold on with hopeful hearts. And while
we may feel like a burden or an annoyance for asking repeatedly,
the truth is that God recognizes the faith it takes to endure. To
Him, it's a powerful step of faith because it says we know that
He can and He will.

But the truth is that endurance is not easy. Even though the
Word tells us that if we ask, God will give; if we seek, He will let us
find what we need in that moment; and if we knock, He will open
the door, it still takes diligence and determination. It still requires

the courage to *keep on* in those times we just want to give up.

The truth is that we often ask God for His help and blessings but don't watch for them. In our mind, we're waiting for Him to answer in the ways we want—the ways we asked. So that's what we're focused on looking for. But God usually has a different plan in mind. And without fail, it's always for our good and His glory. Are you watching in faith?

With His help, we can adopt a holy stubbornness to pursue the Lord until it pays off. We can keep our eyes and ears open to His answers, knowing they could be different than our requests. It's called divine determination. It's glorious grit. It's faithful fortitude. And through God, we can have it.

DEAR LORD, HELP ME DEVELOP A "KEEP ON"
ATTITUDE SO I'M ABLE TO PERSEVERE WITH HOPE
AND EXPECTATION, TRUSTING YOUR WILL TO BE
DONE IN AMAZING WAYS. IN JESUS' NAME. AMEN.

The Four Kinds of Prayers

*First of all, then, I ask that requests, prayers, petitions,
and thanksgiving be made for all people. Pray for kings
and everyone who is in authority so that we can live a
quiet and peaceful life in complete godliness and dignity.
This is right and it pleases God our savior, who wants all
people to be saved and to come to a knowledge of the truth.*

I Timothy 2:1–4 CEB

In this letter to Timothy, Paul is urging believers to pray four kinds of prayers, both in a community setting as well as in private. He knows the value this practice holds for the Father and the follower. And as in so much of his writing, Paul addresses the ins and outs of prayer here in this passage of scripture.

The first kind of prayer listed is *requests*. This is when you're earnestly pleading with God about a very specific issue or need, either for you or someone you care about. It may even come from desperate and broken places where you need the Lord to intervene in significant ways.

The second is just listed as *prayer*, which may encompass the countless general requests that come up each day. It may also be a time when you recognize that you can approach the throne room at any time and commune with your loving and caring Creator. He's not off-limits, and you don't need to pray through anyone else. It's personal and direct.

Third, Paul mentions *petitions*. This kind of prayer is also known as intercession, and it's where you use your position as a child of God and woman of faith to mediate on behalf of others. Maybe they're unable to cry out for help or can't find the words, but you can be there for them as an intercessor. You can confidently bring their needs to God.

Lastly, we're to pray with *thanksgiving*. These prayers recognize the Lord's goodness and mercy in your life. They acknowledge His goodness and kindness and generosity. These are the times you recount God's blessings, showing gratitude for the ways He has powerfully intervened in your life.

Every day let's come before Him with a heart of humility and reverence. Let's ask the Holy Spirit to teach us to pray with compassion for others. Let's show gratitude for His greatness and respect for His position. And let's remember we can approach God with courage and confidence because we are His beloved children and our prayers matter deeply to the Father.

DEAR LORD, THANK YOU FOR THE PRIVILEGE OF TALKING
TO YOU ABOUT ALL THINGS. IN JESUS' NAME. AMEN.

Pray, Follow, Repent

And [if] My people (who are known by My name) humbly
pray, follow My commandments, and abandon any actions
or thoughts that might lead to further sinning, then I shall
hear their prayers from My house in heaven, I shall forgive
their sins, and I shall save their land from the disasters.

2 CHRONICLES 7:14 VOICE

For context, this verse is about Israel and the temple and how tough times were ahead because of God's judgment. He had faithfully entered a covenant with the people of Israel, promising to care and provide for them, but they chose to forsake Him by embracing other gods.

You'll see throughout the Bible that the prosperity of the nation of Israel was directly linked to their obedience and that their hardship was directly linked to their disobedience. They were on a short leash for good reason! And today's verse was (and is) a promise to Israel that if they humbly prayed, followed God's commands, and repented from sinning, He would hear their prayers, forgive their sins, and save them. At every turn, the Lord was looking for opportunities to bring restoration to them even though natural consequences were still a part of sin's aftermath.

While this verse is specifically for the nation of Israel, we can choose to follow suit in our own lives today. We can pray, follow, and repent, which is our duty as believers. We can choose to turn away from earthly idols and people we often find ourselves worshipping and let the Lord restore our hearts of allegiance to Him instead. Let's be on a short leash too! Each time we take a step in the wrong direction, let's be quick to repent. As women of faith, let's make this a daily (if not hourly) practice so that sin doesn't stand between us and God.

Friend, be a gutsy Christian who chooses to walk out obedience to the Lord's will in meaningful ways. Pray for the courage to stand up against groupthink and selfishness that will pull you out of His plans. Take your faith seriously and follow His commands with fervor. Abandon actions or thoughts that will lead you into sin. Instead, seek to live a holy life that points others to God in heaven. And watch how our amazing Father will forgive and restore you in miraculous ways.

DEAR LORD, HELP ME LIVE IN WAYS THAT BLESS
YOU AND FURTHER YOUR KINGDOM HERE
ON EARTH. IN JESUS' NAME. AMEN.

Good Works or Good Looks

So here's what you tell them; here's what I want to see: Men,
pray wherever you are. Reach your holy hands to heaven—
without rage or conflict—completely open. Women, the same
goes for you: dress properly, modestly, and appropriately.
Don't get carried away in grooming your hair or seek beauty
in glittering gold, pearls, or expensive clothes. Instead, as is
fitting, let good works decorate your true beauty and show
that you are a woman who claims reverence for God.

I Timothy 2:8–10 voice

Sometimes we get too caught up in our outward appearance.
Not that there's anything wrong with wanting to put our best foot
forward and look nice, but Paul is telling us where true beauty
comes from. He says to dress properly, modestly, and appropriately. This isn't a call to revert our appearance back to the days
of covered wagons and dusty trails. We're not to be uninterested
in personal hygiene or to dress in rags. And coloring our hair,
doing our nails, and putting on makeup each day isn't sinning or
being disrespectful to God. Rather, consider the bigger picture
of what Paul is suggesting.

It's our good works—not our good looks—that should define
our true beauty. It's the fruit that comes from our faith (not our
features) that is most attractive. And if we're putting more time

into our earthly exterior than our eternal efforts, our heart is way out of balance.

So how can we keep our focus on what matters most? It all starts with digging into God's Word and letting it transform you from the inside out. Every time you open the Bible, He will use it in strategic ways to open your eyes to His will. The Lord lets scripture settle into your spirit and challenge old ways of thinking. Key verses will jump out and speak directly to your heart, bringing a good word needed in that moment. And as you connect with God in these kinds of ways, your faith will mature supernaturally as your desire to do good works grows.

Then, when the doors of opportunity open, you'll boldly and faithfully follow God's will right through them and be His hands and feet to those around you. Your true beauty will shine forth!

DEAR LORD, LET MY GOOD WORKS BE MY FOCUS RATHER THAN JUST LOOKING GOOD. GIVE ME CONFIDENCE TO EMBRACE THE CALL YOU'VE PUT ON MY LIFE TO BE COURAGEOUS IN MY FAITH. IN JESUS' NAME. AMEN.

Called to Something Higher

You have been taught to love your neighbor and hate your enemy. But I tell you this: love your enemies. Pray for those who torment you and persecute you. . . . It is easy to love those who love you—even a tax collector can love those who love him. And it is easy to greet your friends—even outsiders do that! But you are called to something higher: "Be perfect, as your Father in heaven is perfect."

MATTHEW 5:43–44, 46–48 VOICE

As believers, we are called to something higher. While the world teaches us to hate those who oppose us, God's plan is something completely different. Hating is easy. Living with bitterness is often effortless. It's not hard to hold on to an offense with gusto. But choosing to love those considered your enemies takes His supernatural strength and your obedience.

Why do you think the Lord would ask us to love our enemies? Why would He tell us to pray for those who hurt us? Think about how difficult it is to stay angry with the person you bring to the throne room of grace. Placing someone before God and asking Him to show them His blessings and favor changes our hearts in short order. Before long, our anger has dwindled and we've forgiven them in our heart. It's an amazing and powerful exchange.

Why don't you try it today? Has someone in your life hurt

your feelings or perhaps hurt a close friend of yours? Did someone spread a rumor about you or betray a secret? Was a person of trust reckless with their words, saying things that shocked and upset you? Are you tired of being preached to by someone who thinks differently than you do and won't let it go? Have you faced rejection that cut to the core? Have you reached your limit with a coworker? Friend, pray for them.

Boldly ask God to bring restoration. Ask Him to bring reconciliation. Pray with hope and expectation that the Lord will help you release the anger inside. Pray with thanksgiving, knowing He will hear you and act faithfully. Pray over and over again until peace is restored in your spirit. And pray for your enemies earnestly, because you are called to something higher than hating.

DEAR LORD, HELP ME EMBRACE THE CALL TO PRAY
FOR THE ONES WHO'VE HURT ME. I KNOW IT'S THE BEST
(AND HARDEST) THING TO DO. IN JESUS' NAME. AMEN.

Salt and Light

"You are the world's seasoning, to make it tolerable.
If you lose your flavor, what will happen to the world?
And you yourselves will be thrown out and trampled
underfoot as worthless. You are the world's light—a city
on a hill, glowing in the night for all to see. Don't hide your
light! Let it shine for all; let your good deeds glow for all
to see, so that they will praise your heavenly Father."

MATTHEW 5:13–16 TLB

Jesus frequently used the ideas of salt and light to describe the role of His believers in the world. These images were timely and relatable, and we see Him unpacking each of them in today's verse.

Let's consider salt. Back in the first century, it had two main purposes. First, people used it to preserve their food since they didn't have refrigerators or freezers. Without it, meat especially would spoil quickly in the arid environment. Jesus is telling believers that we're like salt because we are preservatives in this world. We are what keeps evil at bay. And second, just as we do now, the people back then used salt as a flavor enhancer. It added oomph to make their meals taste better. We're called to be enhancers here too. Believers who embrace their faith add flavor to life by exerting a good and godly influence.

Regarding light, we're called to shine God's goodness into the world. Through the things we do and the words we speak, we can point others to the Father in heaven. The way we live preaches whether we realize it or not. So stand strong and understand we must be bright lights to illuminate the dark places—because if not His followers, then who? Shining bright isn't about bringing attention to us but about pointing the spotlight on God alone.

Pray for the courage to be salt and light. Yes, it will take intentionality to make sure we live righteous lives that look different than what's happening in the world. So ask God every day to guide this pursuit and trust that He will do so. And ask for the spiritual eyes and ears to recognize opportunities to enhance and shine where it's needed most.

DEAR LORD, I HUMBLY ACCEPT THE CALL TO BE SALT AND LIGHT TO A BITTER AND DARK WORLD. GUIDE MY STEPS SO I BRING GLORY TO YOUR NAME THROUGH THE WAY I LIVE MY LIFE. IN JESUS' NAME. AMEN.

Stepping Boldly and Honestly

Since we have a great High Priest, Jesus, the Son of God
who has passed through the heavens from death into new
life with God, let us hold tightly to our faith. For Jesus is not
some high priest who has no sympathy for our weaknesses
and flaws. He has already been tested in every way that
we are tested; but He emerged victorious, without failing
God. So let us step boldly to the throne of grace, where we
can find mercy and grace to help when we need it most.

HEBREWS 4:14–16 VOICE

How do we "step boldly to the throne of grace"? Recognize first that it's about having confidence and not cowardice. How can we have confidence? By trusting in Jesus as our great High Priest. And while the high priest at the temple would normally be the one to offer the sacrifice and intercede on behalf of the people, Jesus Himself was the final sacrifice. So he was both and is both, and that gives us the privilege of approaching the throne ourselves.

Under the Mosaic law, every sacrifice for sin had to die, and then new sacrifices were required to cover new sin. And so the offering of sacrificial animals happened on a regular basis because sin was regular. But when Jesus came to earth and died on the cross for our sins—past, present, and future—as our High Priest, He brought a different kind of sacrifice. His death paid for our sins once and for all.

But keep in mind that Jesus lived as a man. Because He experienced all we do here on earth, He developed great sympathy for the trials and tribulations we walk through. Jesus understood our human condition. He was tested and tried. He had to navigate temptation. And even though He came through sinless, Christ has a full understanding of what we face.

So yes, we can step boldly to the throne of grace and receive help when we need it most. Be honest as you pray. Tell Him the truth of what's going on in your life. The Lord recognizes every challenge and can sympathize in real ways.

DEAR LORD, WHAT A PRIVILEGE TO TALK TO YOU ABOUT MY CHALLENGES, REALIZING YOU UNDERSTAND THEM ALL. YOU KNOW THE PITFALLS OF LIFE. YOU KNOW MY FLAWS AND SHORTCOMINGS. AND IN YOU I CAN FIND COMPASSION AND HELP FOR ALL I'M FACING, AS WELL AS STRENGTH AND WISDOM TO MOVE FORWARD IN FAITH. IN JESUS' NAME. AMEN.

Faith to Move Mountains

The disciples were utterly amazed and asked, "How did the fig tree wither so quickly?" Then Jesus told them, "Truly, if you have faith and don't doubt, you can do things like this and much more. You can even say to this Mount of Olives, 'Move over into the ocean,' and it will. You can get anything—anything you ask for in prayer—if you believe."

MATTHEW 21:20–22 TLB

. . . .

As they were walking by a fig tree, Jesus cursed it, and the disciples watched the branches wither without delay. They were amazed by how quickly it responded to Him, and they wondered why. Jesus said it was because of His faith and then went on to tell them they could accomplish things like this if they believed and didn't let doubt interrupt their faith. They could even make the Mount of Olives—a hill of rock that was 2,652 feet above sea level and about thirty miles from the shore of the Mediterranean—move over into the ocean. Can you imagine that?

In saying this, Jesus wasn't trying to teach His disciples how to razzle and dazzle others. This wasn't a chance to impress or show off. Instead, He was training them to do the great works prepared for them in advance. He was teaching them to use their faith to overcome fear and any other barriers to their ministry. And Jesus knew that some of what they'd face would be mountain-sized obstacles that only faith could move. Then, He told them to pray and boldly ask for God's help with both expectation and unshakable belief.

Are any mountains standing in your way today, friend? Are they keeping you stuck or stunted? Are you intimidated by their size or influence? Have they shut you down or shut you up? Do you feel outmatched or outwitted? Do you feel hopeless to move forward? Ask God for the courage to believe they can be moved. Pray with hope, trusting that He will bring the *super* to your *natural* and empower you. Pray unceasingly, waiting for the path to be cleared. And pray with thanksgiving because you know God is with you each step of the way.

DEAR LORD, HELP ME MORE FULLY UNDERSTAND THE
POWER OF FAITH AND HOW I CAN WIELD IT IN MY LIFE.
HELP ME BELIEVE IN YOUR PROMISES AND STAND FIRM
IN THEM WITHOUT DOUBT. IN JESUS' NAME. AMEN.

Allegiance to God

You long for something you don't have, so you commit murder. You are jealous for something you can't get, so you struggle and fight. You don't have because you don't ask. You ask and don't have because you ask with evil intentions, to waste it on your own cravings. You unfaithful people! Don't you know that friendship with the world means hostility toward God? So whoever wants to be the world's friend becomes God's enemy.

JAMES 4:2–4 CEB

The book of James talks a lot about the practical side of living as believers. In today's passage, James is addressing his readers' desire to get what they want from God. And he points out some bad behavior we can relate to today.

They wanted something they didn't have, so they killed for it. This could have been actual murder or just acting hatefully toward others. They were filled with jealousy for what they couldn't get, so they caused strife and argued with those around them. They turned away from God, refusing to pray with a humble heart. Or they did ask but did so with evil intentions. And their motives were selfish and focused on all the wrong things. James may have written this letter a long time ago, but it's spot-on with where many Christians are today. Too often, when we don't get what we want, we behave badly and take out our frustration on others.

If our craving is to be courageous women of God who stand boldly in our faith, then it's important we get this right. We need to remember to take our focus off ourselves and, instead, lean into the Lord with pure intentions. This doesn't mean we can't pray for ourselves or ask for our heart's desire. We can want things and work toward them. But let's make certain our eyes and hearts are turned toward the eternal and not the earthly. Let's align our longings with the Lord's so we don't fall into one of the categories James warns about. Remember, we are *in* the world but not *of* the world. And our allegiance should always rest with God alone.

Friend, we can simply ask for what we want and trust Him with the method and timing.

DEAR LORD, HELP ME CHOOSE TO LIVE IN WAYS THAT
BLESS OTHERS, BENEFIT ME, AND ALWAYS BRING
GLORY TO YOUR NAME. HELP ME REMEMBER TO KEEP
MY EYES AND HEART ON FOLLOWING YOUR WILL AND
WAYS. AND EVERY DAY, LET MY LIFE PREACH LOUDLY
ABOUT MY FAITH IN YOU. IN JESUS' NAME. AMEN.

The Humble versus the Proud

Do you think it is empty rhetoric when the Scriptures say, "The spirit that lives in us is addicted to envy and jealousy"? You may think that the situation is hopeless, but God gives us more grace when we turn away from our own interests. That's why Scripture says, God opposes the proud, but He pours out grace on the humble.

JAMES 4:5–6 VOICE

A bold woman of faith understands the need to surrender to God. Without doing so, we will live in ways that glorify ourselves. Our fleshly desires will rule the day and direct our steps. And that sin nature will keep us separated from our Father. Scripture says that when we turn away from our own interests, we'll receive the hope and grace needed to navigate life. We can't be faithful to the world and to the Lord at the same time. One or the other will always be in the driver's seat.

Do you need to repent of selfishness today? If so, why not go ahead and do it? When we mess up, the only way to get a fresh start is to humble ourselves in the Lord's presence. It's time to confess and draw near so He can bring about much-needed restoration. And that, in turn, will usher in grace—even more grace—as we realign ourselves with His will. It's not that He expects perfection but that He blesses a purposeful heart.

Remember that the proud are self-seeking. Their paths follow their own desires and cravings. Their ways are based on what they want, when they want it. But the humble are kingdom-seeking, and they choose to walk the road of righteous living, trusting God to meet their needs in the right ways and at the right times. These believers exhibit a powerful dependence on the Lord as provider.

Every day, ask God for the courage and confidence to be humble so grace flows freely from you. As you ask, expect the Lord to answer. You can have hope for a redirected heart. Humility isn't easy, friend. And it requires some deliberate choices on your part. But when those self-centered thoughts arise, be quick to confess and realign yourself with the Lord's will once again.

DEAR LORD, I WANT TO LIVE IN HARMONY WITH
YOU AND NOT IN OPPOSITION. HELP ME SEEK
HUMILITY OVER PRIDE SO GRACE WILL PROFOUNDLY
MARK MY LIFE. IN JESUS' NAME. AMEN.

The Command to Resist

So give yourselves humbly to God. Resist the devil and he will flee from you. And when you draw close to God, God will draw close to you. Wash your hands, you sinners, and let your hearts be filled with God alone to make them pure and true to him.

JAMES 4:7–8 TLB

. . . .

James gives us strong advice on how to take the devil's advantage away. He boldly says we can make him flee from us! So what does it look like to *resist* the devil?

First, let's understand what that word means. To resist means to act in opposition to. It's taking action to defeat or thwart. It's to remain unaffected. This can be either a defensive or offensive response.

In a defensive stance, resistance helps us battle all kinds of temptation. We ask God to give us the fortitude and willpower to stand strong. It's active and in real time. But resistance can also be an offensive weapon, especially when we're diligent to pray on the armor of God every morning. Anytime we use scripture as a weapon against the enemy's schemes, it's a win. Truly, scripture is our greatest asset in the battles we face. And with the Lord's help, we can resist.

But notice what comes before our ability to resist the devil. James tells us that we must *give ourselves humbly to God*. We must submit to His authority. If we don't, finding the grit and guts to resist will be hard to do. And if we're not prepared for the devil's attacks, we will fall prey to them every time. And he knows this. But fully equipped and ready, believers scare him. He sees our divine protection.

Before your feet even hit the floor in the morning, be quick to ask God for courage to resist the devil. Pray for His armor to cover you. Throughout the day, pray every time temptation comes your way. Anytime a thought pops into your head that leads you away from His perfect will, take it straight to the Lord. If you feel too weak to battle those strong, fleshly feelings that seem overwhelming, let Him know and then wait with expectation for an extra measure of strength. Be hopeful for God's help, because He will provide it.

DEAR LORD, I NEED YOUR STRENGTH AND WISDOM TO
RESIST THE ENEMY, WHOSE ONLY PLAN IS TO STEAL,
KILL, AND DESTROY. HELP ME REMAIN FAITHFUL
IN ALL MY WAYS. IN JESUS' NAME. AMEN.

Planning with God, Not without Him

The reality is you have no idea where your life will take you tomorrow. You are like a mist that appears one moment and then vanishes another. It would be best to say, "If it is the Lord's will and we live long enough, we hope to do this project or pursue that dream." But your current speech indicates an arrogance that does not acknowledge the One who controls the universe, and this kind of big talking is the epitome of evil.

JAMES 4:14–16 VOICE

James is speaking a big truth when he says we're clueless as to where life will take us. We can hope. We can plan. We can think through ideas and options. But the reality is that we really have no idea what tomorrow holds. But take heart! Nothing's wrong with dreaming for the future. We just need to involve God in those plans from beginning to end.

James isn't being critical or condemning. He is, however, warning us to seek God's guidance. Our plans and projects should never be entertained if they're outside of His will for our lives. If we feel a check in our spirit, it may be the Lord telling us to take a step back and be prayerful about it. To ignore such a warning and move forward is foolish. It's arrogant. We're not independent and sovereign, so pushing ahead as if we are will inevitably land us in a messy situation with painful consequences.

In His sovereignty, God has the supernatural ability to see the whole picture. He sees the details we're not even considering and understands how they will affect the outcome of what we're planning. And rather than overwhelm us, He lets situations unfold day by day. That way, as we seek Him, He can provide daily instruction to help us navigate our next steps with confidence.

Let's not script out our life without His valuable input. Be prayerful! Boldly invite God into your decisions about marriage, the timing of children, building a home or renting, careers and job opportunities, saving and spending, and everything in between. Let's be intentional to live every day according to His will. And if we're unsure, let's pray with expectation and a hopeful heart. We can trust Him to show us the way as we humbly pursue His direction.

DEAR LORD, I DON'T WANT TO TAKE ONE STEP OUT
OF YOUR WILL FOR MY LIFE. I'M INVITING YOU INTO
EACH DECISION AND PLAN. IN JESUS' NAME. AMEN.

Why It's Good to Admit Sin

*If we go around bragging, "We have no sin," then we
are fooling ourselves and are strangers to the truth. But
if we own up to our sins, God shows that He is faithful
and just by forgiving us of our sins and purifying us from
the pollution of all the bad things we have done.*

1 JOHN 1:8–9 VOICE

There's something powerful about admitting we're wrong. To say that we've fallen short or just plain failed is cathartic because it helps to release expectations that we must be perfect. Maybe those are our expectations or ones we feel from those around us. Regardless, choosing to be bold and own up to our sins brings us peace. The weight of the world falls off our shoulders, and those obnoxious internal messages—the ones that say we have to be more or perform better—begin to dissipate.

But let's be honest. It's hard to admit we're not Wonder Woman. It takes a humble heart to fess up when we've tripped and fallen. So, at times, we decide to keep those flaws and sins hidden and act like we have it all together. We might even brag about how well we're doing. But the truth is that we've all fallen short of God's glory. We're all battling a sinful nature riddled with selfishness. And when we act holier-than-thou, we're being foolish. We're actively deceiving ourselves and others, hiding what is true.

This kind of behavior isn't God's best for us.

If we want to be gutsy girls, then we need to make peace with imperfection. The Lord isn't looking for us to be faultless, so neither should we. It's okay to flounder and flop. Friend, we will mess up! But when we do and own up to it, God will restore us in supernatural ways. We will find the freedom to be both flawed and fabulous. So each time we miss the mark, let's go to the Lord in prayer, confessing and asking for comfort.

We are sinful creatures! But we are also deeply loved and forgiven.

DEAR LORD, I ADMIT THAT I'M A MESS AT TIMES. I FALL SHORT MORE TIMES THAN I CARE TO ADMIT. BUT I KNOW THAT OWNING MY SINS AND SHORTCOMINGS ALLOWS YOU TO FORGIVE AND PURIFY. THANKS FOR THE REMINDER THAT I DON'T NEED TO BE PERFECT. IN JESUS' NAME. AMEN.

Perseverance in Prayer

Bend Your ear to me and listen to my words, O Eternal One;
hear the deep cry of my heart. Listen to my call for help,
my King, my True God; to You alone I pray. In the morning,
O Eternal One, listen for my voice; in the day's first light, I will
offer my prayer to You and watch expectantly for Your answer.
PSALM 5:1–3 VOICE

David understood the need to persevere in prayer. He knew it could take time to see God's response to his requests. In this psalm, he's crying out for help, asking the Lord to direct his steps. Like many of us, David had faced intense suffering and was desperate to hear from God. And notice that his prayers and pleas started in the morning and likely continued throughout the day. But also recognize David's resolve to watch expectantly for God's answer. He may have started out this psalm feeling desperate and looking for hope, but these verses end with confidence in the Lord's goodness. We can have that confidence too!

In what struggles are you asking God to hear the deep cry of your heart? What are you praying for in hopes of bending His ear to you? What is making you call for His help? Well, friend, keep on keeping on! Go to the Lord in prayer with a hopeful heart, believing that He hears you and will respond. Pray with expectation because the Bible says He will answer in the right way and at the right time. Pray without ceasing, knowing it lightens your load and brings comfort as you wait. Pray with thanksgiving that God is who He says He is and will do what He says He will do. And pray that the Lord's will be done, because you can trust it's always for your good and His glory.

Like David, we may start out our laments from a weak and worried place. But the more we pray and share our fears and weaknesses with Him, the more courageous we'll feel to stand strong, patiently waiting for God to show up and meet our needs in meaningful ways.

DEAR LORD, I WILL PRAY TO YOU WITH GREAT
EXPECTATION AND RAW HONESTY. AND I'LL WAIT FOR
YOU TO BRING THE HOPE AND HELP I'M NEEDING IN
THOSE TIMES. WHEN I'M FULL OF ANXIETY OR FEELING
WEARY IN THE BATTLE, I WILL PERSEVERE IN PRAYER
AND SIMPLY TRUST. IN JESUS' NAME. AMEN.

Fix Your Gaze on God

My gaze is fixed upon You, Eternal One, my Lord; in
You I find safety and protection. Do not abandon me
and leave me defenseless. Protect me from the jaws of
the trap my enemies have set for me and from the snares
of those who work evil. May the wicked be caught in
their own nets while I alone escape unharmed.

PSALM 141:8–10 VOICE

Friend, where is your gaze fixed today? Too often we look to people and things here on earth to keep us safe and help us walk out tough times and seasons. We may not forget about God, but we decide to trust in worldly rescues instead of heavenly ones. We place our hope in humanity rather than in the one who created us. And what we forget is that they'll never give us what we need the very most—at least not for long.

Think through these questions today: Is my focus on earthly remedies or eternal ones? Am I relying on my boyfriend or husband to be a safety net in the storms that life brings? Am I depending on a parent or other family member to fix my problems? Has a certain friend been a protector of my heart and felt like a safe place? Am I putting my hope in the government, a movement, a church, or the company I work for? Has my anchor been trusting in certain promises, policies, or procedures? Friend, none of these will satisfy in the end.

We can learn from David's steadfast confidence unpacked in this psalm. He was focused on eternal solutions, knowing the only secure place for his gaze was locked on God's promises. That's where his safety and protection came from. Rather than trusting in himself, David saw the Lord as his defense and asked Him to engage and not abandon. He boldly asked for shelter and security from any set snares. And he asked God to expose the wicked while he escaped unharmed.

As women of God, we can have this same confidence by fixing our gaze on the Lord and our expectations on His promises.

DEAR LORD, HELP ME FOCUS MY HEART AND MIND ON YOU BECAUSE I KNOW THIS EARTH HAS NOTHING FOR ME. WHILE I'M SO GRATEFUL FOR MY FRIENDS AND FAMILY, THEY ARE NOT MY SAVIOR. JESUS IS MY SAVIOR, AND MY GAZE IS FIXED ON HIM ALONE. IN JESUS' NAME. AMEN.

God Hears Your Cries

When the upright need help and cry to the Eternal, He hears their cries and rescues them from all of their troubles. When someone is hurting or brokenhearted, the Eternal moves in close and revives him in his pain. Hard times may well be the plight of the righteous—they may often seem overwhelmed—but the Eternal rescues the righteous from what oppresses them. He will protect all of their bones; not even one bone will be broken.

PSALM 34:17–20 VOICE

Sit in the truth that God hears your cries. Let that beautiful promise settle in your heart today, because it will give you hope for divine intervention. It will calm the chaos that keeps you stirred up, assuring you the Lord *will* provide a rescue when you live in righteous and respectable ways that glorify His holy name. God, in His endless goodness, will move in closely when you hurt—even closer than He is right now. He'll revive you when life sucker punches you in the gut. Never forget that the Lord notices the brokenhearted. And scripture says He will save you from *all* trouble, not just certain parched places. Friend, God sees you.

The reality is that we will have painful times. To think any differently only sets us up for huge discouragement and disappointment. Life will come at us ruthlessly at inopportune moments. It'll be smooth sailing until it isn't. Difficult circumstances may overwhelm us, or unexpected calamities may leave us utterly speechless. The weight of grief may exhaust us to the core. Broken relationships may flood us with a roller coaster of emotions leading to hopelessness. Even now, any or all of these may well be our plight! But a rescue is coming.

Feeling overwhelmed or exhausted sometimes is normal and natural in our human condition. It's just a part of life, something we'll all face as long as we're drawing breath on planet Earth. But God promises to rescue the righteous from oppression. He will provide the protection we need at every turn. So be quick to pray. Unpack your fears and worries and ask for what you need. And watch as this practice strengthens you for the battles ahead while also comforting your anxious heart. You are never alone and without an ally.

DEAR LORD, HEAR MY CRIES OF DESPERATION AND FEAR.
HELP ME BE STEADFAST AS I WAIT FOR DELIVERANCE
FROM ALL MY TROUBLES. IN JESUS' NAME. AMEN.

Seeking the Lord

Give thanks to the LORD, call on his name; make his deeds known to all people! Sing to God, sing praises to him; dwell on all his wondrous works! Give praise to God's holy name! Let the hearts of all those seeking the LORD rejoice! Pursue the LORD and his strength; seek his face always!

1 CHRONICLES 16:8–11 CEB

Today's verses tell us to turn our face toward the Lord. It's an intentional move on our part because if we're not deliberate to acknowledge Him, we won't. With everything else going on in our lives, it will simply slip our minds. Maybe you know exactly what I'm talking about.

As many believe Ezra wrote Chronicles, the first of the two books was written to help the exiled children of God understand how to worship Him again as they returned to Israel. It may have been simple advice, but it was necessary to restore their hearts to the Lord. It helped reset their focus in significant ways. Did you notice what they were told to do?

They were told to give thanks because a glad heart delights the Lord. They were instructed to call on God's name, which is a powerful act of surrender, recognizing the need for help. Ezra also commanded them to sing praises as they dwelled on the Lord's goodness and graciousness. The Israelites were to rejoice wholeheartedly, giving thanks where thanks was due. And they were to pursue God's strength and seek His face always. Simply put, Ezra was charging them to go after God's presence with passion and purpose.

Ever wonder what it means to seek the Lord? It's not something we do because He is lost; rather it's the turning of our faces toward Him. It's the choice to set our minds and hearts on God. It's a conscious decision to pursue Him through the Word, where He powerfully reveals Himself, and through prayer, where He meets us deeply and profoundly. And as we focus our attention and our affection on our great Father, we will experience His presence.

We are free to pursue God boldly and humbly because we're assured that He is always pursuing us. A relationship is a two-way street. And we're promised that if we seek Him with our whole heart, we will find Him. Start every day in prayer, then continue with expectation and without ceasing. Pray with thanksgiving and hope. And know God is with you always.

. . . .

DEAR LORD, I WILL SEEK YOU WITH PASSION
AND PURPOSE! IN JESUS' NAME. AMEN.

God Hears the Prayers of the Righteous

The Lord is far from the wicked, but He
hears the prayer of the [consistently] righteous
(the upright, in right standing with Him).

PROVERBS 15:29 AMPC

Prayer is an amazing privilege for believers. What a gift to have direct communication with our Creator—anytime and anywhere! Nothing is sweeter than to have meaningful fellowship with the Lord, and we do that by talking through life's challenges with Him. On a good day, we pray in celebration. On bad days, we pray through tears. And as we pursue righteous living—even if imperfect and messy at times—we can be assured He hears us. He promises it in His Word. So each time we cry out, our words reach the throne room.

In contrast, the Lord is far from the wicked. He's not far away in proximity or out of earshot—remember, God is all-knowing and all-seeing. He is, however, far from comforting them. He's far from helping and blessing them, and He's not inclined to rescue them from their bad choices. The Lord is far from fellowshipping with them in genuine community. And unless they come into a saving relationship with Jesus, they won't enter the kingdom.

The wicked are those who continue sinning even though they know it's wrong. They don't care or confess. Instead of taking note, they refuse to listen to the Holy Spirit's prompting, ignore what scripture says, and pay no attention to a pastor or friend's warning. The wicked think they can get away with their sin and live for today. Others may not see it. Friends and family may think all is well. But these people cannot hide their iniquity from God. He sees it all.

Friend, the most crucial decision you can make is to accept His Son, Jesus, as your Savior. He came to earth to give up His life on the cross, bridging the gap left by sin, and three days later He rose again. And at the moment you make this bold personal decision to accept the invitation to become a child of God, you are righteous. Each day following that decision, your delight is to live in ways that benefit you and glorify God. When you do, your prayers to the Lord are heard and answered.

DEAR LORD, I ACCEPT YOUR GIFT OF SALVATION.
MAKE ME RIGHTEOUS SO MY LIFE BRINGS GLORY TO
YOUR HOLY NAME. HELP ME TO BE UPRIGHT EVEN WHEN
THOSE AROUND ME ARE NOT. IN JESUS' NAME. AMEN.

Boldly Praying and Praising

Are you hurting? Pray. Do you feel great? Sing. Are you sick? Call the church leaders together to pray and anoint you with oil in the name of the Master. Believing-prayer will heal you, and Jesus will put you on your feet. And if you've sinned, you'll be forgiven—healed inside and out.

JAMES 5:13–14 MSG

What a great reminder that we're to pray and praise boldly regardless of the circumstances we're facing. We have the privilege of talking to God whether we find ourselves in a valley or on a mountaintop. We can rejoice in His goodness whether we're "living our best life" or feeling down in the dumps. Being in an active relationship with God provides perspective and creates compassion in believers. And together, prayer and praise are potent.

What does prayer look like in your life? When the migraine headache stops you in your tracks, do you pray for relief? When the words spoken sting, do you talk to God about it? Do you recognize answered prayer by praising the Lord? When others reach out with petitions or requests, do you join them in prayer? When their celebrations come at the mighty hand of God, are you quick to glorify Him together? Do you seek support from your church community, letting them encircle you with believing prayer?

Friend, prayer and praise are two essential parts of walking out a Christian life. And they're also the two parts that often get overlooked. Maybe we get too busy to remember or don't make the time to engage with God. But as godly women who love the Lord with all our hearts, minds, and souls, we should be praying throughout our days and praising without ceasing, with expectation and thanksgiving attached. We should be hopeful for His hand to move and grateful for all the ways it already has. Too often, however, prayer becomes our last-ditch effort to find stabilization. Sometimes we see it as a last resort after trying everything humanly possible to fix our struggles, or we give credit to worldly solutions without considering divine intervention.

But when prayer becomes our default button, our automatic response to whatever life brings, we benefit and the Lord is glorified. Consistent communication with the Father is vital to a faith-filled life.

DEAR LORD, I KNOW IT TAKES GRIT TO MAKE PRAYER
A TOP PRIORITY. IT TAKES INTENTIONALITY. I WANT
YOU TO BE THE ONE I GO TO FIRST FOR HELP OR TO
SHARE A HALLELUJAH. IN JESUS' NAME. AMEN.

The Nine Names

I love You, Eternal One, source of my power. The Eternal
is my rock, my fortress, and my salvation; He is my True
God, the stronghold in which I hide, my strong shield,
the horn that calls forth help, and my tall-walled tower.
I call out to the Eternal, who is worthy to be praised—
that's how I will be rescued from my enemies.

PSALM 18:1–3 VOICE

. . . .

This psalm is one of rejoicing for the victory God has given the psalmist over his enemies. As he is praising with deep love for the Lord, he uses nine names to describe His character. These names not only represented God then, but because He is unchanging, they also describe who the Lord is for us today.

God is our *source of power*, the one our true strength comes from.

God is our *rock*—He is our sanctuary.

God is our *fortress*, a safe place to be.

God is our *salvation*—He saves us and is always ready to rescue us.

God is our *true God*, the one and only Almighty.

God is our *stronghold* where we can find refuge and shelter.

God is our *strong shield* and provides protection.

God is our *horn* that calls for help, bringing deliverance and freedom.

God is our *tall-walled tower* that serves as a defense and fortification.

Sometimes our courage will wane. We may face battles that feel impossible to walk out one minute longer. Circumstances may cause us to lose hope and give in to exhaustion. Relationships are challenging, finances are stressful, and the world often feels downright crazy. But as believers, we realize our God stands with us through it all. He is exactly what we need and gives us all we need to thrive.

So, friend, be quick to pray when those demanding times come. God is with you. He is for you. And you can confidently tell Him all you're facing. Pray with a hopeful heart full of anticipation for His help. Pray with gratitude, knowing God will always come through. And pray without ceasing, waiting patiently until He answers. The Lord has you.

DEAR LORD, THANK YOU FOR LOVING ME AND COVERING ME AS I NAVIGATE THE TOUGH TIMES THIS LIFE BRINGS. THANKS FOR KEEPING ME CLOSE TO YOUR HEART. THANK YOU FOR BEING ALL THESE THINGS FOR ME EVERY DAY AND IN EVERY SITUATION. THERE IS NO ONE ELSE LIKE YOU! IN JESUS' NAME. AMEN.

Pulled to Safety

He reached down His hand from above me; He held me.
He lifted me from the raging waters. He rescued me from my
strongest enemy, from all those who sought my death, for they
were too strong. They came for me in the day of my destruction,
but the Eternal was the support of my life. He set me down in
a safe place; He saved me to His delight; He took joy in me.
PSALM 18:16–19 VOICE

David is once again praising the Lord for being his protector and rescuing him from enemies. In this particular psalm, he undoubtedly felt like a man who was drowning in raging waters. And just as God ensured that Moses would be pulled and saved from actual water in Exodus 2, He also pulled and saved David from situations that he likened to "raging waters." The same is true for you. Rest assured that when the waters of life threaten you, God will save you as well.

So let's think about it. What waters are threatening to overtake you today, friend? Are you being pulled under by challenges in your relationships? Are the seas of discouragement in your career lapping at your heels? Are the waves of frustration in parenting slapping you in the face? Are you tired of treading the deep water of your finances or your health? Has a tsunami of grief washed you away from thriving in life? Is an ocean of chaos rising faster than you can hold it at bay?

No matter the intensity of our troubling circumstances, God is stronger. And as we cry out in heartache or frustration, we can trust that He'll reach into the raging waters and pull us to safety every time. He won't let us drown in the tumultuous situations that come our way. Even more, scripture says the Lord will set us down in a safe place where we can find rest and peace—a place of comfort where we can catch our breath.

The truth is that the waters will rise in our lives from time to time. But as believers, we're anchored to the only one who can keep us afloat. Our faith keeps us buoyant in the most beautiful ways. And if we're tethered to God—spending time in the Word and in prayer—we can be confident that we'll always be pulled to safety.

DEAR LORD, THANK YOU FOR KEEPING ME
FROM GOING UNDER WHEN I FACE THE RAGING
WATERS OF LIFE. IN JESUS' NAME. AMEN.

When a Precedent Has Been Set

The True God who encircled me with strength and made my pathway straight. He made me sure-footed as a deer and placed me high up where I am safe. He teaches me to fight so that my arms can bend a bronze bow. You have shielded me with Your salvation, supporting me with Your strong right hand, and it makes me strong. You taught me how to walk with care so my feet will not slip.

PSALM 18:32–36 VOICE

David was so good about seeing God's hand in his life. He may have missed things from time to time, but overall, David praised the Lord for being his provider and protector. Let's consider the different roles the Lord plays in these verses, and let's personalize this passage to your life right now.

As a woman of God, you can be assured that the Lord's strength and power will surround you each day. He'll be diligent to remove any obstacles that might keep you from moving forward in the call He has placed on your life. The Holy Spirit will prompt you, keeping you alert for what's ahead. And God will keep you safe.

When you find yourself steeped in personal battles, He'll show you how to gain the victory so that you're blessed and He's glorified. He'll help you navigate life with the sword of the Spirit—God's Word. And as you walk the narrow path of righteousness, growing in wisdom and maturity, He'll make sure your steps are certain.

If the Lord did all this for David, He will do it for you too. A precedent has been set in the Bible, which means you can pray with hope and expectation that God will do the same for you. As you approach Him in prayer, humbly ask for a repeat—this time in your life. Show gratitude for the ways He has blessed you in the past, and let Him know that you trust His will to be done.

Then, friend, ask for the spiritual eyes to see His hand move in your circumstances. Watch as God strengthens and straightens, teaches and trains, shields and saves. And be thankful!

DEAR LORD, YOU REALLY DO TAKE CARE OF ME IN
SIGNIFICANT WAYS. WHAT A BLESSING TO UNDERSTAND
WHO YOU ARE IN REAL TIME. MAKE ME EVER AWARE
OF YOUR GOODNESS SO THAT I HAVE COURAGE TO
TRUST YOU AT ALL TIMES. IN JESUS' NAME. AMEN.

A Gentle and Quiet Spirit

*Don't be concerned about the outward beauty that depends
on jewelry, or beautiful clothes, or hair arrangement.
Be beautiful inside, in your hearts, with the lasting charm
of a gentle and quiet spirit that is so precious to God.*

1 Peter 3:3–4 tlb

Sometimes we think that having a gentle and quiet spirit means we're to be doormats. It means we're pushovers and lack spines to stand up and advocate for ourselves. But that's simply not true.

God would never ask a woman of faith to let others walk all over her. We can say no. We can establish healthy boundaries. And we can have confidence rooted in the Lord. Remember, we are made in His image, and the value arising from that beautiful truth can't be removed. If we look at Jesus' time on earth, we'll notice He said no to certain people and opportunities. He even withdrew at times to regroup and recharge through prayer and time alone with the Father.

So how can we have a gentle and quiet spirit that benefits us and brings God glory? Daily, let's choose to remove ourselves from a noisy world so we can sit in His Word and find encouragement. Let's listen for His still, small voice to speak into our hearts. As we read the Bible, let's be sensitive to the places our spirits feel stender, and let's meditate on what each verse is saying. Let's look for examples of men and women who had gentle and quiet spirits and dig deeper into their stories. And let's resolve to obey God's leading.

The more we focus on maturing the inside rather than obsessing about the outside, the more we'll grow in humble confidence. We'll understand what makes someone truly beautiful. We'll recognize what God values most and be encouraged to grow deeper roots with Jesus. We'll become gutsy girls who choose faith over all else. And our gentle and quiet spirits will help us make wise choices, be honest with ourselves and others, and delight God. Our decision to follow His will and ways will be precious in His eyes.

DEAR LORD, I CONFESS THE TIMES I'VE BEEN OVERLY CONCERNED WITH THE WAY I LOOK. I'VE WANTED TO MEET THE WORLD'S STANDARDS OF BEAUTY RATHER THAN FOCUSING ON WHAT MATTERS MOST TO YOU. HELP ME CONFIDENTLY EMBRACE A GENTLE AND QUIET SPIRIT, KNOWING IT'S PRECIOUS IN YOUR EYES. IN JESUS' NAME. AMEN.

Praying for the Unkind

*And now this word to all of you: You should be like one big
happy family, full of sympathy toward each other, loving
one another with tender hearts and humble minds. Don't
repay evil for evil. Don't snap back at those who say unkind
things about you. Instead, pray for God's help for them, for
we are to be kind to others, and God will bless us for it.*

1 PETER 3:8–9 TLB

As believers, we're called to be one big happy family. But sometimes we forget we're on the same team, both locally and as a global church. Rather than being full of sympathy and loving others with tenderness and humility, we argue. We pick sides and campaign against our brothers and sisters. Our words and actions don't bless them or glorify God. Too often we forget that He has called us to unity.

Our lives should point to the Father in heaven. People are watching us, especially knowing we are women of faith. The truth is that how we treat others—what we say and how we respond—is always being watched. Our lives preach one way or the other. So it really does matter how we choose to conduct ourselves when we feel attacked.

Friend, why not take an honest inventory of the past week? Have you spoken mean-spirited words about someone who has hurt you or someone you love? Have you discussed the desire for revenge—even if in a joking manner—in conversations? Have you been quick to react when upset or angry? Have your kids overheard hateful or inappropriate statements coming from your mouth? Deep breath. We're all human and have fallen short of the glory of God. Amen? But let's make changes now and reset our hearts to follow God's call for unity with other believers.

Moving forward, let's choose to pray for the Lord to help those who cause us emotional pain. This may seem counterintuitive, but we're to be kind when they're mean. Yet being kind doesn't mean we're to be a doormat for continued abuse. Healthy personal boundaries are essential. But we need to realize that our response to unkindness can either bring blessings or hinder them. Ask God to make you bold and give you discernment so you're following His will and honoring Him with an end goal of unity.

DEAR LORD, HEAR ME AS I PRAY FOR A KINDER HEART
WHEN I FEEL BACKED INTO A CORNER. MAKE ME HUMBLE.
AND KEEP MY EYES FOCUSED ON LOVING THE UNLOVABLE
AND FORGIVING THE UNFORGIVABLE. IN JESUS' NAME. AMEN.

The Lord Watches Over the Righteous

If you love life and want to live a good, long time, then be careful what you say. Don't tell lies or spread gossip or talk about improper things. Walk away from the evil things in the world—just leave them behind, and do what is right, and always seek peace and pursue it. For the Lord watches over the righteous, and His ears are attuned to their prayers. But His face is set against His enemies; He will punish evildoers.

1 PETER 3:10–12 VOICE

When today's passage of scripture says that "the Lord watches over the righteous," it is referring to those who are believers. These are people who take their faith to heart and want to live a good, long life blessing others and bringing God glory. They persist in doing what He has asked, like promoting unity and loving with purpose. They show compassion to those around them because their kindness comes from humble and tender places. They are careful with their words, not reckless or thoughtless. They refrain from gossip and insensitivity. And since they don't live from a defensive position, they're not repaying evil with evil. The righteous "always seek peace and pursue it" with passion.

Knowing that the Lord's eyes are always focused on us brings comfort by reminding us that He is sovereign over all creation. He is omniscient. The Lord knows everything and sees everything—the good, bad, and ugly. He misses nothing. And if He is always watching, that means He is always with us. We're never alone. We'll never be abandoned. We will never be separated from the Father's love. No matter what happens, we're always in the Lord's care—and that care is personal and individualized because He knows exactly what we need and when we need it. Friend, you are held.

It may be hard to live in the ways Peter unpacks above, but it's well worth our effort. Pray for the Lord's strength and wisdom each day. Ask for a generous heart that chooses love. Ask for the courage to respond with a gentle (yet sometimes firm) answer. When unkind words want to come out, ask God for divine duct tape. Ask for the confidence to walk away from the wrong things.

You can pray with hope and expectation because the Lord sees you, is with you, and promises to equip you to walk in His will. Why? Because God watches over the righteous.

DEAR LORD, GIVE ME THE STRENGTH AND WISDOM TO
WALK IN WAYS THAT BLESS OTHERS AND GLORIFY YOU.
THAT IS MY HEART'S DESIRE! IN JESUS' NAME. AMEN.

Love Covers Many Faults

We are coming to the end of all things, so be serious and
keep your wits about you in order to pray more forcefully.
Most of all, love each other steadily and unselfishly, because
love makes up for many faults. Show hospitality to each
other without complaint. Use whatever gift you've received
for the good of one another so that you can show yourselves
to be good stewards of God's grace in all its varieties.

1 PETER 4:7–10 VOICE

The Lord wants us to love each other steadily and unselfishly because love is vital for forgiveness. Without it, we won't find reasons to let go of offenses and, instead, will cling to them with all we've got. Yet unforgiveness creates bitterness, which leads to a hard heart. And hard-heartedness keeps us trapped in a pit of hate, unable to effectively be in community with others. As believers, when we choose to forgive, we're reflecting God's love.

The admonition in today's scripture passage isn't a way to cover sinful behavior that needs to be stopped. It isn't a command to show love by keeping hurtful or dangerous secrets. Nor is it a call to conceal or hide actions that are unlawful or inhumane. We're not covering sin with love by sweeping abuse or other indiscretions under the rug. Both the one wronged and the wrongdoer matter.

Nor does this concept of love covering sin mean we ignore the pain it may have caused us personally. We don't have to continue letting it happen, especially when it's becoming a habit. We're not to let someone push our buttons whenever they feel like it. We forgive them, but if the cycle continues, we forgive and then erect thoughtful boundaries to keep our hearts protected.

One of the best ways we can love others well is to keep short accounts. We get to choose if we're easily offended or if we let it go. Sometimes it's just not worth confronting another. When they make a snarky comment or are dismissive of your feelings, it may not be the hill to die on. Ask God for perspective. Maybe they had a hard day or just got bad news. Maybe they're battling fear or insecurity. We can love them by extending grace and refusing to be easily offended. And we can pray for God's help to love them steadily and unselfishly.

DEAR LORD, GIVE ME THE KIND OF LOVE THAT IS ABLE
TO COVER MANY FAULTS. GIVE ME DISCERNMENT
TO KNOW WHEN TO SPEAK UP AND WHEN TO LET
AN OFFENSE GO. IN JESUS' NAME. AMEN.

Suffering Is the Norm

Dear ones, don't be surprised when you experience your
trial by fire. It is not something strange and unusual, but
it is something you should rejoice in. In it you share the
Anointed's sufferings, and you will be that much more
joyful when His glory is revealed. If anyone condemns
you for following Jesus as the Anointed One, consider
yourself blessed. The glorious Spirit of God rests on you.

1 PETER 4:12–14 VOICE

Are you often surprised by the fiery trials that have come your way? Chances are you've seen many, and they just keep coming. Maybe the sudden death of a loved one caught you off guard. Maybe your husband's secret life was exposed, and you were clueless about it. Maybe you got a phone call that deeply affected your life in painful ways. Maybe you lost your job unexpectedly and have a stack of bills on your kitchen table. Maybe your child made a horrible decision that you can't undo. Maybe a past indiscretion was uncovered and you're having to face it now.

Scripture tells us not to be surprised by these difficulties. The truth is that suffering is the norm for believers. We may think (and hope) it's more of an exception, but it's not. In this life we *will* have troubles. And when we ask God for His perspective, we'll understand that suffering is both a powerful privilege and a

314

beautiful burden. It's something that should cause us to rejoice.

Peter goes on to remind us that being criticized or slammed for being a woman of faith is actually a blessing. When others make fun of us for trusting God or laugh because our hope is securely in Him or mock that our courage comes from clinging to the Lord, we are blessed. That may be a hard pill to swallow, but it's true. It's in these tough moments that the Holy Spirit literally rests on us.

There is no shortage of hard times these days, friend. But praise God that He finds a way to bless us through them!

Stay close to the Lord. Every day, saturate yourself in His Word and talk to Him through prayer. Pray with hope and expectation that God will bring good from heartbreak. Pray for His comfort and guidance, knowing difficult circumstances connect you closer to Him. And be a gutsy girl of faith, standing strong at every turn because God is always with you.

DEAR LORD, KEEP MY EYES AND HEART FOCUSED
ON YOU NO MATTER WHAT IS HAPPENING
IN MY LIFE. IN JESUS' NAME. AMEN.

The God Who Restores

The Eternal restored the fortunes of Job after he prayed for his friends; He even doubled the wealth he had before. All of his brothers and sisters, along with those he had known earlier, came and shared meals with him at his house. They sympathized with him and consoled him regarding the great distress the Eternal had brought on him. Each guest gave him a sum of money and each, a golden ring. The Eternal One blessed the last part of Job's life even more than the first part. He went on to possess 14,000 sheep, 6,000 camels, 1,000 teams of oxen, and 1,000 female donkeys. He also fathered 7 more sons and 3 more daughters.

JOB 42:10–13 VOICE

. . . .

Be encouraged by the truth that we serve a God who's in the business of restoration. We read in this closing chapter of the book of Job that once Job surrendered to God and reconciled with his friends, the Lord began restoring this broken man. Notice the possessions he once had were doubled by God and he fathered another ten children. His siblings and other friends came, bringing with them sympathy and reestablishing a sense of community he deeply missed. But what comforted Job the most was his mature relationship with the Lord.

One of the smartest things we can do as believers is grow

robust roots in our faith. These are what hold us securely when life beats us up. Think of all that Job went through. It's almost unimaginable, isn't it? Yet what settled his spirit more than anything else was knowing his God. His assets were doubled. He had ten new kids to be dad to. He had renewed fellowship with both friends and family. But Job clung to and was reassured by his established connection with the Father.

Friend, God's heart for restoration is why we can find courage in messy moments. It's why we can be confident that God will always show up. It's why we can pray with hopeful hearts when we make mistakes. And it's why we can endure hardship when it settles on our life. When we choose to surrender our wills to His and yield to His path for our lives, we'll experience the blessings of restoration.

DEAR LORD, THANK YOU FOR THE REMINDER ABOUT
THE CONNECTION BETWEEN SURRENDER AND
RESTORATION. HELP ME LIVE EACH DAY READY TO
FOLLOW YOUR LEAD IN MY LIFE, EVEN IF IT'S NOT THE
EASIEST STEP TO TAKE. IN JESUS' NAME. AMEN.

Praying from the Heart

"Pray like this: Our Father who is in heaven, uphold the holiness of your name. Bring in your kingdom so that your will is done on earth as it's done in heaven. Give us the bread we need for today. Forgive us for the ways we have wronged you, just as we also forgive those who have wronged us. And don't lead us into temptation, but rescue us from the evil one."

MATTHEW 6:9–13 CEB

This passage of scripture is called the Lord's Prayer, and Jesus taught it to His disciples. It's an example we can follow too, but we're not told to pray these exact words, for on their own they hold no power. Reciting this prayer word for word doesn't express our true hearts to God. He would much rather hear fresh prayers that come from deep places than something we've simply memorized. We can, however, look at the ingredients Jesus shared and apply them to our own prayer lives.

Our Father who is in heaven: We pray directly to God.

Uphold the holiness of your name: We praise and worship only God.

Bring in your kingdom so that your will is done on earth as it's done in heaven: We pray for His will (not ours) to be done personally and globally.

Give us the bread we need for today: We ask God for what we need.

Forgive us for the ways we have wronged you, just as we also forgive those who have wronged us: We confess and repent to God and forgive others.

And don't lead us into temptation, but rescue us from the evil one: We ask for His help to overcome sin and for protection from the enemy.

Nothing's wrong with praying this prayer if it's from the heart. You can take bits and pieces and add your own heartfelt flair too. But keep in mind that God wants to hear our authentic thoughts. So be honest as you talk to Him, because nothing is off-limits to unpack in His presence. You can pray about insecurities and fears. You can share celebratory news and anything that has delighted your heart. You can express your frustrations and the things that make you want to scream. You can boldly and confidently pray about anything and everything. And you can pray with expectation and hope because God hears you.

DEAR LORD, THANK YOU FOR WANTING
TO KNOW THE DEPTH AND COMPLEXITY OF
WHAT'S ON MY HEART. IN JESUS' NAME. AMEN.

Sacred Spaces with God

He pulled away from them about a stone's throw,
knelt down, and prayed, "Father, remove this cup from
me. But please, not what I want. What do you want?"
At once an angel from heaven was at his side, strengthening
him. He prayed on all the harder. Sweat, wrung from
him like drops of blood, poured off his face.

LUKE 22:41–44 MSG

By the time Jesus and His disciples had reached the garden of Gethsemane, it had been a long day. He then gathered Peter, James, and John, and they went a bit farther to where they could be alone. Jesus was in anguish because He knew His death was just around the corner, yet His friends couldn't bring Him any peace. So He went to pray alone, because He knew only His Father could bring the comfort needed in that moment. He poured out His heart to God and was strengthened by an angel.

Sometimes that's exactly what we need too. We may run to our bestie to ruminate about our heartbreaking circumstances. We may call our mom or dad to unpack the hurtful events of the day and get advice. We may look to our boyfriend or husband for help to navigate a messy moment. We may even turn to social media to gain sympathy and support. But friend, the only one who can truly meet you in the brokenness is God.

Instead of looking to friends and family, why don't you withdraw to sacred spaces with the Lord? You may have an amazing community of people who deeply love you and want what's best, but even in their awesomeness, they pale in comparison to God. They may have every good intention to guide your next steps, but they simply can't. Only the Lord sees the entire situation from beginning to end. He knows every player and every detail. And when you hide away in His presence and share your struggles, He'll bring you comfort, strength, and direction.

If we're to be gutsy girls of faith, then we need to be gutsy girls in prayer. No better weapon of war is at our disposal, for we know the battle is not of flesh and blood. So pray with passion and fervor. Boldly ask the Lord to equip you with wisdom and perseverance to stand strong. Pray with a hopeful and expectant heart, knowing He is with you always. And pray with thanksgiving for the ways He's already at work to straighten your crooked path.

DEAR LORD, YOU ARE ALL I NEED. IN JESUS' NAME. AMEN.

The Call to Simply Endure

Remember this, and do not abandon your confidence,
which will lead to rich rewards. Simply endure, for when
you have done as God requires of you, you will receive the
promise. As the prophet Habakkuk said, In a little while,
only a little longer, the One who is coming will come without
delay. But My righteous one must live by faith, for if he gives
up his commitment, My soul will have no pleasure in him.

HEBREWS 10:35–38 VOICE

Today's verses tell us to *simply endure*. Did you catch that? And when you read it, did it rattle you a bit? As women, we've faced plenty of challenging circumstances that made us want to give up in frustration. We've had to navigate heartbreaking moments that made us want to give in to despair. We've walked many dusty paths where we wanted to wave the white flag and call it a day. And we have watched our hopes be crushed, our security shaken, and our peace stolen by the struggles life has brought our way. So maybe the idea of *simply enduring* feels too big. But as believers, we can do this!

In our own strength, we are incapable of persevering for long. We have limited resources in our human condition. But when we saturate ourselves in God's Word, we will find the resolve to stand in confidence. As we spend quality time in prayer and talk through our fears and worries with God, He will bless us with exactly what we need for the next step. This is called living by faith.

When the Lord created you, He didn't expect you to navigate the easy parts or the hard parts of life alone. He created you for community, both with those around you and with Him. God knows better than anyone that we need His help. We're not expected to figure life out without Him. We may be smart and skilled, but those advantages only go so far. The worst thing we can do is rely on ourselves for endurance.

Be quick to invite God into the hard spaces of your life. Anticipate His empowerment. Pray with optimism and trust in His promise to be with you always. Pray without ceasing until you feel strengthened to simply endure. And then, by faith, stand with courage through every trial.

DEAR LORD, SOMETIMES I'M INTIMIDATED BY MY
LACK OF ENDURANCE. MEET ME WHEN I'M LACKING
AND EMPOWER ME TO PERSEVERE SO THAT I'LL
RECEIVE THE PROMISE ON THE OTHER SIDE OF THAT
BOLD ACT OF FAITH. IN JESUS' NAME. AMEN.

Being Mindful and Careful

So be careful how you live; be mindful of your steps.
Don't run around like idiots as the rest of the world does.
Instead, walk as the wise! Make the most of every living and
breathing moment because these are evil times. So understand
and be confident in God's will, and don't live thoughtlessly.

<small>EPHESIANS 5:15–17 VOICE</small>

Paul is encouraging believers to be aware of how they're living and make sure their walk aligns with their professed faith. Our life preaches one way or another. And just as there were temptations and risks back in the day, we face countless pitfalls today too. The truth is that this isn't an easy world to live in. Often, the level of evil seems to increase right before our eyes. And while our hope is in the Lord and His imminent return, standing strong takes courage. It requires our eyes to stay focused on God's goodness so we can make the most of our time here. And it means we must live and love with intention.

Each day, we have a choice. Will we embrace the earthly ways, or will we cling to the ways of the eternal? Will we run around like idiots, or will we follow the path of the wise? Will we partner with sinners or link arms with the saved? Unless we think ahead and draw lines in the sand now, making the right choices when temptation comes knocking may be harder than we think. Too often our wishy-washy plans fail and we don't think through real-time decisions with a holy mindset.

God is hoping we live shrewdly so our choices line up with His will for the Christian life. He is hoping we're careful about how we live and mindful of our steps. Consider the truth that we're not meant to fit in; we're created to stand out. And what guides us in this righteous pursuit is opening the Bible and letting God speak to us through His Word. As we seek His direction in prayer, the path forward will become clear. But we must choose this way of living each day and commit to seeking the Lord first.

DEAR LORD, HELP ME PREPARE MY HEART DAILY
SO I CAN BE MINDFUL OF MY STEPS AND WALK
WITH THE WISE! IN JESUS' NAME. AMEN.

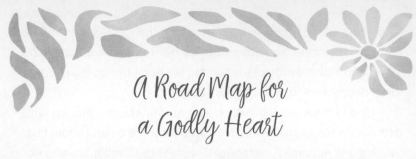

A Road Map for a Godly Heart

He has showed you, O man, what is good.
And what does the Lord require of you but to
do justly, and to love kindness and mercy, and to
humble yourself and walk humbly with your God?

MICAH 6:8 AMPC

. . . .

The sixth chapter of Micah is an imaginary conversation between Israel and God. In the first five verses, the Lord states His case against His disobedient children. Then in verses 6–7, Israel answers with a few questions. And today's verse, verse 8, is God's response. He didn't want the people's religiosity. Instead, His requirement was to do justly, love kindness and mercy, and to embrace humility. Simply put, they needed a heart change.

God wanted them to act justly. They needed to understand right and wrong.

God wanted them to love kindness and mercy. They were to show love to those around them and loyalty in their love toward the Lord.

God wanted them to embrace humility. Their hearts were to be humble before God as they surrendered to His will and ways.

Did you notice that these three responses together make up a godly heart? To act justly is *outward*. To love kindness and mercy is *inward*. And to embrace humility is *upward*. It's a three-part equation that produces a powerful faith that blesses others, benefits us, and brings delight to the heart of God.

If we're going to make a godly heart our goal, then we need to spend time in prayer. We have no greater tool at our disposal to help us as we pursue righteous living. Let's commit today to asking the Lord to make Micah 6:8 a road map we follow, helping us choose to live in ways that reflect our faith and point to our Father in heaven. When all is said and done, that's the reason we're here!

DEAR LORD, I WANT TO BLESS THOSE AROUND ME BY UNDERSTANDING RIGHT AND WRONG AND LIVING BY THOSE TRUTHS. I WANT A HEART THAT'S SET ABLAZE TO SHOW KINDNESS AND MERCY TO OTHERS AS WELL AS LOYAL LOVE TO YOU. AND I WANT TO BE HUMBLE, SURRENDERING MY WILL TO YOURS IN EVERY WAY. CHANGE MY HEART SO IT'S RIGHT WITH YOU AND CONTINUES TO BE EVERY DAY. IN JESUS' NAME. AMEN.

Asking for Discernment

So Jesus told them, "I'm not teaching you my own
thoughts, but those of God who sent me. If any of you
really determines to do God's will, then you will certainly
know whether my teaching is from God or is merely
my own. Anyone presenting his own ideas is looking
for praise for himself, but anyone seeking to honor
the one who sent him is a good and true person."

JOHN 7:16–18 TLB

As women of faith, we must ask God for discernment each day. As much as possible, we must be able to tell the difference between the truth and lies. It's vital that we understand whether the messages we're hearing are God-ordained or self-satisfying. The only way we can walk out the Father's will in our lives is to know the true God and His commands. Otherwise, we will fall prey to false teachings by false teachers. We may have the right attitude and a desire to follow the Lord with passion and purpose, but a lack of discernment will be our downfall.

Every day, ask God to bless you with a greater measure of divine discernment. Be bold as you ask for spiritual eyes to see what is right and what is wrong. Ask for spiritual ears to know when what you're hearing isn't right. And ask for God to nudge you when the one you're listening to has selfish or nefarious plans in place. As believers, we have the gift of the Holy Spirit who lives within us. He is tasked with empowering us, maturing us, and warning us. Are you paying attention to the Spirit's leading?

It may present as a gut feeling. When He's trying to get your attention, you may feel uncomfortable or unsettled. An internal alarm may keep going off inside, telling you to leave or stop. You may not be able to pinpoint why you feel as you do, but you're stirred up nonetheless with a sense of foreboding. Friend, don't ignore it. Instead, go right to God and ask for confirmation. Let Him direct you. Pray for your next steps to be uncovered and illuminated.

Prayer is an essential part of a believer's life because it's a direct connection to God. Never hesitate to bow your head when you need discernment. Listen to His still, small voice and pray for clarity.

DEAR LORD, GIVE ME THE ABILITY TO DISCERN BETWEEN
TRUTH AND LIES, RIGHT AND WRONG. I WANT TO
FOLLOW ONLY YOU. IN JESUS' NAME. AMEN.

God's Word Is
Our Flashlight

No, I haven't turned away from what you taught me;
your words are sweeter than honey. And since only
your rules can give me wisdom and understanding, no
wonder I hate every false teaching. Your words are a
flashlight to light the path ahead of me and keep me
from stumbling. I've said it once and I'll say it again and
again: I will obey these wonderful laws of yours.

PSALM 119:102–106 TLB

In this psalm, the writer is dedicated to declaring the value of God's Word. When he says it's a flashlight for the path ahead, he's making a profound statement of just how much the scriptures guide his steps. The same is true for us today. Just as it lit the path ahead for the psalmist so he wouldn't stumble and fall, the Bible lights up our path too. It illuminates each step forward so we can walk in this dark world with wisdom. It allows us to see clearly so we don't stray from God's plans. We're able to discern the direction we are to go.

But the truth is that sometimes we decide to listen to worldly advice instead. It tells us to look out for number one. It says we have the power within. It says all we need is love. But sinking our teeth into these kinds of untruths will lead us into a pit of confusion and pain.

Or maybe we let counselors or pastors or coaches tell us what to do. We listen to our friends and lean on their understanding. We subscribe to what celebrities or politicians think is best. Or we find comfort in our own wisdom, which is usually self-centered and follows the path of least resistance. Sound counsel may come from some of these sources at times, but for believers, God is the ultimate authority, and the instruction found in His Word is unmatched.

The Bible teaches us right from wrong. It challenges our blind acceptance of cultural values. The Lord uses scripture to reveal our sinful nature and call us higher. It helps us focus on what matters most and live in ways that glorify God and benefit us. And it perfectly equips us to pursue righteousness in our lives.

As you read God's Word, pray for fresh revelation. Pray for its transformational power to bring necessary changes. And pray for scripture to become a flashlight as you walk through your day.

DEAR LORD, THANK YOU FOR YOUR WORD
THAT LIGHTS MY WAY! IN JESUS' NAME. AMEN.

A True Believer

"Not everybody who says to me, 'Lord, Lord,' will get into the kingdom of heaven. Only those who do the will of my Father who is in heaven will enter. On the Judgment Day, many people will say to me, 'Lord, Lord, didn't we prophesy in your name and expel demons in your name and do lots of miracles in your name?' Then I'll tell them, 'I've never known you. Get away from me, you people who do wrong.' "

MATTHEW 7:21–23 CEB

. . . .

Two important questions often accompany these verses. The first is whether this passage is saying a believer can lose their salvation. The second is whether those who perform miracles always do so through the power of God. The Word clearly states that a true believer cannot lose their eternal life, but it also clearly indicates that many can perform miracles through demonic power.

This chapter is the end of the Sermon on the Mount, and in it, Jesus was contrasting the difference between genuine faith and false faith. From sheep and wolves to good fruit and bad fruit, He was unpacking the two groups of people who would come before Him on judgment day. The truth is that many who would identify as Christians today will be unable to enter the kingdom because their faith is not real. These people never honestly embraced a saving faith in Jesus, and their salvation was never solidified in Him.

The major takeaway from today's scripture is the importance of true faith in Jesus. We need to read His words and hear His words and put them into practice in our everyday life. We need to hide them in our hearts and meditate on them daily. We need to choose obedience over self-indulgence, even when it takes every bit of strength. Our desire should be to follow God's will and ways with passion and purpose. We should exercise the gift of prayer to help empower us to live righteous lives, being honest about our challenges and struggles to do what is right. And as true believers, we should trust in the name of the Lord, depend on His help, commit our hearts to loving Him, and know that our salvation and eternal life are secure through His blood alone. Our faith must be genuine.

DEAR LORD, I WANT MY FAITH TO BE TRUE AND AUTHENTIC. ON JUDGMENT DAY AND EVERY DAY AFTER, I WANT TO CELEBRATE WITH YOU IN HEAVEN BECAUSE I WHOLEHEARTEDLY FOLLOWED YOU WITH MY LIFE. IN JESUS' NAME. AMEN.

The Pride of Life

For all that is in the world—the lust of the flesh [craving
for sensual gratification] and the lust of the eyes [greedy
longings of the mind] and the pride of life [assurance in
one's own resources or in the stability of earthly things]—
these do not come from the Father but are from the world
[itself]. And the world passes away and disappears, and
with it the forbidden cravings (the passionate desires, the
lust) of it; but he who does the will of God and carries
out His purposes in his life abides (remains) forever.

1 JOHN 2:16–17 AMPC

The pride of life is anything that leads to haughtiness, pretention, self-centeredness, self-importance, or vanity. The Word is clear that the pride of life, along with lustful cravings of our flesh or our mind, is not from God. All these things are in direct opposition to the Lord. So anything that promotes us as more than we are or gives us a god-like persona is at the core of the pride of life, and it's ugly.

While every believer will be tempted by the three things mentioned in today's verses, the pride of life may be the most evil. Think about it. This is the very sin that got Satan kicked out of heaven: he wanted to *be* God rather than *serve* God. And this lust elevated him to more than he was and fed into a misguided personal desire. Even Eve in the garden of Eden was tempted by the pride of life and eventually took a bite of the forbidden fruit in hopes of being like God in wisdom, knowing good from evil.

We can see the pride of life in operation today through people whose pride stands in the way of their ability to faithfully serve the Lord in meaningful ways. Their perceived superiority separates them from community and eventually renders them ineffective for the kingdom. And make no mistake, the pride of life is an earthly product, not an eternal one.

In time, all of these forbidden cravings will pass away along with the world. But until then, as gutsy girls of God, we're to resist being tempted in these ways. Instead, our focus should be to do the Lord's will and carry out His purposes in our words and actions. And we'll find the strength and wisdom to do so by spending time in the Word and in prayer.

So let's commit to asking God for His help every day so we can live and walk with humility, being content with who the Lord made us to be.

DEAR LORD, REMOVE ANY ARROGANT WAYS IN ME
SO I DON'T FALL PREY TO THE PRIDE OF LIFE AND
SIN AGAINST YOU. IN JESUS' NAME. AMEN.

Saved by Faith Alone

Because of his kindness, you have been saved through trusting Christ. And even trusting is not of yourselves; it too is a gift from God. Salvation is not a reward for the good we have done, so none of us can take any credit for it. It is God himself who has made us what we are and given us new lives from Christ Jesus; and long ages ago he planned that we should spend these lives in helping others.

<small>EPHESIANS 2:8–10 TLB</small>

Today's verse points out God's kindness and grace when it comes to our salvation. We have been saved because of our faith, not by our works. Unfortunately, countless people have that backward. If asked, they would cite their good deeds as a one-way ticket to heaven. They'd brag about how much money they've donated to charities or how many hours they've spent volunteering their precious time. Maybe they would even recite times when they were selfless to help others who were struggling. But God doesn't extend salvation only to the good-hearted and slam heaven's pearly gates on the ones who behave badly. Instead, scripture is clear that we are saved by accepting Jesus as our Savior. It's faith that saves. Not works. And Paul wrote the entire book of Ephesians to make that truth known.

We can be confident, therefore, that salvation is a gift from the Lord and not from our own hand. It's not a result of our good works or selfless efforts or thoughtful actions. God Himself has given us new life through His Son, Jesus. That means we can't take any credit or boast about all we've done to earn salvation. And while these other things—good works, efforts, and acts—may be a result of our faith, they are not what save us from an eternity in hell. God alone brings about our salvation.

And understand that God saved us for a reason, which is to help others. As believers, we have a beautiful calling that He planned for long ago. Friend, you are here for a reason! So let's follow the Lord's path for our lives so we can bring Him glory as we work to share His kingdom with the world.

If you're not certain of your salvation, pray this prayer. . .

DEAR LORD, I KNOW I'M A SINNER AND DESERVE THE CONSEQUENCES OF MY SIN. HOWEVER, I'M CHOOSING TODAY TO TRUST IN JESUS CHRIST AS MY SAVIOR. I BELIEVE HIS DEATH AND RESURRECTION PROVIDED FOR MY FORGIVENESS AND BOUGHT MY SALVATION. THANK YOU FOR SAVING ME AND FORGIVING ME! IN JESUS' NAME. AMEN.

His Plan of Salvation

So never forget how you used to be. Those of you born as
outsiders to Israel were outcasts, branded "the uncircumcised"
by those who bore the sign of the covenant in their flesh,
a sign made with human hands. You had absolutely no
connection to the Anointed; you were strangers, separated
from God's people. You were aliens to the covenant they
had with God; you were hopelessly stranded without God in
a fractured world. But now, because of Jesus the Anointed
and His sacrifice, all of that has changed. God gathered
you who were so far away and brought you near to Him
by the royal blood of the Anointed, our Liberating King.

EPHESIANS 2:11–13 VOICE

. . . .

As Gentiles, we were not part of God's plan of salvation for the nation of Israel. Paul is telling us to remember that before Jesus, we were separated from God. We were strangers without any connection to Him. We were aliens to the covenant Israel had with God. We were stranded in a dark world, alone. There was no hope for us. And then Jesus came to earth. It's through His blood shed on the cross that we were brought to God the Father. In His goodness, God included Gentiles in His plan of salvation.

This is why we can rejoice every day! This is why we can have confidence as we navigate this crazy world. If you have accepted

Jesus as your Savior, then you have become inseparable from God's love and compassion. So grab hold of this truth with fervor and be intentional about growing deep roots of faith. Express your thanks to the Father for bringing you closer to Him through Jesus.

One way you can do this is by reading God's Word, because it is how He reveals Himself. It's where you learn about this amazing Father who cares deeply about you. And it will guide you in living a life of righteousness—one that brings honor and glory to His name.

The other way is to be committed to a robust prayer life. This is your direct line to God. You don't need to pray through a saint or recite a memorized prayer. Friend, you can just open your mouth and your heart and talk to Him. You can pray bold prayers of need or thank God for all He has done to help you. You can pray anywhere and at any time. You can celebrate wins or lament your heartache in His presence. Just be sure to invite God into your life in both the big and the small.

DEAR LORD, THANK YOU FOR INCLUDING ME IN
YOUR PLAN OF SALVATION. IN JESUS' NAME. AMEN.

Choosing What to Think About

Summing it all up, friends, I'd say you'll do best by filling your minds and meditating on things true, noble, reputable, authentic, compelling, gracious—the best, not the worst; the beautiful, not the ugly; things to praise, not things to curse. Put into practice what you learned from me, what you heard and saw and realized. Do that, and God, who makes everything work together, will work you into his most excellent harmonies.

PHILIPPIANS 4:8–9 MSG

The truth is that we can choose what we think about. Today's verses confirm that we have the power to control our thoughts. We get to decide which ones land and which ones don't. And if we're not careful and intentional to keep our mind focused on the best and not the worst, we'll be affected in profound ways.

Every day, we are hit with a million messages. From images to viewpoints to ideals, we are constantly being battered by the world's opinions, which are usually in direct conflict with what God wants for His believers. The world's sound bites aren't conducive to godly living because they preach all the wrong things. They urge us to trust ourselves, to do what's in our own best interests, and to satiate every fleshly desire. And so often, we fall right in line and agree. We match our values with the world's.

But Paul is directing us to live differently. With God's help, we are to continually reject any thought that pulls us away from Him and instead pursue the things that bring us closer to Him. Rather than get bogged down in the world's noise, why don't we focus on what is true and noble? Let's concentrate on what is reputable and authentic. Let's meditate on what's compelling. . .what is gracious. Since we know we *can* control our thoughts, let's think about the beautiful things and not the ugly. Let's put our effort into finding things to praise rather than griping about those things we'd like to curse. It's making an intentional shift in what gets our attention, and it applies to every area of our lives. We can even let it be a filter to help us determine what we watch, what we read, and what we listen to.

As you pray for discernment, the Holy Spirit will guide you to make the best decisions. He will point you to what glorifies God. And as you regularly seek His input, you'll become wise about what to allow your eyes and ears to absorb.

DEAR LORD, GUIDE ME AS I TRY TO KEEP
MY FOCUS ON WHAT BLESSES ME AND
HONORS YOU. IN JESUS' NAME. AMEN.

God's Joyful Singing

The Eternal your God is standing right here among you,
and He is the champion who will rescue you. He will
joyfully celebrate over you; He will rest in His love for you;
He will joyfully sing because of you like a new husband.

Zephaniah 3:17 voice

For context, this verse points to a future time when God's judgment on Israel is over. Israel's enemies are no more, giving the nation a time of blessing and security. It will have been a long road laced with heartache, but a time will come when tears are wiped away and joy abounds. Zephaniah is talking about the millennial kingdom when Jesus will come down and reign with His people.

This verse paints a beautiful picture that is chock-full of emotion and encouragement no matter who reads it. When it mentions that God will sing because of you, it's describing His joy at being reconciled with His chosen people. We can find great comfort in this image. We can cling to the Lord in hopes of better days to come. His love for us is endlessly deep and wide, and His presence is with us always. And in the end, He will make all things right again. That is a promise we can hold on to.

Let this verse direct your prayers and calm your anxious heart right now. Pray it back to the Lord and personalize it, replacing the word *you* with the word *me*. Spend time today asking God to be your champion. Ask Him to rescue you from whatever is holding you too tightly. Ask for evidence of His presence, like feeling a sense of peace sweep over you or a reassurance that you're not alone. Ask to receive a profound sense of the Lord's joy over you, regardless of your imperfections and struggles. Ask Him to guide you into restful times where you know, without a doubt, that His great love for you is real and unshakable. And, friend, boldly ask God to make you aware that He delights in who He made you to be.

DEAR LORD, THANK YOU FOR SCRIPTURES LIKE THIS
THAT COMFORT MY HEART IN CHALLENGING TIMES.
HEAR MY PLEA TO FEEL YOUR PRESENCE TODAY.
HOLD ME TIGHT WITH A FATHERLY GRIP AND
NEVER LET ME GO. IN JESUS' NAME. AMEN.

Soaring on Wings as Eagles

*God strengthens the weary and gives vitality to those
worn down by age and care. Young people will get tired;
strapping young men will stumble and fall. But those who
trust in the Eternal One will regain their strength. They will
soar on wings as eagles. They will run—never winded,
never weary. They will walk—never tired, never faint.*

Isaiah 40:29–31 VOICE

. . . .

Ancient Hebrew culture considered eagles to be mighty warriors because they are very protective of their young. They will even relocate their babies if there is a threat in the area. Today, eagles are known for their strength. They are courageous birds who often fly above the clouds to avoid storms and dangerous weather. When people use the phrase "on wings as eagles," it describes those who exhibit the same characteristics as these majestic creatures.

Isaiah uses the image of soaring eagles to describe those who choose to remain faithful to God and wait on Him patiently. And just as he was hoping this for Israel, we can embrace this principle for us today. If we walk it out in our own lives, the Lord will ensure we regain our strength and find the courage to overcome whatever stands in our way.

When we approach God in faith and humility, He will meet us in our greatest needs. If we need strength to stand up for our convictions, He'll give it. If we need wisdom to know the next right step, He'll provide it. If we need discernment to choose rightly, He'll supply it. If we need boldness to make tough decisions, He'll strengthen our confidence as needed. If we're lacking perseverance to weather the storms, we'll find it through the Lord. If we need resolve to withstand the desire to give up or give in, God will give us just that. And in our weariness and weakness, He'll come alongside us and empower us to trust once again. As we wait for God to move in our situations and circumstances, He will cause us to soar on wings as eagles.

Pray as much and as often as necessary for you to stand in faith. The Word tells us to pray without ceasing! So gather yourself together and unpack everything burdening your heart. Be honest. Be real. And keep waiting and asking until you see His hand move mightily in your life.

DEAR LORD, STRENGTHEN ME TODAY
AS I TRUST YOU WITH ALL MY HEART.
IN JESUS' NAME. AMEN.

No More Pain or Suffering

And I heard a great voice, coming from the throne.
See, the home of God is with His people. He will
live among them; they will be His people, and God
Himself will be with them. The prophecies are fulfilled:
He will wipe away every tear from their eyes. Death
will be no more; mourning no more, crying no more,
pain no more, for the first things have gone away.

REVELATION 21:3–4 VOICE

These verses hold a promise of restoration and hope for the future when this dark world will pass away and a new Jerusalem will come down out of heaven. No more sadness. No more death. No more grief or suffering. No more pain or loss. No longer will there be any reason for tears to run down our cheeks. Even more, the Lord will live with us. We will be in His presence, experiencing His glory for the rest of eternity.

This is not wishful thinking, friend. We don't need to cross our fingers and hope it turns out this way. This is a solid promise of God, and He keeps every one of them. So as we consider the state of our life, our nation, and the world, let's embrace this promise and allow it to bring much-needed comfort to our weary hearts. God will work everything for good in the end. Here is a hope we can confidently hold on to, especially when life feels overwhelming.

Friend, where are you ready for God to wipe away your tears? Have you been through a tough season of grief, losing someone very close to you? Are you watching your child make life decisions that will only bring pain and suffering? Did your life get turned upside down without warning because of a revealed betrayal? Are you walking out the natural consequences of your actions and it's almost unbearable? Has your marriage failed or has a cherished friendship fizzled out? Is the physical pain from a chronic condition too much to manage?

Ask God to sustain you in this hard season while He fills your heart with hope for what is coming! This struggle will not be forever but only for a season. Just a bit longer. And then God will wipe away every tear and usher in everything new.

DEAR LORD, GIVE ME THE COURAGE TO STAND STRONG
AS I ENDURE THIS HARDSHIP. HELP ME KEEP MY EYES
FOCUSED ON YOUR PROMISES. IN JESUS' NAME. AMEN.

Ready to Tell Them Why

Why would anyone harm you if you eagerly do good?
Even if you should suffer for doing what is right, you will
receive a blessing. Don't let them frighten you. Don't be
intimidated, but exalt Him as Lord in your heart. Always
be ready to offer a defense, humbly and respectfully, when
someone asks why you live in hope. Keep your conscience
clear so that those who ridicule your good conduct in the
Anointed and say bad things about you will be put to shame.

1 PETER 3:13–16 VOICE

The reality is that as believers, we will face challenges for trying to do the right thing. Life won't be easy. Having faith doesn't exempt us from pain or heartache. We will experience grief. Sadness will come. We will face disappointment, discouragement, and despair. Even when we pursue righteous living, husbands will leave, children will make bad choices, finances will be strained, health will falter. But we can live in hope. Even more, our suffering done right should point others to God. We should always be ready to share about the Lord and how His death brings us perspective in demanding times.

Each time you demonstrate hope in Him while navigating difficult circumstances, others will notice. Remember, our lives preach one way or the other. You don't have to be happy about each hardship, but your actions can boldly reveal unwavering trust that God will show up. You can use words that show the depth of your trust, your certainty that the Lord is going to make right what others have made wrong. You can get out of bed each morning with the expectation that you will see His goodness, and you can share those goodness sightings in your interactions with others. And when someone asks how you can have such hope in your affliction, you can be ready—with humility and respect—to tell them why.

Prepare your heart now to share your faith in those moments by spending time in prayer. God will equip you with the perfect words when you need them, especially as you've been seeking His help. And because it's the Lord's will for us to share the good news with those around us, asking for His help with this aligns with His desire for our lives. We can have confidence in His presence with us as we continue to trust Him for open doors to speak.

DEAR LORD, MAKE ME READY TO GIVE AN
ANSWER FOR HOW I CAN HAVE HOPE IN THE
HARD TIMES. IN JESUS' NAME. AMEN.

No Reason to Despair

So we have no reason to despair. Despite the fact that our
outer humanity is falling apart and decaying, our inner
humanity is breathing in new life every day. You see,
the short-lived pains of this life are creating for us an eternal
glory that does not compare to anything we know here. So we
do not set our sights on the things we can see with our eyes.
All of that is fleeting; it will eventually fade away. Instead,
we focus on the things we cannot see, which live on and on.

2 CORINTHIANS 4:16–18 VOICE

Paul tells us in today's passage of scripture that even though life is difficult, and we will experience hardship and suffering throughout it, there is no reason to despair. We have hope that outshines any of the temporary hurts and pains we'll have to endure. It's our faith in God that anchors us in the storms and gives us confidence to hold on with expectation. Whether we're on a mountaintop or in a valley, He is with us. And because of that beautiful truth, we don't have to lose heart in the short-lived pains of this life because they're creating for us an unmatched eternal glory.

Paul wrote these words from experience. Did you know he was imprisoned and beaten for preaching the good news? In his travels, Paul faced hunger and thirst as he lacked basic needs; plus he underwent countless other struggles the Bible doesn't tell us about. But this man chose to remain faithful and positive. He didn't focus on his circumstances. He didn't obsess over all he was lacking. Instead, he kept his eyes on God and his faith in action. He wasn't going to let his struggles lead him into despair.

Why not ask God to empower you as He did Paul? This great man continued to preach regardless of his problems. You can have the same resolve in your life too. Ask for a hearty hope that believes without fear. Pray with expectation for the Lord to show up and strengthen you in times of need. Ask for a heavenly perspective so you're able to see the big picture instead of getting lost in the small details. And remember this life is but a breath, followed by an eternity without any decay or discouragement.

DEAR LORD, KEEP MY EYES TRAINED ON YOUR GOODNESS
SO I DON'T GET BROUGHT DOWN BY SHORT-LIVED PAINS
THAT FEEL INSURMOUNTABLE. IN JESUS' NAME. AMEN.

Even Though You're Broken

But this beautiful treasure is contained in us—cracked pots made of earth and clay—so that the transcendent character of this power will be clearly seen as coming from God and not from us. We are cracked and chipped from our afflictions on all sides, but we are not crushed by them. We are bewildered at times, but we do not give in to despair. We are persecuted, but we have not been abandoned. We have been knocked down, but we are not destroyed. We always carry around in our bodies the reality of the brutal death and suffering of Jesus. As a result, His resurrection life rises and reveals its wondrous power in our bodies as well.

2 Corinthians 4:7–10 voice

In this passage, Paul is using a metaphor to say that God stores the beautiful treasure (the gospel) in us, even though we're broken and fragile. It is by design so others can see His power through us. His light shines in our hearts, giving us power to do amazing things. We are ordinary, but God is extraordinary.

And as He empowers us as believers, we can be cracked and chipped by hurtful words and actions but not crushed. We can be bewildered by difficult seasons of life, but we don't give in to despair. We may be persecuted relentlessly, but we are not alone. Life's circumstances may have punched us in the gut and knocked us to the ground, but we'll get right back up. This world may throw everything at us, but we will always persevere. We'll keep standing rather than curling up into a ball. We won't give up or walk away. You see, it's through our suffering that we continue to share the reality of the brutal death and suffering of Jesus so that His resurrection life also is revealed in our bodies.

We're never left without hope. Even the difficulties and struggles we face have eternal purpose. And the glorious goal for us is that through our weakness, God's goodness will be on display. Friend, every heartbreak you'll experience is a chance for His power to be revealed. Don't cover up your challenges, because others will be encouraged as they watch God working in you and through you.

Ask the Lord for this powerful truth to settle in your heart. Pray for a boldness to come upon you—one that gives you courage to let others see God's goodness through your brokenness. You don't have to be all put together because He works best in your weakness. Let those around you see you walk out your testimony by faith.

DEAR LORD, HELP ME LIVE WITH HONESTY
AND AUTHENTICITY SO YOU SHINE THE
BRIGHTEST. IN JESUS' NAME. AMEN.

God's Grace Is Enough

I begged the Lord three times to liberate me from its anguish; and finally He said to me, "My grace is enough to cover and sustain you. My power is made perfect in weakness." So ask me about my thorn, inquire about my weaknesses, and I will gladly go on and on—I would rather stake my claim in these and have the power of the Anointed One at home within me. I am at peace and even take pleasure in any weaknesses, insults, hardships, persecutions, and afflictions for the sake of the Anointed because when I am at my weakest, He makes me strong.

2 CORINTHIANS 12:8–10 VOICE

Paul suffered from something he only described as a thorn. We don't know exactly what it was, but we know he asked God to remove it three times, and the Lord did not. For him to have even included it in his writings means it was noteworthy. Instead of taking away the anguish, God reminded Paul that His grace was enough to cover and sustain him. Paul's ability to preach and spread the gospel wasn't because of his awesomeness. Instead, his faithfulness and stamina to share the good news were because of God's grace. It was sufficient. It was enough.

Friend, in your weakness, God's strength shines brighter. When you cannot, He can. When there's no fight left in you, the

Lord will work through you in supernatural ways. And just as Paul gladly went on and on about it, you too can boast of God's power working in you when you're weak. Regardless of what challenges lie ahead, when you ask, He will give you the strength to withstand and overcome them all.

Where do you need the Lord's grace to cover and sustain you today? Where do you need His power to replace your weakness? What thorns do you need to trust God with? Spend time in prayer unpacking these with Him. Open your heart and share those vulnerable places with honesty. Talk to Him with an expectant heart, believing He will give you the confidence and courage to navigate every weakness, insult, hardship, persecution, and affliction because you just cannot on your own. His grace is all you need.

DEAR LORD, YOU KNOW ALL THE THINGS BOGGING
ME DOWN TODAY. YOU KNOW WHERE I'M FEELING
WEAK. BECAUSE YOU HAVE ALLOWED THESE IN MY LIFE,
I TRUST THAT YOUR GRACE IS ENOUGH TO COVER AND
SUSTAIN ME. THANK YOU! IN JESUS' NAME. AMEN.

yet

Even though the fig trees are all destroyed, and there is
neither blossom left nor fruit; though the olive crops all
fail, and the fields lie barren; even if the flocks die in the
fields and the cattle barns are empty, yet I will rejoice
in the Lord; I will be happy in the God of my salvation.
The Lord God is my strength; he will give me the speed
of a deer and bring me safely over the mountains.

HABAKKUK 3:17–19 TLB

When our world begins to crumble and everything seems hopeless, believers can still rejoice in the Lord. We can still find happiness because we know it's not dependent on our circumstances—it just can't be. We may not be able to choose what we go through, but we can choose how we go through it. So no matter what life brings our way—be it bad times or really bad times—our faith will keep us steady and strong.

Did you notice the three things Habakkuk did to help him better trust God? First, He chose to rejoice in the Lord even though things around him were dire in every way. Second, he rejoiced in God for his salvation through Jesus. And third, he understood it was the Lord God who was his strength. No doubt Habakkuk was walking through tough and trying times, *yet* he chose to trust the Lord completely.

You may have suffered a painful breakup or lost someone very close to your heart, *yet* you can experience joy knowing you are held by the Lord. Maybe you received an unexpected diagnosis that leaves little hope for recovery or are unable to pay the bills stacking up, *yet* you can cling to God for comfort. Have you watched your family fall apart, leaving you brokenhearted? You can feel the pain *yet* find rest through prayer and time in God's Word. Maybe you've had more sad news this week than in the last ten years combined. Friend, you can navigate this pain *yet* have a sense of peace at the same time.

Spend time in prayer today, asking the Lord for a sense of His presence in your struggles. You may not know what lies ahead, *yet* go ahead and pray with thanksgiving for who He is and what He promises to do. And pray with a hopeful heart as you trust God to empower you to stand strong in faith and persevere.

DEAR LORD, HELP ME TO REJOICE IN
YOU ALWAYS. IN JESUS' NAME. AMEN.

How Do We Love God?

The most important commandment is this: "Hear, O Israel, the Eternal One is our God, and the Eternal One is the only God. You should love the Eternal, your God, with all your heart, with all your soul, with all your mind, and with all your strength." The second great commandment is this: "Love others in the same way you love yourself." There are no commandments more important than these.

MARK 12:29–31 VOICE

Loving is hard to do because we're unable to love perfectly like God does. Even so, His most important command is to love Him with all our "heart, soul, mind, and strength." So how do we do this? How do we love Him in these ways?

We choose to put Him first in our lives. We don't let anything or anyone else take that number one place in our day. We prioritize God above all else because nothing here holds a candle to His goodness. And we also love others well because He clearly asks it of us.

We desire a relationship with the Lord. Growing closer to Him, learning more about who He is, shows our love. We spend time in God's Word, which is where He reveals Himself. And we invite the Lord into our days and share our hearts with Him, deepening the bond between us.

We follow His will and ways. When we decide to do what God is asking, our obedience shows Him we care. Our hearts want what His heart wants. And rather than be selfish and do whatever feels good or right at the time, we intentionally walk in His ways with humility.

Let's decide to be women committed to loving God with all our "heart, soul, mind, and strength." No, we won't do it perfectly, but perfection isn't what He's looking for. Instead, God is asking us to love Him and others with passion and purpose.

Today, talk to the Lord about your thoughts surrounding love. Confess your shortcomings and be honest about where you're struggling to love Him or others well. And ask for the ability to love God deeply in ways that bless Him and bring glory to His name.

DEAR LORD, YOU DESERVE MY LOVE AND DEVOTION
IN EVERY WAY. HELP ME PRIORITIZE OUR RELATIONSHIP
DAILY. GIVE ME THE WISDOM AND STRENGTH TO PUT
YOU FIRST ABOVE ALL ELSE. IN JESUS' NAME. AMEN.

Running with Endurance

So since we stand surrounded by all those who have gone
before, an enormous cloud of witnesses, let us drop every
extra weight, every sin that clings to us and slackens our pace,
and let us run with endurance the long race set before us.

HEBREWS 12:1 VOICE

If we love the Lord and follow Him, the writer of Hebrews is telling us two very important things. First, we are to drop every extra weight and sin that clings to us and slows us down. Whatever tangles us up in knots and keeps us from freedom should be released from our grip. And second, we're to run with endurance until the end. We are to persevere patiently through the trials of life so we don't tire out too early and give up.

Friend, God is faithful, and when we press into Him for hope, we will find it. Understand that He uses every difficulty and hardship to strengthen us. Nothing we go through is wasted! Even more, this is how the Lord matures our faith into something powerful. This kind of faith helps us navigate the challenges that come with marriage, friendship, and parenting. It provides an eternal perspective on our worldly woes. And as we endure with grace, it seasons our hearts with hard-won wisdom that will help others stay the course.

But we can also find encouragement from those who have gone

before us—the enormous cloud of witnesses. They understand the essence of the challenges we face, and they are cheering us on to the finish line. They are rooting for our victory. And while we cannot see them with our human eyes, scripture allows us to see them with our spiritual eyes. Together, they are shouting and applauding for us to stand strong. They're offering inspiration and encouragement to push forward through the suffering.

As you pray in those messy moments, lay every burden at the Lord's feet. Confess and repent of the sin that entangles your heart. And ask God, with expectation, for the staying power to endure the long race in which you find yourself. With gratitude, thank Him for those who have gone before you and are cheering you on today. And trust that the will of God will come to pass in the right ways and at the right times. Your job is to endure, trusting that He has equipped you to do so.

DEAR LORD, I DON'T WANT TO GIVE UP WHEN THE TROUBLES START. I DON'T WANT TO THROW IN THE TOWEL BECAUSE LIFE GETS HARD. HELP ME DROP EVERY EXTRA WEIGHT AND SIN AS I FIND ENDURANCE THROUGH YOU TO STAY STRONG. IN JESUS' NAME. AMEN.

Focused on Jesus

Now stay focused on Jesus, who designed and perfected
our faith. He endured the cross and ignored the shame
of that death because He focused on the joy that was
set before Him; and now He is seated beside God on
the throne, a place of honor. Consider the life of the One
who endured such personal attacks and hostility from
sinners so that you will not grow weary or lose heart.

HEBREWS 12:2–3 VOICE

Scripture says we are to stay focused on Jesus because He pioneered the way forward. He's the one who made a way for us to experience God's presence in our lives every day. And Christ also perfected—brought to completion—our faith by enduring the cross for our benefit. Jesus willingly gave up His life, choosing to focus on the joy that was to come and the people who would be saved. He had a divine perspective on His earthly task. And Jesus knew He would be resurrected and seated in the heavens with the Father once again.

He also ignored the shame of His death. Crucifixion was a very painful way to die, and public humiliation came with it. Remember how He was mocked as He hung on the cross? Onlookers said He should save Himself to prove He was the Messiah. But Jesus knew the only way to save humanity was by not saving Himself.

As we face struggles in our lives, let's remember with thanksgiving what Jesus did for us. Let's meditate on how He patiently endured His suffering, and we'll gain a much-needed divine perspective on our circumstances too. Let's think about how Jesus' joy became a tool to keep Him focused. Let's remain diligent, doing what is necessary for our faith to grow and mature. And let's persist in a posture of prayer.

We will battle hard things in this life. We will face loss and grief. Bouts of fear and anxiety will shake us to the core. We'll undergo seasons of doubt. Our hearts will break, and our faith will be challenged. But we can stay focused on Jesus and find peace and comfort every time. We can cling to Him so that we don't grow weary or lose heart.

DEAR LORD, HELP ME KEEP MY EYES ON YOU WHEN LIFE
GETS TOUGH SO I DON'T GIVE IN TO DISCOURAGEMENT.
HELP ME REMEMBER WHAT YOU ENDURED AND BE
ENCOURAGED THAT I TOO CAN WITHSTAND ADVERSITY
IN MY OWN CIRCUMSTANCES. IN JESUS' NAME. AMEN.

God's Correction

*When punishment is happening, it never seems pleasant,
only painful. Later, though, it yields the peaceful fruit
called righteousness to everyone who has been trained by
it. So lift up your hands that are dangling and brace your
weakened knees. Make straight paths for your feet so that
what is lame in you won't be put out of joint, but will heal.*

Hebrews 12:11–13 Voice

Nobody likes to be punished for doing wrong things, but it's important that we develop the right attitude toward God's discipline. The truth is that He only corrects those He loves. As believers, we should expect to be corrected by the Lord. We should expect to be trained by Him through our suffering and struggles. And we should know it is only for our greater good. How else are we to mature in our faith and understanding? How else are we to bear the fruit of righteousness?

Ask God to give you patient endurance to navigate difficulties and a willingness to learn from your life experiences. Ask Him to develop in you an unwavering trust that God always has your best in mind. Ask Him to settle in your spirit the truth that His ways are best and that His discipline is necessary. Correction may not be joyful or feel good, but we can know it will produce in us a rich harvest. If we let it, God's chastisement will grow our faith in deep and wonderful and important ways.

So when those hard moments come, let's choose to embrace them. When we are challenged in parenting or struggling in marriage, let's be quick to humble ourselves in His presence. When our hope is dashed again or the door of opportunity closes hard, let's ask God for clarity so we can regroup with the right expectations. When we stumble in our pursuit of righteous living, let's listen for the Lord's direction back to the path that leads to Him.

If we will choose to have a spirit that is teachable and a heart that is willing to surrender, we'll undergo a powerful transformation that molds us to be more like Jesus. And the more we become like Him, the more we can be a blessing to those around us and bring glory to His holy name.

DEAR LORD, HELP ME EMBRACE YOUR CORRECTION,
KNOWING IT IS OUT OF YOUR LOVE AND FOR
MY GOOD. IN JESUS' NAME. AMEN.

Building Yourself Up

*But you, dear friends, carefully build yourselves up in
this most holy faith by praying in the Holy Spirit, staying
right at the center of God's love, keeping your arms open
and outstretched, ready for the mercy of our Master,
Jesus Christ. This is the unending life, the real life!*

JUDE 1:20–21 MSG

Jude was the brother of Jesus and James. While he grew up in the
same home, he did not believe Jesus was the Messiah until after
His resurrection. In his book, the theme is that the church must
contend for its faith and that people must persevere to the end by
following the truth and resisting false teachers. These are some
power-packed truths that we as believers must lean into today.

Today's verses give us the antidote to false teaching. They
encourage us to live proactively as believers, thereby minimizing
any negative influence it may have on us. As counterfeit messages
continue to creep in quietly and subtly, standing steadfast in the
truth is vital. Unless we know God's Word, these false teachings
may be hard to spot. Their departure from the whole counsel
of God is understated; often they're disguised as feel-good and
self-centered messages. Friend, we must be vigilant so we don't
fall prey to a clever yet devastating deviation from God's unwavering truth.

We can build ourselves up in faith by praying at all times and without selfish desires. We can commit to reading God's Word regularly, being mindful to take its sound doctrine and counsel to heart. We can walk in spirit and truth, being intentional to stay on paths of righteousness each day. We can choose to depend on the Lord for all things rather than look to our own understanding. And we can be obedient to His leading and willing to be disciplined with a surrendered spirit.

In these last days, we must stay focused on keeping our faith so the enemy can't knock us off course. Clothe yourself in God's armor. Pray for discernment to know truth from lies. Pray for wisdom to spot false teaching. Confess your sins and repent. And keep your arms open and outstretched toward the loving Father who will protect those who seek Him.

DEAR LORD, I WANT TO KNOW YOU MORE AND MORE
SO I CAN STAY AT THE CENTER OF YOUR LOVE. HELP ME
HOLD ON TO WHAT IS TRUE. IN JESUS' NAME. AMEN.

Changing Your Where

Early in the morning, Jesus got up, left the
house while it was still dark outside,
and went to a deserted place to pray.

MARK 1:35 VOICE

Jesus' life gives us a beautiful understanding of what prayer looks like. Not only does He teach us how to pray and what to pray, but also He gives us examples of where to pray. The Bible doesn't leave us to figure out the Christian life on our own. It's our playbook, if you will. A complete guide to help set our hearts and minds in the right direction.

Notice the three descriptions of Jesus' prayer practice in today's verse. He got up early. He left the house. And He went to a deserted place. Do you find it curious that Jesus didn't just stay put? Why didn't He stay warm in bed and pray from there? Why didn't He brew some of His favorite coffee and sit at the kitchen table? Why not sit on the porch or rooftop and talk to the Father from there? We may understand the early morning choice because we've experienced what a busy and loud house can be like, but why did Jesus need to go to a deserted place? We may never know the answers this side of heaven, but we can trust they had great purpose.

The takeaway is that there may be times when we need to

change up *where* we pray. There are times we offer up liquid prayers, where tears fall down our face and we want to be alone. We may need to lament and want that to be private. We may want to pray aloud and have the freedom to say what we need to say without others hearing. Our prayers may be guttural or spoken out of frustration, and their content may be something you only want to share with God. Or maybe you want to shake things up so you can get out of a prayer rut. Regardless, Jesus shows us that changing our *where* is okay and serves a purpose.

Think of some places where you might want to spend time with the Lord. Are there certain times of day or night that appeal to you? Is there a mountain stream or a valley of flowers or a park down the street that calls to you? Friend, let the Spirit lead your heart to new places and processes of connecting with the Father. Be open to a fresh way of praying. God just wants to be in a relationship with you, and He is always ready and willing to listen.

- -

DEAR LORD, HELP ME FIND THE FREEDOM TO MEET
YOU IN FRESH NEW PLACES. IN JESUS' NAME. AMEN.

New Every Morning

*How enduring is God's loyal love; the Eternal has
inexhaustible compassion. Here they are, every
morning, new! Your faithfulness, God, is as broad as
the day. Have courage, for the Eternal is all that I will
need. My soul boasts, "Hope in God; just wait."*

LAMENTATIONS 3:22–24 VOICE

Jeremiah authored the book of Lamentations as the nation was grieving the loss of Jerusalem to Babylon in 586 BC. In its pages, you will read heartfelt laments for the city. You'll see raw expressions of their mourning and pain. But in the verses above, you will see a shift.

Jeremiah's tone changes from gloom and despair to one full of hope and confidence in God. Even in demanding times, he knew God was good. He believed in the Lord's faithfulness toward His children. Even in His discipline, the Lord was steadfastly devoted to His chosen people. Jeremiah knew this because he knew God's loyal love and inexhaustible compassion are new every morning. God is unchanging, and His heart toward us is unwavering. It was true for the Israelites, and it is true for Gentile believers too.

No matter what we may be facing, the Lord is faithful. We may have gone to bed broken and overwhelmed, but every morning we can wake up to a new batch of freshly made love and compassion.

What a blessing to know these will never run out. They will never be backordered or out of stock. And even more, we have access to them every day. We sin and make mistakes daily, but God's mercy is waiting.

Have you thanked Him for His fresh mercy? Have you told the Lord how much you appreciate that His love and compassion are new every time the sun comes up? Today, take time to meditate on this powerful truth and then tell Him why it blesses you. Thank Him that His goodness is something you can expect with certainty each morning, and share how it encourages your heart today. And express how, in the middle of your difficulties, this gift helps shift your outlook from gloom and despair to hope and confidence, just as it did for Jeremiah.

DEAR LORD, I LOVE HOW YOU ALWAYS KNOW EXACTLY
WHAT I NEED AND WHEN I NEED IT. THANK YOU FOR
NEVER RUNNING SHORT ON YOUR LOYAL LOVE AND
INEXHAUSTIBLE COMPASSION! IN JESUS' NAME. AMEN.

God Is Good

It is good. The Eternal One is good to those who expect Him, to those who seek Him wholeheartedly. It is good to wait quietly for the Eternal to make things right again. It is good to have to deal with restraint and burdens when young. Just leave in peace the one who waits in silence, patiently bearing the burden of God; just don't interfere if he falls, gape-mouthed in the dust. There may well be hope yet.

LAMENTATIONS 3:25–29 VOICE

God is good. And He is good to those who expect—who wait on—Him. The Lord is good to those who seek His presence with all their heart. God does not hide, and He will be found. He is good to those who surrender to His perfect will. He is gracious to those who trust in Him.

We need good in our lives, don't we? We hear of wars and rumors of wars. We see sickness, disease, and death take their toll. We struggle in relationships that sometimes end in heartbreak. We lose people we deeply love, sometimes unexpectedly. Finances ebb and flow, and so does our stress level. We collaborate with people who are difficult at best. We battle anxiety that keeps us destabilized. We get tangled up in local and world news, which keeps us stirred up and scared. And unless we seek God wholeheartedly, these things will overwhelm us and rob us of peace and joy.

Jeremiah, the writer of Lamentations and often called the weeping prophet, was mocked and ridiculed by his fellow Israelites. They were spiteful and refused to embrace his message of God's grace and goodness. But he still penned the verses above, believing with all his heart that the Lord is good to those who expect and seek Him. Jeremiah was faithful to submit to God and follow His ways.

Even with all the hardship we'll face and the trials that will come our way, we can choose to trust that God is good. We can seek Him through the Word and through time in prayer. In our heartache, we can sit in His presence and receive significant comfort. And we can choose to wait patiently as the Lord moves in our circumstances. Life will continue to be grueling, but God will continue to be good.

DEAR LORD, I KNOW YOU ARE GOOD. AND I KNOW THAT AS I SEEK YOU WHOLEHEARTEDLY AND WAIT WITH PATIENCE FOR YOU TO ACT, I WILL EXPERIENCE YOUR GOODNESS IN BEAUTIFUL WAYS. LET ME REMEMBER THIS TRUTH WHEN LIFE FEELS HARD. IN JESUS' NAME. AMEN.

Bringing Grief to the Holy Spirit

It's time to stop bringing grief to God's Holy Spirit;
you have been sealed with the Spirit, marked as His own
for the day of rescue. Banish bitterness, rage and anger,
shouting and slander, and any and all malicious thoughts—
these are poison. Instead, be kind and compassionate.
Graciously forgive one another just as God has forgiven
you through the Anointed, our Liberating King.

EPHESIANS 4:30–32 VOICE

How we live matters to God. And as believers, we have His Spirit within us to direct us in His ways. We have been sealed and marked for eternity, and the Holy Spirit provides guidance and comfort. As we pursue righteous living, we find that the Spirit's prompting is vitally important. When we're intentional to acknowledge His role in our lives, we live in a beautiful relationship together where He leads and we faithfully follow. But when we grieve the Spirit, our actions disrupt that harmony.

So how exactly do we grieve God's Holy Spirit? When we don't live peacefully with other believers, showing kindness and compassion, but instead treat them in hurtful ways, we bring grief. When we do not banish bitterness, rage, anger, shouting, slander, and all malicious thoughts, we bring grief. When we fail to forgive as God has forgiven us, we bring grief. You see, suppressing the Spirit keeps Him from being able to reveal Himself as He desires through our words and actions. And it prevents us from living a godly life that benefits us, blesses others, and brings glory to the Lord.

Let's choose to be women who welcome and embrace the Holy Spirit's influence. Let's follow His leading so we grow closer to God and our faith matures. Let's step far away from the world's influence and sin's snare. And let's not shut down or shut out the Spirit by refusing to follow His leading.

Friend, be quick to pray with a humble and surrendered heart, asking for the strength to love others well. We simply cannot do this—at least not for long—without His help. And as we are called to love God first and our neighbor next, we need to lean into the Spirit's help so we obey the Lord and bless His Holy Spirit.

DEAR LORD, THANK YOU FOR THE GIFT OF THE HOLY SPIRIT IN MY LIFE. GIVE ME THE ABILITY TO HEAR HIS LEADING AND FOLLOW HIS WAYS SO I CAN LOVE AS YOU HAVE ASKED ME TO DO. IN JESUS' NAME. AMEN.

Scripture Index

OLD TESTAMENT

NEW TESTAMENT

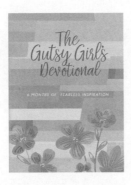